# ENGLAND AND THE LOW COUNTRIES
## IN THE LATE MIDDLE AGES

EDITED BY
CAROLINE BARRON AND NIGEL SAUL

SUTTON PU

D1212606

First published in the United Kingdom in 1995 by
Alan Sutton Publishing Limited, an imprint of Sutton Publishing Limited
Phoenix Mill · Thrupp · Stroud · Gloucestershire GL5 2BU

Paperback edition first published in 1998 by Sutton Publishing Limited

A catalogue record for this book is available from the British Library

ISBN 0 7509 1834 9

*Cover illustration from* Livre de Merveilles *(1410), Fr 2810 f. 86v
(Bibliothèque Nationale, Paris/photograph Bridgeman Art Library, London/New
York)*


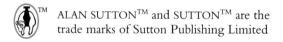

Typeset in 10/11 Bembo.
Typesetting and origination by
Sutton Publishing Limited.
Printed in Great Britain by
MPG, Bodmin, Cornwall.

# Contents

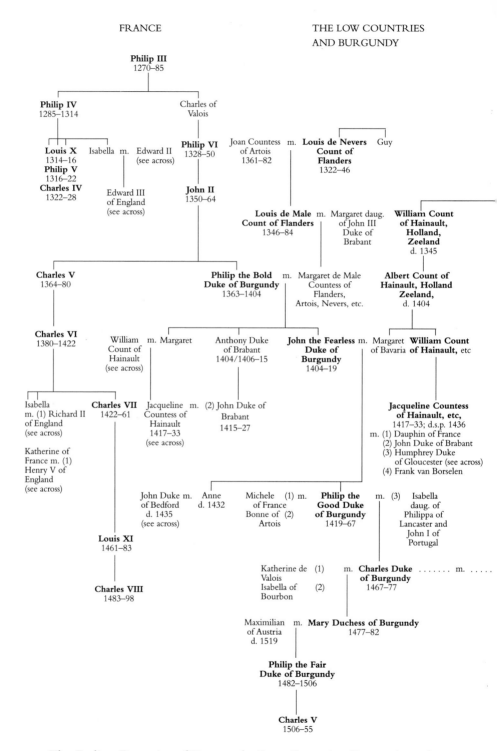

The Ruling Dynasties of France, the Low Countries, Burgundy and England 1300–1500

# ENGLAND

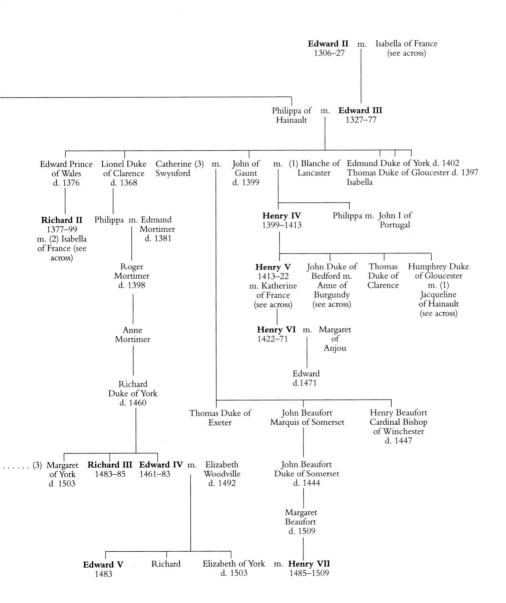

**Edward II** m.  Isabella of France
1306–27        (see across)

Philippa of  m.  **Edward III**
Hainault          1327–77

Edward Prince    Lionel Duke    Catherine (3)  m.  John of   m.  (1) Blanche of   Edmund Duke of York d. 1402
of Wales         of Clarence    Swynford           Gaunt          Lancaster        Thomas Duke of Gloucester d. 1397
d. 1376          d. 1368                            d. 1399                         Isabella

**Richard II**   Philippa  m. Edmund                **Henry IV**        Philippa m.  John I of
1377–99                      Mortimer                1399–1413                        Portugal
m. (2) Isabella              d. 1381
of France (see
across)

                 Roger                              **Henry V**    John Duke of   Thomas    Humphrey Duke
                 Mortimer                           1413–22        Bedford m.     Duke of   of Gloucester
                 d. 1398                             m. Katherine   Anne of        Clarence  m. (1)
                                                     of France      Burgundy                 Jacqueline
                                                     (see across)   (see across)             of Hainault
                                                                                             (see across)

                 Anne                               **Henry VI**  m.  Margaret
                 Mortimer                           1422–71           of
                                                                      Anjou

                 Richard                                          Edward
                 Duke of York                                     d.1471
                 d. 1460

                             Thomas Duke of         John Beaufort           Henry Beaufort
                             Exeter                 Marquis of Somerset     Cardinal Bishop
                                                                            of Winchester
                                                                            d. 1447

. . . . . . (3) Margaret   **Richard III**  **Edward IV**  m.  Elizabeth      John Beaufort
of York                    1483–85          1461–83            Woodville      Duke of Somerset
d. 1503                                                        d. 1492        d. 1444

                                                                              Margaret
                                                                              Beaufort
                                                                              d. 1509

             **Edward V**      Richard      Elizabeth of York  m.  **Henry VII**
             1483                           d. 1503                1485–1509

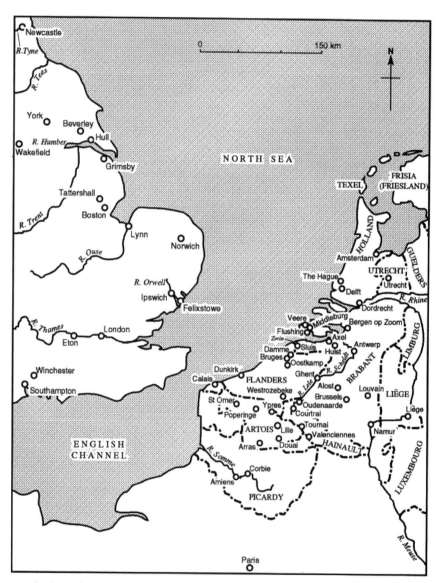

England and the Low Countries *c.* 1400.

# Introduction: England and the Low Countries 1327–1477[1]

Caroline Barron

*Royal Holloway College, University of London*

In September 1991 the ninth conference for historians of the fifteenth century was held at Royal Holloway and Bedford New College. Papers given at the conference ranged widely in that several dealt not only with England and the Low Countries, but also with England's relations with Italy and Spain. This published volume, however, focuses on England and the Low Countries where the links between eastern England and the northern European seaboard were, in the Middle Ages, so close as to render the area a coherent region (see map, opposite). A traveller in London would have found it as easy, if not easier, to cross the water to Calais or Sluys or Middelburg, as to travel overland to Wales or Lancashire or the Lake District. The channel tunnel may, indeed, restore an easy familiarity with the Continent which has not existed since the sixteenth century.

The papers printed here fall within a span of 150 years and cover a wide range of topics: from linguistic influence to the exchange of musical talent, and from the comparatively mundane trade of the port of London to the expensive gifts exchanged at the highest social level. It may be that the extent to which England was culturally and economically dependent upon the sophisticated and wealthier economies of the Low Countries in the later Middle Ages has been obscured by later English nationalism. In the fifteenth century, in spite of the Hundred Years War (or because of it?), England was truly a part of northern Europe, bound by language, religion and interdependent economies, into a single community and a common market. It was the rulers, Edward III and the later dukes of Burgundy, who attempted to raise the formal barriers of economic sanctions, bullion restriction and protected markets to secure their military and political ends.

This introduction aims to provide a background for the more specialised chapters produced by contributors. In the first part the political and economic relations between England and the Low Countries are sketched, from the accession of Edward III in 1327 to the death of Charles the Bold, duke of Burgundy, in 1477. The footnotes are intended to direct readers to the rich, but scattered, secondary writing on various aspects of this chequered relationship. The second part of the introduction explores the social and cultural exchanges, and addresses two negatives: some areas of interchange not covered by the essays in this volume, and some areas in which the influence of the two regions upon each other was comparatively slight. There is much that needs further exploration, and by historians competent in the vernacular languages of both countries. This volume is but the end of a beginning.

The Low Countries in a convenient, but vague, term used to describe, in the medieval period, a multitude of political units. The essays in this volume discuss aspects of the relationship of Englishmen with the people who lived in the low-lying areas stretching from the river Somme in the south-west to the Zuider Zee in the north-east (see map). At the heart of this area lay the county of Flanders, bisected by the rivers Leie and Scheldt and dominated by the great weaving towns of Ypres, Ghent and Bruges. To the north-east of Flanders lay the separate counties of Holland, Zeeland and Guelders, and to the east the duchy of Brabant (with Antwerp at its core controlling access to the Scheldt) and the county of Hainault, and to the south-west Artois and Picardy. At the point where this land most nearly touched England, Calais was situated, in the northern tip of the county of Artois, but closely nudging the weaving towns of Flanders. It was the great water-logged, over-populated, industrially advanced and economically precocious basin of land stretching from Calais in the west to Antwerp in the east which absorbed English wool, English armies and English merchants for three hundred years. The shift in importance from Calais, in the fourteenth century, to Antwerp, in the sixteenth, symbolised the transformation of the military presence to the predominantly mercantile. But the loss of Calais, and the decline of Antwerp in the middle of the sixteenth century marked the end of an economic era: England now turned her attention westwards across the Atlantic to new trading patterns and New World empires.

At the beginning of the fourteenth century the Low Countries were still several separate political countries, but by the end of the century many of them had been swept into the control of the expansionist Burgundian state, a process of accretion and consolidation which was to continue in the fifteenth century until the Burgundian state was itself swallowed up in the Hapsburg empire.[2] Louis of Nevers, who was count of Flanders from 1322 to 1346, married Joan, countess of Artois, and thus linked the rich area around Arras with the county of Flanders. The men of Artois spoke French, and Louis' policy was significantly francophile. This aggravated the developing separatism of the weaving towns of Bruges, Ypres and Ghent, who were organised in their opposition to their count by Jacob van Arteveldt, the dominating and charismatic leader from Ghent. Van Arteveldt's policy was to unite the three towns under the hegemony of

Ghent against their francophile count. Instead, they were to form an alliance with the more distant king of England, who was likely to prove a less interventionist overlord and whose kingdom was closely linked economically with the fortunes of the Flemish cities. Indeed the Flemish weaving towns had become almost completely dependent upon the supply of English wool for their prosperity. This was a natural alliance and it offered diplomatic advantages to Edward III in his impending struggle to assert and make good his claims to the French crown.[3]

Edward's entente with the Low Countries had begun early, while he was still Prince of Wales. In January 1328 he had been married to Philippa, the daughter of the count of Hainault, in return for Hainaulters to accompany Edward's mother Isabella in her successful bid to oust her husband, Edward II, from the throne.[4] The alliance of Hainault was thus secured for Edward, but it proved more difficult to persuade the other rulers of the Low Countries to cooperate. Reginald, count of Guelders was secured for an anti-French alliance, but John, duke of Brabant, and Louis, count of Flanders, resisted. For Brabant and Flanders, the links with France were both natural and traditional. In order to persuade Brabant and Flanders into an English alliance, and to foment discontent in the weaving towns, Edward in August 1336 prohibited the export of English wool to Flanders. A year later the duke of Brabant made an alliance with Edward and English wool entered Antwerp, but the blockade of Flanders continued.[5] In 1337 Edward referred to Philip 'who calls himself king of France',[6] and in January 1340 Edward formally claimed the French crown and was recognised as king of France in Ghent. In this way the defection of the count of Flanders from his French overlord was made easier and a treaty of economic and political alliance between England and Flanders was agreed.[7] But in fact this treaty was between Edward and the Flemish towns (led by van Arteveldt), and Count Louis of Flanders remained true to the French alliance, while his illegitimate brother Guy was recognised by Edward as count. This alliance was crucial to Edward and he had to pay heavily for it. The staple for English wool was established at Bruges, subsidies amounting to some £140,000 were paid to the weaving towns, and there was to be free trade between England and Flanders which meant, in particular, that Flemish cloth could be imported into England freely. Moreover, Edward agreed to issue a common coinage which would circulate freely in Brabant, Flanders and in his realms of England and France. Edward's financial problems had been prodigious,[8] but this alliance was a triumph of diplomacy, sealed in June 1340 by the victory of the English fleet over the French at Sluys, the outport of Bruges. But this marked the high point of Edward's success in Flanders: he was unable to take Tournai from its pro-French defenders in spite of a long and costly siege; his financial troubles escalated to such an extent that he was forced to flee secretly from Ghent to evade his creditors; he was abandoned by William, count of Hainault, and John, duke of Brabant; the duke of Guelders died; and Louis of Flanders remained true to his French overlord. Moreover, the independent Flemish towns resented the leadership of Ghent, which was itself rent by bitter rivalries between the guilds. In July 1345 Jacob van Arteveldt was murdered. But at the battle of Crécy, in Artois, in August 1346, Edward won a notable victory over the French king; Count Louis of Flanders was killed, leaving his sixteen-year-old son as his heir. Louis de Mâle, who was count of Flanders from 1346 until his death in 1384, managed to avoid a marriage with Isabella, the daughter of Edward III, and instead attached himself to Margaret, the daughter of the duke of Brabant. In this way he kept his options open and continued to be sought as an ally by both England and France.

The year after Crécy, Edward's alliances seemed to be in ruins.[9] Only the Margrave of Juliers and the Flemish towns remained faithful to their English alliance.[10] As Malcolm Vale has pointed out, Edward's allies 'were not prepared to risk their lives, capital assets and equipment in a war against superior numbers, led by a ruler who had not yet proved his abilities in continental warfare'.[11] In 1348 Louis de Mâle invaded Flanders and re-established his authority over his rebellious county: he made peace at Dunkirk with the towns and with Edward III.[12] But the defection of the Flemish towns was less serious than it might have been, for in August 1347, after a long siege, Edward had taken the town of Calais which was to play a vital role in the dissemination of English armies and English wool in the Low Countries. The English now had a base from which they could harass both the French and the Flemings should they need to do so. Louis de Mâle had a particularly difficult hand to play. He could not afford openly to abandon the English alliance because the Flemish towns depended for their prosperity upon imported English wool (although the English economy also depended, but to a lesser extent, upon the export of wool to Flanders) and to abandon England was likely to bring the towns out in revolt.[13] But these Flemish towns, also, and Bruges in particular, depended upon the import of French grain for survival. The English victory over the French at Poitiers (1356) made the Flemish towns particularly restive. Louis had one trump card that he could play: he had only one child, his daughter Margaret, who was his heir, and so her hand was eagerly sought in marriage. To keep the English happy, Louis agreed in a treaty drawn up at Dover in October 1364 that Margaret should marry Edward III's fourth son, Edmund Langley.[14] But a papal dispensation was needed for this marriage and a francophile Pope could be easily persuaded to take his time over this.[15] In 1369 Margaret was instead married to Philip, duke of Burgundy and brother of the French king Charles V. Thus with a twist of a wedding ring, Flanders slipped out of the English sphere of influence. But the 'bonnes villes' or great towns of Flanders fought against this turn of events, not least because the English vented their feelings by perpetrating acts of mass piracy upon Flemish shipping. But not all Flemish towns were as anglophile as Ghent, and Louis began to foster a better relationship with Bruges as an antidote to the rebellious Ghenters.

Since 1362 Philip van Arteveldt, whose father had been murdered in 1345, had been receiving an English pension, and in January 1382 he seized power in Ghent and proclaimed the city's independence from the count and an alliance with the English.[16] The support of the English, however, on which the success of the Arteveldt rising depended, came too little and too late.[17] At Roosebeke, on 27 November 1382, the men of Ghent, Bruges and Ypres were soundly defeated by an army of Frenchmen led by their count. Philip van Arteveldt was killed and the men of Bruges and Ypres submitted to Louis, although Ghent continued to hold out. In support of the beleaguered Ghenters, the English sent a motley crusading army led by Bishop Henry Despenser of Norwich in the summer of 1383. The expedition achieved nothing except the destruction of some of the outlying suburbs of Ypres and the humiliation of the English.[18] When Louis de Mâle, the last count of Flanders, died in February 1384, he knew that his daughter and her husband would be able to take control of Flanders. The men of Ghent finally made peace with their new count, duke Philip of Burgundy, at the Peace of Tournai in December 1385. Philip had restored all the commercial privileges of the Ghenters and they were free to trade where they wanted, except that all political relations with England were ruptured and the English were forbidden access to the Flemish towns.[19]

The union of Flanders with Burgundy was momentous for the configuration of power in Europe for the next hundred years, but the Peace of Tournai failed to sever Flanders from England as Philip had intended. As Prevenier has observed, 'La réalité commerciale était sans doute plus forte que la théorie des mandements ducaux, et comme souvent, la politique suit la voie tracée par les impératifs économiques'.[20] The problem was that Philip had wider concerns than Flanders alone, and the political and economic interests of the different parts of his dominions were not always in harmony. In particular, the Flemings needed English wool and an English alliance, which conflicted with Philip's French loyalties. In Brabant, economic needs and, in particular, the rising fortunes of the town of Antwerp, militated agaist a wholesale ban on imported English cloth, whereas the Flemish towns needed to protect the markets for their own cloth. Philip could not ignore the economic needs of the Flemish towns because their prosperity was important to the prosperity of the Burgundian house: it has been calculated that 24 per cent of the gross income of the Burgundian dukes came from Flanders alone − more than from Burgundy itself.[21] So it was in Philip's interest to foster peace, and hence prosperity, in Flanders. But this was no easy task. In deference to his French loyalties, Philip allowed a French army to muster near Bruges in preparation for an invasion of England in 1386. Francis Ackerman of Ghent took up the pro-English mantle of van Arteveldt, and tried to recreate the traditional alliance, but he was murdered in 1388. Meanwhile, Flemish trade with England was disrupted and piracy was rife. [22]

The twenty-eight year truce between France and England drawn up in 1396 removed one of the main complicating political difficulties in the relations between England and the Low Countries: at least the duke of Burgundy was no longer obliged to take an anti-English stand. But the economic difficulties remained. England needed a market for her wool and, to a lesser extent, a market for her developing cloth output. But the English economy was less dependent upon the export of wool than the Flemish towns were upon its receipt. The economies of Ghent and Ypres (and to a lesser extent Bruges) were essentially dependent upon the weaving of English wool into fine cloth.[23] They found alternative, but less satisfactory sources of supply in Scotland and Spain.[24] So the Flemish towns needed the unfettered import of English wool and a ban upon the import of English cloth.[25] Brabant, by contrast, and especially Antwerp, required a good supply of English cloth to export southwards into the hinterland of Germany. The various prohibitions and bans were never completely successful, and trade with Flanders and in Flemish ships captained by 'doche' masters certainly persisted throughout the later fourteenth century, as Vanessa Harding's essay demonstrates, not least because these ring-fenced economies were punctured by the free enterprise of the Italians. Genoese and Venetian galleys came directly to Southampton and London and carried away English wool to supply their native cloth industries, and also, to a lesser extent, English cloth.[26] Clearly the English were in a stronger position than the Flemings since they could feed themselves without the export of either wool or cloth. Moreover, in these two commodities they had goods which they could market outside Flanders. On the other hand the Flemings, and particularly the men of Bruges, had a monopoly of the complex network of banking and credit upon which the English merchants, and those with whom they did business, depended.[27] Just as the British economy today is underpinned by the hidden exports of insurance and banking, so the financial expertise and banking skills of the men of Bruges drew merchants and their factors to Flanders and thus diversified and strengthened the industrial economy, which was overly dependent upon the manufacture of cloth.

Apart from the problem posed by the burgeoning English cloth export, the economic interests of Flanders and England were complementary. When the political conflicts had been resolved by the Anglo-French truce of 1396, it was possible for duke Philip's son, John the Fearless (1404–19) to come to a commercial agreement with the English king which was embodied in a treaty drawn up on 10 March 1407.[28] By the terms of this agreement there was to be free passage for both English and Flemish merchants in each other's countries. Merchants from Flanders, Brabant, Holland and Italy were all empowered to buy English wool at the Calais staple. English cloth was still banned from sale in Flanders, but although this may have been some sort of sop to the Flemings, in practice English cloth could be taken to Antwerp and distributed to the markets of Europe from there. Walter Prevenier has characterised this treaty as 'presque un miracle', and perhaps it was:[29] miraculous not in what it achieved but in what it openly recognised. Certainly the next thirty years were comparatively calm ones in the stormy history of Anglo-Flemish relations. The political situation within Flanders itself, however, remained volatile. Duke John the Fearless was conciliatory towards the Flemish towns because he was primarily concerned with the rivalry between his house and the house of Orleans for political dominance in French affairs during the recurrent insanity of the French king, Charles VI. The rivalry between Burgundy and Orleans (Armagnacs) culminated in the murder of duke John at Montereau on 10 September 1419. He was succeeded as duke of Burgundy and count of Flanders by his son, Philip the Good.

The murder of his father by the supporters of the French dauphin drove duke Philip into an alliance with the English. For the first time for nearly a hundred years, the economic interests of the Flemings coincided with the political concerns of their rulers. In 1423 Philip's sister Anne married John, duke of Bedford and uncle of the English king Henry VI, thereby perpetuating (although not by heirs, since the marriage was childless) the Anglo-Burgundian alliance.[30] But Philip had territorial ambitions nearer to home and these brought the alliance with England under strain. Philip's cousin John was count of Brabant; he was also married to Jacqueline of Bavaria, the countess in her own right of the desirable counties of Hainault, Holland and Zeeland. The couple were childless and so, in the fullness of time, Philip would inherit their joint lands and thereby immeasurably enrich his already rich domains. But in the same year that the diplomatic duke of Bedford cemented the Burgundian alliance by his marriage to Anne, his impetuous and undiplomatic younger brother Humphrey seized the opportunity to carry away Jacqueline, and persuaded the Pope to dissolve her marriage to John of Brabant. Humphrey then married Jacqueline himself and raised money and an army in England to reclaim his wife's territories. Philip prepared to help his cousin to fend off the English attack which turned out to be a fiasco and not a serious threat.[31] Bedford smoothed Philip's ruffled feathers and, in due course, John of Brabant died in 1427 and was succeeded by a childless heir (his brother, Philip), who passed the duchy of Brabant to Philip, duke of Burgundy, at his death in 1430. Meanwhile, Jacqueline agreed by the Treaty of Delft in 1428 to recognise Philip as the heir to her three counties and promised not to remarry. But in 1433 she broke the agreement by a fourth marriage, so Philip forced her to abdicate and took over her three counties. Philip now controlled not only Burgundy and Flanders, but also Brabant, Holland, Zeeland and Hainault.[32]

Not surprisingly, since he now had so much to lose, Philip of Burgundy began to move more openly towards a French alliance, and the comparative peace which had characterised Anglo-Flemish relations since 1407 was shattered. A complicating impediment to trade between England and Flanders was the shortage of bullion which affected the whole network of European trade in the second quarter of the fifteenth century. In 1429 the English government promulgated the Calais ordinances which instructed English Staple merchants to accept only bullion or English coin (the Flemish coin was much debased) in return for English wool and also required full payment 'on the nail' from aliens in ready money.[33] This disrupted the credit mechanisms on which the wool trade was based and also provoked Philip of Burgundy in October 1433 to issue an ordinance imposing a uniform currency upon his heterogeneous lands.[34] Philip also, in June 1434, prohibited the sale of English cloth in any of his dominions, which most crucially deprived the English of access to the Antwerp market. But English cloth could still be sold directly to Italians for sale in the southern Mediterranean and to the Hanse merchants for sale in the Baltic lands.[35] At Arras, in September 1435, Philip publicly renounced the English alliance and accepted Charles VII as king of France.[36] The English and the Flemings were once again in opposing political camps, and Philip decided to launch an attack on Calais, an English outpost encircled by Burgundian territory. To do this Philip needed the support of the Flemish towns and so he made strenuous efforts to secure their allegiance. He promised to maintain the ban on the sale of English cloth in his lands (although this prohibition was damaging to Antwerp and to the duchy of Brabant), to maintain a stable coinage for twenty years and to allow the Flemings to buy English wool at Calais.[37] In fact, in June 1436, the militias of Ghent and Bruges were defeated by English sorties and the fleet which Philip sent to blockade Calais came and left within two days, so when Humphrey, duke of Gloucester, arrived in August he was able to raid into western Flanders at will. He took Poperinge, had himself declared count of Flanders, and then destroyed the town and returned to England.[38]

The disruption of the commercial relations between England and Flanders in pursuit of French interests led the Flemish towns into revolt against their Burgundian lords. Perhaps as a result of the Bruges uprising of 1438, Philip was prepared to negotiate a commercial treaty with the

English at Calais in September 1438. By this treaty free trade and safe conducts were restored to the merchants of both countries, although the problem of the Calais staple and the issue of the import of English cloth into Burgundian lands were not tackled.[39] In the following December Philip promulgated an interdict on the sale of English cloth in Flanders which, by implication, allowed it to be sold in the rest of his dominions. The Treaty of Calais, however, did diminish the acts of piracy and 'rétablissait les échanges commerciaux et instituait une neutralité de fait entre les Etats de Philippe le Bon et l'Angleterre'.[40] By this treaty, peaceful, if limited, trade was secured for a further thirty years. The political difficulties, the hostility to English cloth and the bullion shortages had all contributed to a contraction in production and in trade in northern Europe in the middle years of the fifteenth century. English wool exports continued to decline,[41] although the cloth industry developed albeit primarily for domestic consumption. The Flemish weavers, starved of English wool, made cloth from imported Scottish and Spanish wool which was of lower quality and the resulting product was less saleable. English cloth was, however, finding its way into the European markets.

The middle years of the century were characterised by the exchange of threats and bans relating to wool, cloth and bullion between England and Burgundy.[42] Duke Philip's ban on the sale of English cloth in his lands (good for the Flemings and bad for the men of Antwerp) was countered by English bans on Burgundian imports.[43] Before his death in 1467 Philip finally, if tacitly, allowed English cloth to be sold at Antwerp: indeed, English cloth had become so important to the prosperity of Antwerp that the Burgundian dukes had to recognise that 'the merchants who dealt in English cloth (i.e. the men of Antwerp) were more important politically than the artisans (i.e. the Flemings) whose markets were, supposedly, being protected'.[44] Moreover, duke Charles the Bold (1467–77) who succeeded as duke of Burgundy in 1467, was much more anglophile than his father had been. He secured a treaty of friendship with England and, in the year after his accession, married Margaret of York, the sister of Edward IV, as his third wife.[45] English cloth was flooding into the Low Countries and the rest of Europe via the Antwerp market;[46] Flemish manufactured goods were flooding into England, and when Edward IV was in need of a refuge in 1470–71 he found it in Bruges and under the protection of the Burgundian duke.[47]

Duke Charles was killed at the battle of Nancy in 1477 and his only surviving legitimate child, the duchess Mary, died in a hunting accident five years later. The Burgundian lands became the prize in a dispute between Louis XI of France and Mary's widowed husband, Maximilian of Hapsburg, fighting for himself, and for the interests of his only son Philip. It was Philip's son who became Holy Roman Emperor as Charles V and

swept Flanders and the other Burgundian lands into a vast empire which
extended across the Atlantic. In his European dominions, Antwerp had
succeeded Bruges as the commercial and financial capital: few ships now
passed through Sluys and along the Zwin to Bruges. Almost all the
merchants had shifted their operations from Bruges to Antwerp: even the
Hanse finally moved their business headquarters there in 1500.[48] But in the
sixteenth century Antwerp would decline, as Bruges and Ghent had done
earlier, to be supplanted by Amsterdam, the great town of the county of
Holland which would, in time, break free from the Hapsburg empire and
become the heart of its own sea-borne empire. But artistic achievements
are not always directly linked to the political and economic successes which
provoke and inspire them. Thus the craft skills and artistic achievements of
the Flemings and the men of Brabant were still admired and sought after in
the sixteenth century. The influence of the Low Countries upon England
remained pervasive at all levels of society.

It is perhaps remarkable that the endemic political strife in the Low
Countries, strife much more pervasive and acute than that which overtook
England in the mid-fifteenth century, was not more damaging than it was
to the prosperity of the area. It was, originally, the scant agricultural
resources in proportion to the high population density which drove the
Flemings into developing their industrial skills. Since they were forced to
import grain to live, so they had to make goods for export and impelled in
this way, they developed their woollen cloth-weaving industry, as well as
numerous other 'light industries', such as linen-weaving (especially in
Hainault, Tournai, Lille and Courtrai), latten work,[49] brick-making and
beer-brewing, to be followed later by the making of spectacles and
watches, manuscript illumination and printing. The population suffered
acutely in the great famine of 1315–17 and in the outbreaks of plague in
1348–9 and 1368–9, yet the numbers seem to have built up again with
remarkable resilience. It has been estimated that perhaps a sixth to a quarter
of the population of Flanders died in 1348–9, which is rather less than the
rate of devastation in France, Germany and England.[50] It may be that the
extreme over-population in Flanders blunted the impact of the plague
upon the economy of the area. Moreover the population seems to have
been able to reproduce itself and maintain urban populations, which was
certainly not the case in England. By 1469 the population of Flanders has
been estimated at 661,000.[51]

Even if the population was reduced somewhat by the plagues of the later
medieval period, it was still too large for the agricultural resources of the
area, and the Flemings continued, throughout this period, to depend upon
imported grain (in spite of the early invention of the single-handed
plough). Ghent established an important grain staple to which grain from

Hainault, France, and also from Prussia, was brought for distribution throughout Flanders.[52] Indeed, French grain was almost as important to Flanders as English wool and thus a French alliance made quite good economic sense. The Flemings also depended upon imported fuel and much of their coal came from Newcastle upon Tyne.[53] To pay for these imports the Flemings developed a range of manufactured goods, and not only cloth: pickled herrings, linen (about half a million yards of linen was imported into London in 1480–81), beer, building bricks and lattenwork of all kinds were exported in large quantities.[54] There was also developed, at Bruges, a highly sophisticated service centre where money could be exchanged or banked, letters of credit could be drafted, exchanged or honoured, and bargains and deals drawn up and facilitated.[55] All the Italian trading companies had branches at Bruges and for about a century from 1350 the city was the commercial capital of Europe, and the centre of a financial network which extended throughout the Hanse towns to the north-east, and to England, France, Spain, Italy and Germany.[56] The financial services that could be bought in Bruges were as sophisticated, and as important to the economic prosperity of the area, as the cloth-weaving skills had been to the pre-eminence of Ghent and Ypres. It was the ability of the Flemings to keep one jump ahead of current technology, or financial wizardry, which enabled them to live, and to live well, on inhospitable land which was over-populated and often over-run by floods or by invading armies.

In these circumstances it is, perhaps, surprising that there was so much immigration of Flemings and 'Lowlanders' into England. Over-population certainly provides part of the explanation. But there were other 'pushing' factors. Whereas in England the incidence of the Black Death, and subsequent outbreaks of plague, seem to have ushered in a period of comparative prosperity when the real wages of both rural and urban workers rose, in Flanders this was not the case. Although some workers did better after the Plague, the improvements were rarely sustained, and it has been argued that 'poverty was a serious and growing problem in fourteenth-century Flanders'.[57] By the mid-fifteenth century, various different assessments suggest that at least 10 per cent of the population of Ypres, Courtrai, Ghent and Bruges were reckoned to be poor to the extent of needing free fuel (peat) or exemption from taxation.[58] There are no comparable records for English towns, but, even so, there is little indication, even impressionistic, of poverty on this scale between the mid-fourteenth century and the population rise of the early sixteenth century. In addition to over-population and poverty, or perhaps because of them, there was a great deal of civic violence in the Flemish towns.[59] Men were frequently beheaded in reprisals following political coups and towns were divided into armed camps. Much of this was due, not to class warfare nor to the hostility between artisan wage-earners and their employers but, rather, to family blood-feuds exacerbated by economic rivalry. London, and indeed other English towns, were at times turbulent, but no-one was executed by mob violence or lynch law on the streets of London between 1381 and Cade's Revolt in 1450.[60] The strong, and immediate, presence of the king contained the violence of the mercantile factions of the 1380s. Moreover, although there were factions, the English towns did not nourish dynastic elites: rivalries were bitter but not inherited. The successful English merchant moved his heirs (if he had them) out of town into the countryside and so removed also his quarrels and rivalries.[61] There were Montagues and Capulets but not in the second generation.

The Flemish towns were, certainly, fitfully prosperous, and although there was considerable poverty, there was also great wealth. The rulers of Flanders, and in particular the Burgundian dukes, taxed the wealth of the Flemish towns ferociously. The rate of taxation was much heavier than that borne by English towns. From 1407 onwards the duke taxed Bruges at the rate of a seventh of its civic income. Between 1435 and 1467 the municipal accounts balanced only four times.[62] In 1473 Flanders produced 25 per cent of the ducal income (Brabant 22 per cent, Holland 18 per cent); moreover the price of rebellion was high: Bruges was fined £480,000 in 1438 and Ghent had to pay £840,000 in 1447–53.[63] (N.B. if these sums were livres tournois, they should be divided by nine, which produces *c.* £54,400 and £94,500; both prodigious sums by English standards since the grant to the king of a tenth and fifteenth yielded *c.* £34,000 from the whole country). By the use of the trade embargo for political ends and by heavy taxation, the Burgundian dukes in the fifteenth century were effectively killing – albeit slowly – the geese that laid the golden eggs.

By contrast with Flanders, England was, in the period 1350–1500, a comparatively undeveloped and unsophisticated economy. After 1350 the country was underpopulated and there was a shortage of labour. There was sufficient food (the recurrent fears of grain shortages never materialised) and a marked rise in per capita wealth.[64] The highly centralised government prevented rampant and violent competition between towns and contained the worst excesses of street violence. It was possible for most Englishmen to eat well without being inventive and so they were happy to accept imports from Flanders; high-quality cloth, processed food and technological innovations, such as printing. In short, England was an economy and a market ripe for development, and the Flemings duly came. Driven by floods, warfare, taxation, hunger, poverty and violence, they came to England in large numbers to settle and to earn a good living by employing the skills which they had learnt in their more technologically advanced homeland.

Doubtless men and women from the Low Countries had been coming to England for many centuries, but their immigration appears to have been particularly encouraged by Edward III who, as early as 1331, offered letters of protection to immigrants from Flanders and encouraged these men to pursue their 'mesteri'.[65] It is not clear to what extent such immigrants contributed to the development of the English cloth industry, but they played a part in Edward III's plan to starve Flanders of wool, prohibit the import of Flemish cloth and develop the home industry. The immigrants were not always welcomed with open arms and, on occasion, the king had to issue special letters of protection.[66] The Flemish weavers seem to have organised themselves into guilds separate from the native weavers and in London the weavers from Brabant had a guild separate from the Flemings.[67] This alien separatism was punished by the murder of some thirty or forty Flemings who had taken refuge in the church of St Martin Vintry in London, in June 1381.[68] Although there were men from the Low Countries to be found in most English towns by the end of the fourteenth century (e.g. in York and Winchester),[69] they seem to have been particularly numerous in London. In 1436 when the duke of Burgundy's defection to the French led to the demand that all 'Lowlanders' should swear an oath of allegiance, 400 of those who did so came from the London area, the majority came from Holland and Brabant and only 10 per cent from Flanders 'proper'.[70] Many of these 'Lowlanders' lived in the suburbs of London, beyond the jurisdiction of the mayor and the wardens of the crafts: about 10 per cent of Westminster's population of 2,000 in the mid-fifteenth century were 'doche'[71] and in Southwark the percentage may have been even greater: 44 per cent of the aliens who lived in the London area in 1436 came from Southwark.[72] But whereas in the fourteenth century the majority of those who came as immigrants to England may have been from Flanders, with a considerable number from Brabant, by the fifteenth century by far the largest number of immigrants came from Holland. Thielemans counted all the immigrants from the Low Countries into England mentioned in the Patent Rolls between 1435 and 1467, a total of 1,547 Lowlanders: 34 per cent came from Holland and then in descending order Brabant (25 per cent), Zeeland (9 per cent), Guelders (8 per cent), Flanders (6 per cent), Liège (5 per cent), Utrecht (4 per cent) and the remaining 9 per cent divided between Hainault, Artois/Picardy, Limburg, Frisia and Tournai.[73] Nearly a quarter of these Lowlanders settled in London, and a further 40 per cent were to be found in the counties of Norfolk, Suffolk, Kent, Essex and Surrey, i.e., in the counties closest to the lands from which they came.[74] Only a very small number of these immigrants (203) were identified by their craft, but over 25 per cent of these were cordwainers: weavers by this date comprised only 10 per cent. The other notable groups were haberdashers, tailors and jewellers.[75] It must have been these men and women, together with the more transient merchants and shipmen described by Vanessa Harding, who made the significant linguistic contributions to the English language analysed by Laura Wright.[76]

For the reasons already described, the English had little reason or inclination to emigrate to live in the towns of the Low Countries, apart from Calais. But English merchants had been travelling there on business and living together in English hostels since the thirteenth century. The duke of Brabant had granted a charter to 'the merchants of the realm of England' in 1305 to elect their own Governor in Antwerp, and the count of Flanders granted similar privileges to the English at Bruges in 1359.[77] By the second half of the fifteenth century, this community at Bruges was effectively controlled by the Merchant Adventurers Company, in itself under the control of the Mercers' Company of London.[78] William Caxton was Governor of the English company of merchants at Bruges in the 1460s. There is no doubt that English merchants travelled frequently to Calais, and many went further into Flanders and Brabant. For many English men and women, Middelburg in Zeeland was their first landing point on the Continent, and for a period in the 1380s it was used as the staple town for English wool. In 1415 Margery Kempe returned to England from her pilgrimage to the Holy Land and Rome via Middelburg whence her company 'took their journey into England'.[79]

There was contact and exchange between England and the Low Countries at every level. Whereas more 'doche' probably came to settle in England than vice versa, yet more Englishmen and women are likely to have passed through the Low Countries as travellers and pilgrims. At the highest social level, aristocratic marriages facilitated the exchange of people, expensive artefacts, ideas and skills between countries. Edward III was the first English king for two hundred years to take a wife from the Low Countries.[80] Although Edward's mother, Isabella, may have had short-term objectives, in fact the alliance with Hainault was to be of considerable consequence in the development of English foreign policy and in the evolution of aristocratic style and alliances within England. Philippa turned out to be both fertile and faithful, and her death in 1369 was a serious blow to the stability of the royal household which became the focus of faction and rumour. Philippa appears to have avoided filling her own household and the royal court with men and women from her homeland and there was no xenophobic protest about the prevalence of Hainaulters in high office. But Philippa was responsible for bringing to England Sir Walter Manny who started his career as an esquire in her household and became one of Edward III's most trusted war captains, a member of the Order of the Garter and the founder of the London Charterhouse in 1371;[81] and also the chronicler Jean Froissart who first visited England in 1361 at the invitation of Queen Philippa. Froissart came from Valenciennes in Hainault. He wrote admiringly of chivalric feats of arms, but also of the less heroic aspects of the first phase of the Hundred Years War.[82] Both Manny and Froissart made a notable contribution to English life. Philippa was also responsible for bringing to England Philippa and Katherine Roet, daughters of Payne de Roet of Hainault, and wives, respectively, of Geoffrey Chaucer and John, duke of Lancaster.[83] The influence of Philippa Chaucer upon her husband's poetry remains obscure, but Katherine's legitimised children, the Beauforts, were to play a notable part in the politics of the fifteenth century. Her great-great-grandson became king of England as Henry VII.

In the 1360s it looked as if the rich prize of the county of Flanders might fall under English control through the projected marriage of the heiress Margaret de Mâle with Edmund Langley, the fourth son of Edward III. Unfortunately for England, Philip the Bold of Burgundy secured her hand and Flanders was destined to slip into the French sphere of influence. But high-level marriages between members of the English royal family and those of the rulers of the Low Countries continued to be eagerly negotiated and, less often, secured. Some marriages of great political potential were arranged in the fifteenth century: John, duke of Bedford married first Anne of Burgundy, and then Jacquetta of Luxembourg; Jacqueline of Bavaria and countess of Holland, Zeeland and Hainault married Humphrey, duke of Gloucester; and Margaret of York became the third wife of Charles the Bold of Burgundy.[84] All four of these marriages were childless. But these marriages simply mark high points in the endless process of negotiation: diplomatic embassies seeking political alliances or commercial advantages were not rare and special, rather they were in continuous motion and, occasionally, achieved a higher profile because a treaty was secured or a marriage arranged.[85] The continuous diplomacy of late medieval Europe was one of the most important agents of cultural exchange. The essays by Andrew Wathey, Scot McKendrick and Malcolm Vale demonstrate the importance which these meetings of the rich and powerful, the lettered and the influential, had upon the interplay of ideas across the channel, the exchange of rich gifts (tapestries from Arras and gold and jewels from London)[86] and the purchase of manuscripts and printed books.[87] While at one level the intermittent and destructive warfare interrupted the free flow of people and goods between England and the Low Countries, at another level the incessant search for peace and for alliances encouraged contacts of a different kind.

In a way that was not, perhaps, true of English towns in the fourteenth century, the towns of the Low Countries were cultural centres where the rulers, their courtiers, the landed aristocracy and the rich merchants intersected.[88] From the early fourteenth century, it was customary for the Flemish towns to offer notable processions or 'joyeuses entrées' to visiting monarchs or to their count on his first visit to their city. Edward III was received in this way when he entered Ghent in 1340 and in 1384 Philip of Burgundy was ceremonially received at Bruges and installed as count in the church of St Donatian.[89] Such ceremonial was not at first so highly developed in England, nor was it stimulated by the acute rivalry between different towns. But the English courtiers and merchants who observed these festivities in the Low Countries must have filtered the ideas back to England. The first detailed account of any 'joyous entry' anywhere is the chronicler Thomas Walsingham's account of the Coronation procession offered by the city of London to Richard II in 1377.[90] There may have been political disadvantages in ruling over a heterogeneous collection of different towns and states, but the duke of Burgundy was likely to receive more 'joyous entries' than the king of England, who was crowned only once and had only one important city. For this reason, Richard II may well have contrived a second 'joyous entry' into the city of London following his quarrel in 1392.[91] There must have been a lively exchange of ideas, for urban spectacles and the ceremonial development of the Mayor's Riding to take his oath in London must have owed much to Flemish urban processions.[92] Alexandra Johnston's essay demonstrates how public drama in English towns was influenced by the urban drama of the Low Countries, riding on the back of mercantile exchange.

But in one respect, at least, the English towns did not follow the example of the towns of the Low Countries. In Ghent, Lille, Douai, Bruges, Tournai and elsewhere, the citizens participated alongside the local nobility in 'communal' tournaments, although this was more the case in the pre-Burgundian period than subsequently. But such tournaments were never a feature of English civic life. In the 1370s duke Philip sponsored tournaments in Ghent in order to win over the citizens, and there is considerable evidence that the local urban oligarchies themselves organised and promoted tournaments and participated in them.[93] By contrast, the Londoners seem never to have jousted themselves, and merely tolerated the use of Smithfield as a tournament site.[94] As Dr Juliet Vale has shown, many of Edward III's tournaments were held in country palaces and not in urban centres.[95] The 'bourgeois' tournament, so popular in the Low Countries, seems never to have been transplanted across the channel.

It is clear that when members of the royal family, the nobility, courtiers, bishops and clergy visited the Low Countries on embassies they took the opportunity to buy Flemish cloth, or tapestries and hangings, to recruit musicians,[96] commission manuscripts,[97] order funeral brasses,[98] hire painters[99] or simply commission paintings on the spot. Andrew Martindale reflects upon the possible routes whereby Flemish painters might have come to decorate the walls of Eton College chapel in the 1480s.[100] But these men were certainly not alone. Flemish painters and sculptors were hired alongside Englishmen to paint English walls, glaze English windows[101] and carve statues for English churches.[102] A few of the painted panels commissioned by English patrons in the Low Countries still survive: for example the panels of a triptych presented by Prior Weston (1476–89) to the high altar of the Priory church of the Hospitallers in London,[103] or the altar piece, perhaps by Jan Prevost, which was commissioned by Sir Robert Tate (Mayor of London 1488, d. 1500) and now in the church of All Hallows by the Tower where Tate was buried,[104] or the triptych by Hans Memling, now in the National Gallery, London, which depicts Sir John Donne and his wife Elizabeth, the sister of William, Lord Hastings, with their patron saints.[105] The Ashwellthorpe Triptych, now in the Castle Museum in Norwich, was probably painted for Christopher Knyvett (d. *c.* 1520), a member of the notable Norfolk family, and his wife Catherine Van Assche, by a Netherlandish painter. The triptych has as its central theme the Seven Sorrows of the Virgin.[106]

Painters and painting from the Low Countries flooded the English market in the fifteenth century and it seems, sometimes, as if the English painter is almost invisible.[107] It is often argued that Flemish painters enjoyed a higher status and were employed upon more sophisticated work than their English counterparts. Gilbert Prince, who was for many years the court painter of Richard II, was a wealthy man when he died in 1397. His only recorded commissions were for banners, tournament fittings, heraldic devices and banquet decorations. Such a man could not, it is argued, have been responsible for 'real' paintings like the Wilton Diptych.[108] But if we look, for example, at the work of his contemporary, Melchior Broederlam from Ypres, who was responsible for the wings of the altarpiece for the Charterhouse where Philip the Bold was buried, we find that he – or his workshop – was also commissioned to paint banners displaying the Burgundian ducal arms, to provide painted jousting harness and to decorate the ducal barge in 1378.[109] Such tasks, the Dijon work apart, are not so different from those for which Gilbert Prince was paid. Moreover, in 1467 Hugo van der Goes was paid to paint coats of arms for the city of Ghent.[110] In the Low Countries, as in England, painters formed guilds and most of their work, whether religious or secular, was ordered for a specific purpose.[111] The apparent difference between England and the Low Countries in this respect may be due to the different rates of survival rather than to any real difference in the public esteem in which painters were held.

In the course of the later Middle Ages, English towns came to look more like the towns of the Low Countries as they copied the Flemish fashion for using bricks. For lack of stone the Flemings had developed brick-making from the thirteenth century and the city of Bruges had its own brick kiln by 1331.[112] Flemish bricks were imported into England in large quantities (over 100,000 Flemish bricks were used in building the curtain wall at the Tower of London in the 1280s[113]) and Vanessa Harding's essay illustrates the continued import of Flemish bricks into the port of London. But a hundred years later bricks were no longer such a significant imported cargo. Bricks began to be manufactured locally in England (rather as cloth had been) and then the industry developed. The accounts of the Wardens of London Bridge record the purchase of bricks between 1404 and 1421 from a works at Deptford where craftsmen from Holland were employed.[114] Bricks were used extensively in major building works in the fifteenth century: at the royal palace at Sheen, at Eton College, Tattershall Castle, Crosby Hall and Lincoln's Inn and at the gatehouse of Lambeth Palace.[115] The style of these buildings remained distinctively English and Perpendicular but, unsurprisingly, they moved closer to the architectural environment of the towns of the Low Countries. Even those buildings which were still constructed in stone – for example the Guildhall and Leadenhall in London – look much like similar buildings to be found in Bruges.[116]

In a great many different ways, beyond the scope of these essays, Flemish institutions and customs can be seen to have influenced English practice. From 1382 innkeepers in Bruges were required to furnish the city government with lists of foreigners who had entered their hostelries, and a similar ruling was introduced in England by Parliamentary statute in 1390.[117] The craft guilds were organised for corporate action in the great towns of Bruges, Ypres and Ghent by the early years of the fourteenth century, perhaps a half century before such groups can be found acting together in a systematic way in London.[118] Moreover, six of the guilds of Ghent were already running almshouses for their poor and decayed members by 1373, but the first almshouses to be established in England and run by a guild were those of the Tailors of London endowed by the grocer, John Churchman, in the early fifteenth century.[119] The sexual mores in the Flemish towns, in particular Ghent and Bruges, were much more 'advanced' than in England: according to David Nicholas, 'women and men did what they pleased and generally went unpunished'.[120] Attitudes to sexual licence were never as relaxed as this in England (although they were certainly more relaxed than they were later in Protestant England), but they were sufficiently relaxed to allow Flemish women to run English brothels and to earn their living as prostitutes.[121] Oddly enough there was little hostility to Flemish women acting as prostitutes, but a great deal of hostility to Flemish men and women running brothels: for some reason it was thought to be preferable that these should be run by native Englishmen.[122]

In almost every manufacturing skill the men of the Low Countries led the way, in beer-brewing using hops, in cloth weaving and dyeing, in the manufacture of brass and latten, in techniques of oil-painting, in shipbuilding, brick-making, the manufacture of spectacles and surgical implements and in surveying, hydraulics and map making. But it is worth remembering that the introduction of the printing press in the towns of the Low Countries came only shortly before its arrival in England. Johannes Gutenberg began to print with moveable type in Mainz in about 1450 and by 1465 a printing press was established in Rome. By 1473 there were presses in Utrecht, Alost and Bruges, and three years later in 1476 William Caxton set up his press at Westminster. Because Caxton learnt to print in Bruges, it is possible that the role of the Low Countries in the introduction of printed books into England has been exaggerated. In 1480–81 as many as 900 books were imported into London by alien merchants, largely shipped in from the Low Countries.[123] But Dr Lotte Hellinga has demonstrated that of the surviving identifiable books owned in England or Scotland before 1500 (probably the more expensive printed books), over 40 per cent were printed in Italy, 31 per cent in Germany and only 11.6 per cent were printed in the Low Countries, although it is likely that most of the English-language books were printed in Bruges, Antwerp or Deventer.[124] The two most notable printers after Caxton were immigrants, but not from the Low Countries. Wynken de Worde came from the duchy of Lorraine and Richard Pynson from Normandy. The failure of the cities of the Low Countries to take the lead in the development of this new technology is, perhaps, symptomatic of their loss of economic pre-eminence.

When so much of English urban life in the fourteenth and fifteenth centuries appears to have been borrowed from, or influenced by, the Low Countries, it is perhaps worth noting those areas where the influence appears to have been minimal, or non-existent. The religious climate of late medieval Flanders as characterised by Toussaert is not one that is familiar to the student of the fifteenth-century Church in England.[125] In Flanders he characterises the higher clergy as French and often absentee, the local curates as poor and engaged in secular crafts to make ends meet, and the population largely indifferent to the moral teaching of the Church (hence the widespread sexual licence mentioned earlier).[126] If Toussaert is correct – and his picture has been questioned – it may have been this climate of religious apathy which provoked two important spiritual movements in the Low Countries: the Beguines in the thirteenth century and the *Devotio Moderna* in the second half of the fifteenth. Beguine communities flourished in the Low Countries and Germany for a century or so from 1220. They were predominantly groups of pious women who chose to live together in little 'towns within towns', which can still be seen in Bruges. It was the extreme mysticism of some of these women which finally brought the censure of the Church, although the purged

communities were allowed to continue under town control. Some of the
most famous female mystics and writers came from Low Countries:
Beatrice of Nazareth wrote in Flemish, Hadewijch came from Antwerp
and Marguerite Porete, who was burned for heresy in 1310, came from
Hainault.[127] Two female communities have, however, been identified in
mid-fifteenth-century Norwich which seem to resemble beguinages. In
them, small groups of women, known as sisters and dedicated to chastity,
lived together. One of the groups may have been founded by John Asgar, a
merchant from Bruges, who established himself in Norwich and became
mayor in 1426. As Norman Tanner suggests, 'it may well be that the
communities in Norwich had at least a tenuous link with the Low
Countries, the heart of the beguine movement'.[128] In many ways the
*Devotio Moderna* movement which was initiated by Geert Groote (d. 1384),
the son of a cloth merchant from Deventer in Holland in the 1370s, was
similar in its aims to that of the early Beguines. The adherents, who
formed themselves into Sisters – or Brothers – of the Common Life, hoped
to live a practical and devout life without the legal and formal structures of
monastic vows and orders. The most famous brother was Thomas à
Kempis (1380–1471) who wrote the *Imitatio Christi*. Both of these pious
movements were predominantly urban and they were widely successful in
the Low Countries, but neither movement seems, so far as we are yet able
to tell, to have attracted much support in England. The reasons for this
might be worth exploring.

There were, of course, many other differences. The greater
populations, greater wealth and sharp rivalry of the Flemish towns
produced much that was grander and finer than anything to be found in
London, their nearest English rival. There was nothing in London like
the guilds of rhetoricians in Bruges which performed plays, sang masses,
composed and read poetry.[129] Nor did English towns commission great
mural paintings such as the representation of the guild militias of Ghent
which once decorated the hospital there.[130] One cannot find in English
towns great free-standing belfries or towers such as that now attached to
the Cloth Hall at Bruges.[131] There is an ebullience and exaggeration
about these manifestations of urban pride which cannot be found in the
sober urban environments of late medieval England. But the similarities
between England and the Low Countries are more striking than the
differences. The trading links between the two countries continued
throughout the period in spite of wars, piracy, plague, urban violence,
floods and economic sanctions. The commercial interdependence of the
two areas led to a homogeneity in their culture and life styles. The
'doche' spoke a language which could be understood (as Laura Wright
demonstrates) – and ridiculed – in England. Large numbers of men and
women from Flanders, Holland and Zeeland settled in England and

reinforced the trading links between the areas. High-quality artefacts such as tapestries, paintings, monumental brasses and illuminated manuscripts found their way into England and enriched the culture of the aristocratic and mercantile elites. Likewise, lower down the social scale, there were few English households which did not have a Flemish knife or a brass pot or a cheap printed ABC.[132] For much of the period, and in many respects, England was the junior partner in this symbiotic relationship with the precocious industrial communities of the Low Countries, but these essays serve to illustrate the complexity and the importance of this partnership at every level.

## Notes

1    I am very grateful to Andrew Martindale, Nigel Saul, Jenny Stratford and Malcolm Vale, who all read drafts of this introduction and made many helpful corrections and improvements.

2    An excellent general introduction is provided by David Nicholas, *Medieval Flanders* (London and New York, 1992). There is no single work which deals with the relations between England and Flanders (or England and the Low Countries in general) in the period 1300–1500.

3    For the political and economic relations between England and Flanders, see E. Varenbergh, *Histoire des relations diplomatiques entre le comté de Flandre et l'Angleterre au Moyen Age* (Brussels, 1874). Varenbergh surveys the whole period from the eleventh century to 1500. For the ways in which Edward III and his successors, could manipulate the wool export trade to Flanders, see Herman van der Wee, 'Structural changes and specialization in the history of the Southern Netherlands 1100–1600', *Economic History Review*, 28 (1975), pp. 203–21, esp. 210.

4    See Henry Stephen Lucas, *The Low Countries and the Hundred Years War 1326–1347* (Ann Arbor, Michigan, 1929), pp. 52–72.

5    *Ibid*, p. 200.

6    *Ibid*, p. 239.

7    For the terms of this treaty, and its importance, see Varenbergh, pp. 333–7; Lucas, p. 362 *et seq*.

8    For a discussion of Edward's financial problems in Flanders in 1338–40, see E.B. Fryde, 'The Financial Resources of Edward III in the Netherlands', *Revue Belge de Philologie et d'Histoire (RBPH)*, 45 (1967), pp. 1142–216, esp 1175; also *idem, William de la Pole, Merchant and King's Banker* (London, 1988), esp. chap. 9.

9    Lucas, pp. 565–6.

10    *Ibid*, p. 592.

11    Malcolm G.A. Vale, 'The Anglo-French Wars 1294–1340: Allies and Alliances' in Philippe Contamine, Charles Giry-Deloison, Maurce H. Keen eds., *Guerre et Société en France, en Angleterre et en Bourgogne XIVe–XVe siècle* (Lille, 1991), p. 25.

12    Varenbergh, pp. 381–4.

13    For an analysis of the conflicting economic and political interests facing Louis de Mâle in the years 1363–79, with particular reference to Bruges, see David Nicholas, 'The English Trade at Bruges in the last years of Edward III', *Journal of Medieval History*, 5 (1979), pp. 23–61.

14   Varenbergh, pp. 398–400.

15   For a detailed discussion of the frantic, quadrangular negotiations between England, France, the Papcy and Louis de Male between 1361 and 1369, see J.J.N. Palmer, 'England, France, the Papacy and the Flemish succession', *Journal of Medieval History*, 2 (1976), pp. 339–74.

16   See Walter Prevenier, 'Les Perturbations dans les relations commerciales Anglo-Flamandes entre 1379 et 1407: causes de désaccord et raisons d'une reconciliation' in *Economies et Sociétés au Moyen Age: Mélanges offerts à Edouard Perroy* (Paris, Sorbonne, 1973), pp. 477–97.

17   Varenbergh, pp. 424–7; for an excellent analysis of the relations between England and Flanders in the opening years of the Papal schism, see E. Perroy, *L'Angleterre et le Grand Schisme d'Occident* (Paris, 1933), chapter 5.

18   See Margaret Aston, 'The Impeachment of Bishop Despenser', *BIHR*, 38 (1965), pp. 127–48.

19   Prevenier, p. 478.

20   *Ibid*, p. 479.

21   Nicholas, *Medieval Flanders*, p. 339.

22   For figures for cases brought by Flemings for restitution of goods confiscated at sea, see Prevenier, pp. 486–90; see also Nicholas, 'English Trade', pp. 34–45. In 1387 the earl of Arundel made a spectacularly successful series of raids on 'enemy' shipping, see L.C. Hector and Barbara F. Harvey eds., *The Westminster Chronicle 1381–94* (Oxford, 1982), pp. 350–53.

23   See the pie charts showing the proportion of the inhabitants engaged in different craft activities in Bruges, Ypres and Ghent, Walter Prevenier and Wim Blockmans, *The Burgundian Netherlands* (Cambridge, 1986), pp. 392 and 34.

24   In a petition of 1438 the men of the Low Countries complained to the English that, for lack of access to English wool, they were constrained to buy inferior Spanish and Scottish wools, John H. Munro, 'Bruges and the abortive staple in English cloth', *RBPH*, 44 (1966), pp. 1137–1159, esp. 1142. See also, *idem*, 'Monetary contraction and industrial change in the late medieval Low Countries', in N.J. Mayhew ed., *Coinage in the Low Countries* (British Archaeological Record, 1979), pp. 95–137, esp. pp. 119–21. From 1493 the Spaniards maintained a wool staple at Bruges, Munro, 'Bruges and the abortive staple', p. 1158.

25   Munro, 'Bruges and the abortive staple'; J.A. van Houtte, 'The Rise and Decline of the Market of Bruges', *Economic History Review*, 2nd series, 19 (1966), pp. 29–47.

26   For the Genoese galley trade with Southampton, see Alwyn A. Ruddock, *Italian Merchants and Shipping in Southampton 1270–1600* (Southampton, 1951), chapters 1 and 2; for the Florentine galley trade with Southampton and London and the important role played by Bruges in that trade, see W.B. Watson, 'The structure of the Florentine galley trade with Flanders and England in the fifteenth century', *RBPH*, 39 (1961), pp. 1073–91; 40 (1962), pp. 317–47; from 1397 Venetian galleys began to come directly to London, Helen Bradley, 'The Italian Community in London *c*. 1350–*c*. 1450' (London PhD thesis, 1992), chapter 2 and appendix 5.

27   The classic study of the Italian merchant bankers, pawnbrokers and moneychangers is to be found in Raymond de Roover, *Money, Banking and Credit in Medieval Bruges* (Cambridge, Mass., 1948).

28   For the tortuous steps leading up this agreement, see Prevenier, pp. 480–81, 493–7; for the terms of the treaty, see Varenbergh, pp. 497–9, 548–73; see also M.-R. Thielemans, *Bourgogne et Angleterre: relations politiques et économiques entre les Pays Bas Bourguignons et l'Angleterre 1435–1467* (Brussels, 1966), p. 57 and n. 51.

29   Prevenier, p. 481.

30   See Jenny Stratford, *The Bedford Inventories: The Worldly Goods of John, Duke of Bedford,*

*Regent of France (1389–1435)* (The Society of Antiquaries, 1993), pp. 7–8, 380–81; C.A.J. Armstrong, 'The Golden Age of Burgundy: dukes that outdid kings', in A.G. Dickens ed., *The Courts of Europe: Politics, Patronage and Royalty 1400–1800* (London, 1977), pp. 55–75, esp. 55; also *idem*, 'La Double Monarchie France-Angleterre et la Maison de Bourgogne 1420–1800', in *England, France and Burgundy in the Fifteenth Century* (London, 1983), pp. 343–74.

31   Stratford, pp. 9–10; K.H. Vickers, *Humphrey duke of Gloucester* (London, 1907), pp. 91–6, 125–70, 202–4. Vickers was distressed by, and critical of, Gloucester's self-interested and callous treatment of Jacqueline.

32   John H. Munro, *Wool, Cloth and Gold: the Struggle for Bullion in Anglo-Burgundian Trade* (Brussels, 1973), pp. 67–8.

33   *Ibid*, pp. 84–92; T.H. Lloyd, *The English Wool Trade in the Middle Ages* (Cambridge, 1977), pp. 257–61; Peter Spufford, *Monetary Problems and Policies in the Burgundian Netherlands 1433–1496* (Leiden, 1970), pp. 98–100; for the impact of the credit restrictions on English merchants, see Wendy Childs, '"To oure losse and hindraunce": English Credit to Alien Merchants in the Mid-Fifteenth Century', in Jennifer Kermode, ed., *Enterprise and Individuals in Fifteenth-Century England* (Stroud, 1991), pp. 68–98, and Pamela Nightingale, 'Monetary contraction and mercantile credit in later medieval England', *Econ. Hist. Rev.*, second series, 43 (1990), pp. 560–75.

34   Spufford, *Monetary Problems*, pp. 3–8; Munro, *Wool, Cloth and Gold*, pp. 101–2.

35   Thielemans, pp. 56–61; Munro points out that although this ban was 'protectionist', its concern was also to improve the flow of bullion to the Burgundian mints, a flow which had dried up since the Calais ordinances of 1429, *Wool, Cloth and Gold*, pp. 93–109.

36   The price of Philip's allegiance was the formal cession of the Somme towns in Picardy (including Boulogne and Ponthieu) by the French king, see David Potter, *War and Government in the French Provinces, Picardy 1470–1560* (Cambridge, 1993), chapter 1. It was the consistent policy of the French kings, but especially Louis XI, to repossess the Picardy towns and to prevent them from falling within the Hapsburg sphere of influence.

37   Thielemans, pp. 80–9; on the problems of the coinage, see Peter Spufford, 'The Burgundian Netherlands', in Alain Arnould and Jean Michel Massing, *Splendours of Flanders* (Cambridge, 1993), pp. 221–3.

38   Thielemans, pp. 90–107; Munro, *Wool, Cloth and Gold*, p. 114; for Philip's elaborate, but unsuccessful, preparations, see Monique Somme, 'L'armée Bourguignonne au siège de Calais de 1436', in *Guerre et Société*, pp. 197–219.

39   Thielemans, pp. 129–33; for the terms of the treaty, *ibid*, pp. 443–53; Munro, *Wool, Cloth and Gold*, pp. 114–118.

40   Thielemans, p. 133; Munro notes that Philip promulgated bans on English cloth in 1434–9, 1447–52, 1461–7, 'Bruges and the abortive staple', p. 1141.

41   For the adverse effect of the 1429 Calais ordinances and, in 1435, the war with Burgundy, see E.M. Carus-Wilson and Olive Coleman, *England's Export Trade 1275–1547* (Oxford, 1963), p. 123; also Lloyd, *Wool Trade*, p. 263 *et seq*.

42   Nicholas, pp. 387–389; Munro, *Wool, Cloth and Gold*, chapters 5 and 6.

43   *Rotuli Parliamentorum*, 5, pp. 565–8; *Statutes of the Realm*, 1 pp. 411–413; Thielemans, p. 414 and n. 264.

44   Nicholas, p. 388.

45   Thielemans, pp. 421–24.

46   Between 1440 and 1480 Antwerp's share of the total English cloth export rose to 35–40%, which meant, as Munro says, that 'Flemish protectionism had killed Bruges', 'Bruges and the abortive staple', pp. 1143–1444. In the first half of the sixteenth century, England exported 130,000 cloths to Antwerp annually.

47    Munro, *Wool, Cloth and Gold*, pp. 175–6. For the links between England and
      Burgundy under the Yorkists, see S. Thurley, *The Royal Palaces of Tudor England* (New
      Haven and London, 1993) pp. 15–18.

48    Munro discusses the final attempts by Bruges to persuade the foreign merchant
      communities to return, 'Bruges and the abortive staple, 1147–1159'. The ban on
      English cloth was finally lifted in 1489, but this was too late to save Bruges.

49    For an excellent discussion of the metal-working industries in the Low Countries, see
      Spufford in *Splendours of Flanders*, p. 6.

50    Nicholas, p. 266; the population of Picardy (especially Amiens) seems to have dropped
      dramatically in the late fourteenth and early fifteenth centuries; the average number of
      households fell from 100 per parish in 1328 to 30 in 1469, Potter, *Picardy*, pp. 22–3.

51    Nicholas, pp. 305–7, 368; for a map showing the density of population in the Low
      countries at the end of the fifteenth century, see Prevenier and Blockmans, *Burgundian
      Netherlands*, p. 391. Flanders and Holland had more than 60 inhabitants per square
      kilometre; Brabant and Holland had 39–58 per square kilometre.

52    Nicholas, pp. 292–5; much grain was produced in Picardy, Potter, *Picardy*, p. 23.

53    Nicholas, p. 288; the most important coal mines in Europe, however, were at Liège,
      Spufford in *Splendours of Flanders*, p. 6.

54    Whereas in 1420–21 a great variety of miscellaneous manufactured goods had been
      exported from London (e.g., metal and leather goods), by 1480–81 the trade was
      reversed. Cloth completely dominated the export trade of London, and to pay for the
      cloth, alien merchants imported raw materials, linen in vast quantities and kitchen
      ware and armour, see H.S. Cobb, ed., *The Overseas Trade of London Exchequer Customs
      Accounts 1480–81* (London Record Society, 1990), xxxiv–vi. For the influence of
      Dutch on English beer-brewing terminology, see Laura Wright, ch. 8.

55    de Roover argues that there existed in Bruges 'around 1400 a well-developed and
      organised money market, sensitive to changes in business conditions and monetary
      policy', *The Bruges Money Market around 1400* (Brussels, 1968), p. 76.

56    Watson, 'Florentine Galley Trade', pp. 1081–5; 322–7; for an analysis of why Antwerp
      supplanted Bruges, see Munro, 'Bruges and the abortive staple'; for the cultural
      importance of Bruges, see Spufford in *Splendours of Flanders*, pp. 8–9.

57    Nicholas, pp. 268–73, esp. 269. See also R. Van Uytven, 'Splendour or wealth: art and
      economy in the Burgundian Netherlands', in *Trans. Cambridge Bibliographical Society*,
      10 (1992), pp. 101–24 esp. 102.

58    *Ibid*, pp. 367–370; on the poverty and decline of Ypres, see Munro, 'Bruges and the
      abortive staple', p. 1147.

59    Nicholas, pp. 312–13. The economic problems of the Flemish towns may have been
      partly aggravated by the damage inflicted by the Ghent war of 1451–3.

60    For turbulent times in London, see Ruth Bird, *The Turbulent London of Richard II*
      (London, New York, Toronto, 1949); A.J. Prescott, 'The accusations against Thomas
      Austin', in P. Strohm, *Hochon's Arrow* (Princeton, 1992), pp. 161–77; Caroline M.
      Barron, 'Ralph Holland and the London radicals, 1438–1444', in Richard Holt and
      Gervase Rosser eds., *The Medieval Town 1200–1540* (London, 1990), pp. 160–83;
      Isobel M.W. Harvey, *Jack Cade's Rebellion of 1450* (Oxford, 1991).

61    For a study of the 'gentrification' of two successful London merchants, Adam
      Fr3nceys and John Pyel, see Stephen J. O'Connor, *A Calendar of the Cartularies of
      Adam Frauncys and John Pyel* (Camden Soc. 5th series, ii, 1993), Introduction.

62    Nicholas, pp. 339, 374–5.

63    *Ibid*, pp. 328–32.

64    Christopher Dyer, *Standards of Living in the Later Middle Ages* (Cambridge, 1989), esp.
      chapters 6–8.

65    Henri-E. de Sagher, 'L'immigration des tisserands Flamands et Brabaçons en

Angleterre sous Edouard III', in *Mélanges d'Histoire offerts à Henri Pirenne 1881–1926* (Brussels, 1926), pp. 109–26. De Sagher argues that there were immigrants from Flanders, but that they were not skilled artisans and did not contribute to the development of the English cloth industry. T.H. Lloyd discusses the various charters of privileges granted to merchants of the towns of the Low Countries, e.g. Ypres (1232), St Omer (1255), Ghent (1259), Bruges (1260), Douai (1260), *Alien Merchants in England in the High Middle Ages* (Brighton, 1982), p. 107.

66    e.g. in 1355, R.R. Sharpe ed., *Letter Book G* (London, 1905), p. 42.

67    *Ibid*, p. 265 (1370); H.T. Riley, *Memorials of London and London Life* (London, 1868), pp. 345–6.

68    All the chronicle accounts of the Revolt in London mention the massacre of the Flemings, see R.B. Dobson, *The Peasants' Revolt of 1381* (2nd edn. 1983), part 3.

69    P.M. Tillot ed., *The History of Yorkshire: the City of York* (Victoria County History, Oxford, 1961), p. 108; Derek Keene, *Survey of Medieval Winchester* (Oxford, 1985), vol. i, pp. 380–84.

70    Sylvia Thrupp, 'Aliens in and around London in the Fifteenth Century', in A.E.J. Hollaender and William Kellaway eds., *Studies in London History presented to Philip Edmund Jones* (London, 1969), pp. 251–72, esp. 259; see also *idem*, 'The Alien Population of England in 1440', *Speculum*, 32 (1957), pp. 262–73.

71    Gervase Rosser, *Medieval Westminster 1200–1540* (Oxford, 1989), p. 193.

72    Martha Carlin, *Medieval Southwark* (London, 1994), forthcoming, chapter 6.

73    Thielemans, pp. 548–9.

74    *Ibid*, p. 551.

75    *Ibid*, pp. 554–5. In Southwark in the mid-fifteenth century, the predominant 'doche' crafts were tailoring, goldsmithing, cordwaining and haberdashery, Carlin, *op. cit*.

76    See below, ch. 8.

77    George D. Painter, *William Caxton* (London, 1976), pp. 23–24; Nicholas, pp. 304–305; Nicholas, 'English Trade', pp. 24–5.

78    E. Carus-Wilson, 'The origins and early development of the Merchant Adventurers' organization in London as shown in their own medieval records', in *Medieval Merchant Venturers* (London, 1954), pp. 143–82.

79    W. Butler-Bowden ed., *The Book of Margery Kempe* (Oxford, 1954), pp. 129–132.

80    King Stephen married Mathilda, daughter of Eustace III, count of Boulogne in *c.* 1125.

81    For Manny see *Dictionary of National Biography*; J. Venn, *Biographical History of Gonville and Caius College,* iii (1901), p. 3; D. Knowles and W.F. Grimes, *Charterhouse* (London, 1954), pp. 5–8. At about the same time, Philip the Bold (d. 1404) founded the Charterhouse at Dijon where he is buried. Manny was one of five men from the Low Countries who became Knights of the Garter in the reign of Edward III. Richard II made two counts of Holland and one duke of Guelders Knights of the Garter in the 1390s, but the custom lapsed in the fifteenth century. Duke Philip the Good was nominated in 1422, but he was never installed. Duke Charles the Bold became a Knight of the Garter in 1468 when he married Margaret of York. I am grateful for this information to Hugh Collins, who is completing an Oxford DPhil on the Order of the Garter.

82    J.J.N. Palmer ed., *Froissart: Historian* (Woodbridge, Suffolk, 1981); see also M. Galway, 'Froissart in England', *University of Birmingham Historical Journal*, 7 (1959–60), pp. 18–35. Andrew Wathey notes the presence of Mattheus de Sancto Johanne (Mayshuet) as a clerk in the chapel of Queen Philippa, see below, ch. 1.

83    For Katherine, see Anthony Goodman, *John of Gaunt* (London, 1992), pp. 361–4 and refs. there cited; Derek Pearsall, *The Life of Geoffrey Chaucer* (Oxford, 1992), pp. 49–51.

84   For Margaret of York, see Christine Weightman, *Margaret of York, Duchess of Burgundy 1446–1503* (Alan Sutton, 1989). For Jacquetta of Luxembourg's subsequent career, see below, ch. 5.

85   The detailed works of Varenbergh, Lucas and Thielemans cited above, demonstrate the continuous exchange of diplomatic embassies between the English king and the rulers of the Low Countries throughout this period.

86   See, for example, the crown which Margaret of York took with her on her marriage to duke Charles the Bold in 1468, illustrated in Prevenier and Blockmans, *Burgundian Netherlands*, p. 361.

87   See below, ch. 3.

88   Nicholas, pp. 254–5, 351–4; Reinhard Strohm, *Music in Late Medieval Bruges* (rev. edn. Oxford, 1990), esp. chapter 5.

89   Lucas, p. 364; Reinhard Strohm, pp. 18, 79–85. When Louis XI retook Amiens he was ceremonially received there in 1464, Potter, *Picardy*, p. 8.

90   E.M. Thompson ed., *Chronicon Angliae* (Rolls Series, 64, 1874), pp. 153–6.

91   For the development of this idea, see Caroline M. Barron, 'Richard II and London', A. Goodman (ed.) in *Richard II: Power and Perogative* (Oxford, 1995) forthcoming. In 1440 Philip the Good demanded a similar 'joyous entry' of reconciliation, from Bruges, see Reinhard Strohm, pp. 80–83.

92   Johnston draws attention to the pageant welcome provided by the city of York for Richard III in 1483, below, ch. 4.

93   Nicholas, pp. 254–5; Juliet Vale, *Edward III and Chivalry: Chivalric Society and its Context 1270–1350* (Woodbridge, Suffolk, 1982), chapter 2; Reinhard Strohm, p. 69.

94   For the great Smithfield tournament of 1390, see Sheila Lindenbaum, 'The Smithfield Tournament of 1390', *Journal of Medieval and Renaissance Studies*, 20 (1990), pp. 1–20.

95   Juliet Vale, Appendix 12.

96   See, for example, the exchange of musical talent between the English and the Burgundian courts, Reinhard Strohm, pp. 77–79.

97   There survive at least 200 liturgical manuscripts produced in the Low Countries for the English market, see Nicholas Rogers, 'The Miniature of St John the Baptist in Gonville and Caius College MS 241/127 and its context', *Trans. Cambridge Bibliographical Society*, 10 (1992), pp. 125–38, esp. 125. See also Edmund Colledge, 'South Netherlands Books of Hours made for England', *Scriptorium*, 32 (1978), pp. 55–7.

98   High quality Flemish brasses, probably from Tournai, were imported into England in the fourteenth century: the latest surviving Flemish brass in England is that of Robert Thornton, mayor of Newcastle-on-Tyne, who died in 1429, but commissioned his own brass in the 1420s, see H.K. Cameron, 'The fourteenth-century school of Flemish brasses', *Trans. Mon. Brass Soc.,* 11 (1970), pp. 50–81; *idem*, 'Fourteenth-century Flemish brasses to Ecclesiastics in English churches', *ibidem*, 13 (1980), pp. 3–24; *idem*, 'The Fourteenth-century Flemish brasses at King's Lynn', *Archaeological Journal*, 136 (1979), pp. 151–72; *idem*, 'Flemish brasses to Civilians in England', *ibidem*, 139 (1982), pp. 420–40.

99   Armstrong draws attention to several English commissions of paintings in the later fifteenth century such as by Edward Grymstone who, while on a mission to Burgundy, had his portrait painted by Petrus Christus in 1446 or 1449, 'Golden Age', p. 56.

100  See below, ch. 6.

101  Many of the windows in grand English buildings (e.g. Eton and King's College, Cambridge) were filled with grisáille glass imported from Flanders or the Rhineland, and often put in place by Flemish craftsmen. Barnard Flower, a Fleming, was the King's Glazier from 1505–17 and received £24 p.a., Richard Marks, 'Window Glass',

in John Blair and Nigel Ramsay eds., *English Medieval Industries* (London, 1991), pp. 265–94, esp. 279, 281.

102  See below, ch. 5.

103  Geoffrey Agnew has suggested that the two panels are the work of Colijn de Coter of Brussels (d. 1506), see Government of Malta and Council of Europe eds., *The Order of St John in Malta* (Valetta, 1970), pp. 255–6.

104  John Durham, *A Short History of All Hallows by-the-Tower* (privately printed, 1955, rev. edn. 1976), no pagination.

105  K.B. McFarlane, *Hans Memling* (Oxford, 1971), part i. Two panels of a diptych, showing the Annunciation, were painted *c.* 1480 for Abbot Fascet of Westminster (1498–1500), now in a private collection, see Pamela Tudor Craig, *Richard III* (National Portrait Gallery, London, 1973).

106  Andrew Martindale, 'The Ashwellthorpe Triptych', in D.T. Williams ed., *Early Tudor England: Proceedings of the 1987 Harlaxton Symposium* (Woodbridge, 1989), pp. 107–23.

107  For Flemish painters and craftsmen at the court of Henry VII, see Gordon Kipling, *The Triumph of Honour: Burgundian Origins of the Elizabethan Renaissance* (Leiden, 1977), esp. chapter 3.

108  For the most recent discussion of Gilbert Prince as a possible artist of the Wilton Diptych, see Dillian Gordon, *Making and Meaning: The Wilton Diptych* (National Gallery, London, 1993), pp. 72–3.

109  M. Le Chanoine Dehaisnes, *Documents et extraits divers concernant L'Histoire de L'Art dans la Flandre, L'Artois et le Hainault avant le XVe Siecle* (Lille, 1886), pp. 621, 636, 678. Broederlam, like other painters, also decorated furniture, see Penelope Eames, *Furniture in England, France and the Netherlands from the 12c to the 15c, Furniture History*, 13 (1977), pp. 243–4.

110  Nicholas, pp. 350–51; Prevenier and Blockmans, *Burgundian Netherlands*, p. 316; see also below, ch. 6.

111  Nicholas, p. 350.

112  *Ibid*, p. 149.

113  John Schofield, *The Building of London from the Conquest to the Great Fire* (London, 1984), p. 126; Nicholas J. Moore, 'Brick', in Blair and Ramsey, *Medieval Industries*, pp. 211–36, esp. 214–16.

114  Schofield, p. 126.

115  Vale points out, however, that whereas the church of Our Lady, the Gruthuyse mansion and the passage which linked the two, were all built of brick, Edward IV's chapel and oratory at Windsor were built of stone, see below, ch. 5.

116  Caroline M. Barron, *The Medieval Guildhall of London* (London, 1974); Mark Samuel, 'The Fifteenth-Century Garner at Leadenhall', *The Antiquaries Journal* 69 (1989), pp. 119–53.

117  Nicholas, p. 297.

118  Nicholas, p. 202; George Unwin, *The Guilds and Companies of London* (London, 1908), esp. chaps. 4 and 5; Elspeth Veale, ' "The Great Twelve": mistery and fraternity in thirteenth-century London', *Historical Research*, 64 (1991), pp. 237–63.

119  Nicholas, pp. 269–70.

120  Nicholas, p. 315.

121  Ruth Mazo Karras, 'The Regulation of Brothels in Later Medieval England', *Signs*, 14 (1989), pp. 399–433.

122  *Ibid*, pp. 415–16.

123  Cobb, *Overseas Trade*, xxxvi; Elizabeth Armstrong, 'English purchases of printed books from the Continent 1465–1526', *English Historical Review*, 94 (1979), pp. 268–90, points out that printed books appear in the London customs accounts from 1477; many were service books and books of hours printed for the English market.

Armstrong also notes the growing importance of France as a source for printed material in England and the consequent decline in the trade with Italy.

124   Lotte Hellinga, 'Importation of Books Printed on the Continent into England and Scotland before c. 1520', in Sandra Hindman ed., *Printing the Written Word: the Social History of Books c.1451–1520* (Ithaca and London, 1991), pp. 205–24.

125   J. Toussaert, *Le Sentiment religieux en Flandre a la fin du Moyen Age* (Paris, 1960), *passim*. The conclusion provides a hectoring synthesis of his pessimistic view of the role of the Church in promoting Christian attitudes in fourteenth- and fifteenth-century Flanders, pp. 585–606.

126   Nicholas, pp. 354–6.

127   Ernest W. McDonnell, *The Beguines and Beghards in Medieval Culture* (New Brunswick, 1954); Elizabeth Alvida Petroff, *Medieval Women's Visionary Literature* (New York and Oxford, 1986), chapters 4 and 7.

128   Norman P. Tanner, *The Church in Late Medieval Norwich 1370–1532* (Pontifical Institute of Medieval Studies, Toronto, 1984), pp. 64–6, esp. 65.

129   Reinhard Strohm, pp. 68–70, where the involvement of the Gruthuyse family is described. For the short-lived London Puy in the early fourteenth century, see Anne F. Sutton, 'Merchants, Music and Social Harmony: the London Puy and its French and London Contexts, circa 1300', *London Journal*, 17 (1992), pp. 1–17.

130   Nicholas, p. 256.

131   *Ibid*, p. 257.

132   See Vanessa Harding, below, ch. 7.

# 1

# John of Gaunt, John Pycard and the Amiens Negotiations of 1392

Andrew Wathey

*Royal Holloway College, University of London*

The years between 1389 and 1394 witnessed a continuous stream of diplomatic meetings between England and France in search of peace.[1] The agreement of a three-year truce at Leulinghen in May 1389 heralded Richard II's commitment to a lasting resolution of the conflict. A short meeting in 1390 and a series of larger conferences, at which John of Gaunt, Duke of Lancaster was appointed chief English representative, resulted in successive renewals of the truce. These discussions also laid the foundations of a more permanent settlement, finally reached in 1396 and embodied in agreements for a twenty-eight-year truce and in the marriage of Richard II and Isabella, daughter of Charles VI. At all of the larger meetings, at Amiens in 1392 and Leulinghen in 1393 and 1394, diplomacy was pursued through direct discussion between Plantagenet and Valois princes. This practice provided an important vehicle for display, which ensured the presence of musicians serving at the courts of the principals, and, through the close proximity in which the negotiations were conducted, facilitated contacts between them. In Gaunt's case, the heightened importance given to ostentation also gave rise to a more lasting contact between English and French musicians, marked by a striking instance of cultural assimilation. In what follows I aim to trace the political background to this case and to comment on its consequences for the surviving English repertories of the early fifteenth century.

By contrast with periods of diplomatic activity earlier in the century, the conferences of the 1390s were narrowly focused in subject matter. Two central issues dominated proceedings: the geographic limits of the duchy of Aquitaine, shifted and blurred by French gains in the 1370s, and the long-disputed homage that the king of England, as duke of Aquitaine, owed to the French sovereign for the duchy, which was still subject to the full appellate jurisdiction of the French crown.[2] Consideration of these issues was overshadowed by the Treaty of Brétigny, concluded by Edward III in 1360, which set generous boundaries to the territory, while affording some latitude in the performance of feudal services. It was also influenced by the life grant of Aquitaine made to John of Gaunt on the eve of the first meeting at Leulinghen, which both linked the two central points in the debate and invested the duke with a personal stake in its outcome. The terms of the grant, confirmed in 1392, and again in 1394 and 1397, make clear that Gaunt, formerly royal lieutenant in Aquitaine, would hold the duchy from, and owe homage to, Richard II as king of France. From the standpoint of the English crown, therefore, the grant established a means by which Richard could avoid the personal homage due to Charles VI, even if French sovereignty were ultimately conceded. Gaunt's own position is harder to assess: it may well be that he was drawn by the promise of an appanage for his illegitimate offspring the Beauforts, although at no time was he granted the duchy in perpetuity. Of more immediate concern perhaps was the confirmation, implicit in the grant, of the major role intended for the duke in English foreign policy even before his return to England in October 1389. The grant established a clear continuity between Gaunt's past standing and ambitions in Europe, as 'a European prince with pretensions to a throne of his own',[3] and those to which he could look forward in the future. Taken together with his appointment as royal lieutenant in Picardy, it also shouldered him with the rights and duties of the English kingship in its remaining Continental dominions. The ceremonial needs entailed by Gaunt's position were in themselves considerable. But it can be argued that they were made more urgent by the visible connexion between his tenure of the duchy and the issues under discussion with the French. The projection of an image of personal magnificence cast in the mould of kingly values was crucial to Gaunt's credibility as the legitimate substitute for the English king in rendering homage for Aquitaine. In the context of the negotiations, ceremonial and other forms of display could similarly be used to emphasize the duke's standing as the rightful heir to his father's territorial settlements. In addition, the convincing representation of ducal magnificence, important in domestic English politics, also remained a necessity abroad as Gaunt later sought to vindicate his position in the duchy and to re-establish his authority following the Gascon revolt of 1394–5.

The conference held at Amiens in March and April 1392 was organized as a meeting between rulers, and in terms of display was probably the most demanding of the three major embassies in which Gaunt was personally involved. Both Charles VI and the duke made solemn entries into Amiens on 25 March (respectively during and after *diner*), the former accompanied by the king of Armenia, the royal uncles and all of the princes of the blood.[4] Gaunt's official reception into the court of the French king followed, with formal embraces, mutual professions of fraternity and offerings of spice and wine. On the next day a dinner was held at which the duke and Walter Skirlaw, bishop of Durham were seated in the places of honour; subsidiary positions were accorded to John Holland, Earl of Huntingdon and Edward, Earl of Rutland, respectively Gaunt's son-in-law and nephew, paralleling and symbolizing those taken by the dukes of Bourbon and Touraine as Charles VI's supporters. A series of small occasions followed, interspersed between diplomatic discussions, at which both the English and French parties received gifts of wine from the town.[5] The costs of these festivities were substantial: Louis, Duke of Touraine alone apparently received the greater part of 30,000 fr. from Charles VI to meet his expenses at Amiens, and all of the major French participants spent heavily on jewels and plate.[6] Some of the items purchased were clearly designed as presents, reciprocating those made by the English in the course of the formal ceremonies.[7] But several were equally clearly intended for the French princes' own use, and to intensify the splendour of the French party as a whole. The king in particular appears to have taken a leading role in their provision. Several items not normally part of the household baggage, among which a 'grand carrik d'argent' took pride of place, were fetched for use at Amiens from the royal treasury at Paris immediately before the opening of the negotiations. Charles also made gifts – particularly of plate – to his brother and uncles, and lent them precious objects, including a doublet decorated with pearls and fleurs-de-lis in gold which was returned by the duke of Touraine to the royal *argentier* in the following December.[8]

The French party made extensive preparations for the negotiations at Amiens. Billets were selected for the English party, and shields bearing the arms of individual nobles were placed on their doors.[9] Repairs were made to the fortress, and a night watch drawn from the town waits mounted to 'corner pour les perilz des feux'.[10] The duke of Burgundy was solemnly despatched from the king's presence at Corbie at the head of a delegation to receive Gaunt *en route* from Calais. And in the fortnight preceding the negotiations, Charles twice visited the Abbey of Saint-Denis, possibly as part of a programme of display designed to enhance the public perception of royal splendour. It may well be, as the monk of Saint-Denis remarked, that the English sought to disrupt the public reception of some of the French ceremonial, dressing simply, 'vel quia Francorum statum parvipendebant pomposum'.[11] Yet there is little doubt that Gaunt's entourage (said by the monk to number over a thousand) both engaged in the ritual of the more formal encounters, and engineered side-shows of its own, outside the main arena of the negotiations but intended for French eyes nonetheless. An occasion on 9 April, when the duke presented the Cathedral Chapter at Amiens with a 'chief d'or' to cover their reliquary containing the head of St John the Baptist, provides a case in point.[12] This gift, made 'pour lonneur de dieu et decoracion dicelle eglise', not only marked out the duke's veneration

1a (above) and 1b (opposite)   London, British Library, Additional MS 57950 (the Old Hall Manuscript), fols. 21ᵛ–22. Pycard, three- (possibly four-)voice canonic *Gloria*.

of a favourite saint but also laid claim to local loyalties through a timely
intervention in the chapter's dispute with their bishop.[13] The significance
of this event, with its hints at local clientage associated with Gaunt's
position, was not lost on the French: Charles stepped in as the chapter's
rightful protector a few months later.

In addition, informal exchanges and meetings more social than
diplomatic in character played a significant role in creating opportunities
for display at the Amiens conference, no less than at the other major
meetings in this series. As royal and ducal *dieta* records make clear, the
English representatives, their knights and senior gentry were accorded a
ready reception within the social *milieux* of the French courts, at meals and
for other events.[14] Such encounters, running parallel to the main series of
the negotiations, doubtless also resulted on a smaller scale when, during
preparations at Amiens for the marriage of Richard II and Isabella in 1396,
English and French esquires were lodged in the same billets.[15] But a pattern
of informal sociability on the fringes of diplomatic meetings, offering a
range of opportunities for conspicuous display, was probably almost
inevitable, particularly in the days or weeks bordering the main event: as
royal and ducal itineraries reveal, major meetings often saw even the
principals waiting for an important individual to arrive.

John of Gaunt's involvement in the diplomatic conferences of the early
1390s presents a range of potential situations in which contacts between
English and French musicians may have taken place. It is likely that the
ducal minstrels were present for all of these meetings, and with those in the
service of the other principal negotiators took a prominent role in
processions as players of wind instruments, as the monk of Saint-Denis
records. They were also paid for performing at the great secular feasts and
on other occasions.[16] Rewards and gifts to minstrels, from the French royal
dukes in particular, abound during these meetings, and may have been
made not only for playing and for dancing, but also for the smaller tasks of
diplomacy, the carriage of letters and messages.[17] More important,
however, are the chaplains and clerks of royal and ducal household chapels,
both for their involvement with repertoires of written polyphonic music,
and for their potential as agents in its transmission. The entourage of John
of Gaunt at Amiens in 1392 included the clerks of his chapel, some of
whom were probably also present later at the Leulinghen conferences of
1393 and 1394. Other comparable establishments present at these meetings
include the chapels of Charles VI, and the dukes of Berry and Burgundy.[18]
At the major ritual and liturgical events, where the image of the kingship
was on public display, members of these chapels were highly visible, as a
uniformed clerical corps in processions, and occasionally as officiants at
mass. These occasions also emerge as important venues for the
performance of celebratory polyphony; both here and in more private and

sociable settings, where clerks and, occasionally, chamber valets may have sung secular polyphony, there were opportunities for exposure to the musical cultures of other establishments.

By far the most important source of musical contacts deriving from Gaunt's diplomatic activity, however, lies in the recruitment of five French singers as clerks for his household chapel: Jehan Houseau, Pierre de Harcomonte, Ivo de Bonefoy, Jacob Musserey, and a Jehan Pycard, *alias* Vaux. Most of this group, variously styled 'francoys' and 'alienigenis', were engaged in 1390 or 1391, when both Gaunt's chapel and the household that it served peaked in size.[19] A further singer, Lawrence de Dyeppe, was recruited in the course of the Amiens negotiations in 1392 (at either Amiens or Calais), probably to replace Ivo de Bonefoy, who took this opportunity to quit the duke's service. The remaining clerks, however, appear to have served Gaunt continuously into the late 1390s, when the duke withdrew into relative retirement and abandoned his overseas interests. In a general sense, therefore, their presence served to enhance the cosmopolitan aura surrounding the duke's following at the diplomatic meetings, and to underline the European dimension of his political interests. More specifically, they enable the duke's entourage to meet special ceremonial needs arising out of his diplomatic role, and to contribute to the dialogue of display on a footing comparable to that of the French principals attending these negotiations. The recruitment of these clerks can thus be viewed in the same light as other shifts in the composition of Gaunt's entourage: as a response to changing personal needs and circumstances.[20] With the sale of Gaunt's interest in the Castilian throne, the retaining policies of the 1370s and 1380s, geared to supplying the duke with experienced war captains and sheer military manpower, gave way to a different set of demands at home. New patterns of service to the duke in the 1390s most notably reflected his need for personal security and the desire to lay a secure foundation for the following of his eldest son. But they were also intended to support his new role abroad, to underpin his administration in Aquitaine, and to lend credence to his leading position in diplomacy with France.

The most influential results of the clerks' employment within the duke's chapel arose from their sustained proximity with English musicians while serving in England, and the opportunity which this gave them to absorb the liturgical and musical practices of their native counterparts. The detail of this process is inevitably lost, but two important conclusions about the larger patterns in their activities can be drawn from the day-rolls of the duke's household.[21] First, the clerks were seldom absent from the main household while in England, either singly or as a group. As individuals they lacked the private interests in the localities that took English members of the chapel away from the duke's domestic establishment, and it may also be that they regarded its physical setting as a necessary protection against the native population.[22] These singers' close adherence to the household, constituting a pattern of almost permanent service at Gaunt's residence at Hertford, also points to the continuous availability of their musical abilities, and thus to the extent of their potential participation in domestic festivities. Their presence is also at one with Gaunt's massive building programme at Hertford during these years.[23] The second conclusion is that Gaunt's French clerks appear to have been used with discretion at major public events in England, particularly in the period preceding the Amiens negotiations. The French members of the chapel, unlike the duke's minstrels, were taken neither to the parliament that sat at Westminster between 3 November and 2 December 1391, nor to the great council of 12–15 February 1392. It is likely, however, that they were present with the duke and the rest of the household for a ceremony at Westminster Abbey on 18 December 1393, which may have run into royal festivities for Christmas. Their primary opportunities for contacts with English musicians thus lay in Lancastrian and royal circles. As a gift of robes made by Henry, Earl of Derby to two of the clerks shortly before their departure for Amiens reveals, these contacts also provided additional sources of patronage.[24]

It is possible to identify a shift in the French clerks' social standing during the period of their service with the duke. The conditions under which they served during the early 1390s broadly reflected their status as aliens. By contrast with the native English members of the chapel, whose annual fees were frequently assigned on the revenues of local estate officials, the French clerks were paid directly by the duke's receiver general, and received daily wages at lower rates.[25] In the later years of the decade, however, they appear to have become more fully assimilated within the career structures of the household, taking fees and daily wages on a par with the other clerks. Individual French clerks also secured ecclesiastical preferments in England under Gaunt's patronage, and on one occasion one of them acted as the proctor of a native member of the chapel.[26] This shift in status gave them access to networks of connexion and advantage, both within and outside the Lancastrian court, comparable to those frequented by their English colleagues. It may also bespeak a closer integration between their professional and musical activities and those of the chapel as a whole, and possibly greater influence over and assimilation within its services and musical practices.

What lasting results did these contacts produce? In the Old Hall manuscript, and in a fragment at the Shakespeare Birthplace Trust in Stratford-upon-Avon, a total of eight pieces survive ascribed to 'Pycard' or 'Picart', all polyphonic settings of sections of the mass ordinary.[27] As Margaret Bent demonstrates in a recent study, all of Pycard's works make

1c   London, British Library. Additional MS 57950 (the Old Hall Manuscript), fol. 100ᵛ. Pycard, four-voice canonic *Sanctus Marie filius*.

extensive use of English musical techniques (in particular canon) that, despite the origins implied by his name, 'show him to have been thoroughly assimilated as an English composer'.[28] It seems likely moreover that this 'Pycard' can be identified with the French clerk serving in Gaunt's chapel.[29] Sharing in the musical activity of this establishment over a period of eight or more years, and based mainly at Hertford Castle, Pycard thus emerges in part at least as culturally English, as a foreign musician turned native. This case, defying analysis in terms of simple constructs of 'influence', presents a clear instance of enculturation, although a comparable flow of musical expertise and even repertory may also have taken place in the opposite direction.

It remains unclear when the surviving works by Pycard might have been written. An early date seems unlikely on stylistic grounds; they may perhaps have been composed during the seven or eight years which John Pycard spent as a clerk in Gaunt's service, or at a slightly later date, if the composer had remained in England after the duke's death. Yet it is evident that they continued to be copied well into the second decade of the fifteenth century (and possibly beyond), and the manuscript context of their survival may help to confirm their origins in circles surrounding the Lancastrian household.[30] The original layer of pieces in the Old Hall manuscript is now widely thought to have been copied for the household chapel of Thomas, Duke of Clarence, probably between *c.* 1415 and his death in 1421.[31] (An added second layer of pieces by composers working as clerks in the royal household chapels of Henry V and Henry VI reflects its later acquisition by these establishments.) The music of the book's original corpus includes several items by the instructor of the choristers in Clarence's chapel, Lionel Power. It also includes representatives of older repertories with a distinct pedigree in royal foundations, very likely copied from sources that were still available within the circles of chaplains and clerks serving Henry V and his brothers. The composers whose works appear here include John Tyes, a secular *organista* at Westminster Abbey in 1399–1400, and subsequently at Winchester, and a 'Gerveys', who may possibly be identifiable with the Roger Gerveys who was a junior clerk of the royal household chapel 1376–7.[32] In addition, the composer Mattheus de Sancto Johanne, commonly identified with the Old Hall composer 'Mayshuet', served a part of his early career as a clerk in the chapel of Queen Philippa, for a short period immediately before her death in 1369.[33] Works written for use by singers in the service of Gaunt and his son Henry in the 1390s may thus have shared in a direct line of transmission into the repertories of royal foundations (including the royal household chapel) in the reign of Henry IV, and finally into those of the household chapels maintained by his own sons. Alternatively, they may have entered these repertories at a slightly later date, particularly if their author, aided by the impeccable recommendation of service with Gaunt, subsequently found employment elsewhere within royal circles, for example with the Beauforts. A past attachment to Gaunt in itself might also underwrite the later reception of these works in repertories used by singers in royal or Lancastrian employ.

The role sought by John of Gaunt after 1389 in Anglo–French diplomacy provided a clear rationale for display; the new-found wealth from his Castilian pension provided the means with which to support it. The engagement of French clerks to serve in his chapel formed part of this broader programme, and the circumstances under which they were employed disclose the origin of a significant cultural transmission. They also afford a starting point from which to explain the preservation of works by Pycard in English sources, and to locate a part at least of the pre-history of the repertories of the Old Hall manuscript. It may well be that this case provides paradigms for similar musical receptions, and for the mechanics of some other cross-channel cultural transmissions. Here, as in the more clearly political sphere, English political ambitions in Europe, traditionally devoted to fanning the embers of the Angevin empire, possess a major structural importance.

## Notes

1    For the following, and for more detailed accounts of the events sketched here, see C.J. Phillpotts, 'John of Gaunt and English Policy Towards France, 1389–1395', *Journal of Medieval History*, 16 (1990), pp. 363–86; J.J.N. Palmer, *England, France and Christendom, 1377–99* (London, 1972), pp. 142–51; A. Goodman, *John of Gaunt: The Exercise of Princely Power in Fourteenth-Century Europe* (London, 1992), pp. 144–74, 188–200; N.E. Saul, 'The Quest for Peace', *Richard II*, forthcoming. I am very grateful to Dr Saul for allowing me to see a copy of his chapter in advance of its publication. See also G.L. Harriss, *Cardinal Beaufort: A Study of Lancastrian Ascendancy and Decline* (Oxford, 1988), pp. 2–3, 7; S. Walker, *The Lancastrian Affinity, 1361–1399* (Oxford, 1990), pp. 39–80.

2    See Phillpotts, 'John of Gaunt', pp. 368–76.

3    Walker, *The Lancastrian Affinity*, p. 39.

4    For this and what follows see M. Bellaguet, ed., *Chronique du Religieux de Saint Denis* (Paris, 1839), i, pp. 734–43; Amiens, Archives Communales, CC 7, fol. 59v. See also Goodman, *John of Gaunt*, pp. 150–1.

5    Amiens, Archives Communales, CC 7, fols. 39rv, 57v, 59v, 60v, 67.

6    BN, p.o. 2152 'Orléans' (MS français 28636), No. 104. The expenditure of Louis's argentier in March and April 1392 totalled 10,995l. 13s. 7d. *tournois* (Orléans, Archives Départementales du Loiret, 6 J 3, Nos. 34–36); by contrast, average monthly spending under this head in surrounding months rarely exceeded 2,000l.t. (see for example BN, p.o. 2152 'Orléans', Nos. 94, 98, 109, 110; A.D. Loiret, 6 J 4, No. 2; 6 J 3, Nos. 94–97; BL, Add. Ch. 4251). For purchases made by the duke of Burgundy see Dijon, Archives Départementales du Côte-d'Or, B 1486, fols. 6, 28v, 30 ff. For those made by the King, see Paris, Archives Nationales, KK 23, fols. 174v–5.

7   For example the ring presented by Thomas Percy to Charles VI on behalf of Richard II (PRO, E 403/537, m. 22, payment *sub* 5 March 1392).

8   AN, KK 23, fols. 7, 87, 90, 174v–5.

9   *Chronique du Religieux de Saint Denis*, i, pp. 736–7; Dijon, A. D. Côte-d'Or, B 1486, fol. 30.

10  Amiens, Archives Communales, CC 7, fol. 39v. For works executed in preparation for Gaunt's arrival at the Malmaison, where his party was to lodge, see CC 7, fols. 113, 138. See also Goodman, *John of Gaunt*, p. 150.

11  *Chronique du Religieux de Saint Denis*, i, pp. 736–8.

12  For which see Amiens, Archives Départementales de la Somme, G 1133, No. 1. Chapel goods acquired at Amiens were bequeathed by Gaunt to Lincoln Cathedral at his death (see A. Wathey, *Music in the Royal and Noble Households in Late Medieval England: Studies of Sources and Patronage* (New York and London, 1989), p. 181, and Goodman, *op. cit.*, p. 248 for details).

13  A.D. Somme, G 1133, Nos. 2 and 3.

14  For example, BN, p.o. 2860 'Touraine' (MS français 29344), No. 4. See also Petit, *Itinéraires de Philippe le Hardi et de Jean sans Peur, ducs de Bourgogne (1363–1419) d'après les comptes de dépenses de leur hôtel*, Collection des Documents Inédits (Paris, 1888), pp. 226–30.

15  See Amiens, Archives Communales, CC 8, fols. 52v–53.

16  For example, *Chronique du Religieux de Saint Denis*, i, pp. 734–5.

17  See, for example, the gifts made by Philip, Duke of Burgundy to the minstrels of Edward, Earl of Rutland at Paris in late 1395 and those of Richard II at Compiègne in August 1396 (Dijon, A. D. Côte-d'Or, B. 1508, fols. 108, 151v, 152); that made by Louis, Duke of Orléans to five minstrels of the Earl Marshal in June or July 1396 (Orléans, A.D. Loiret, 6 J 5, No. 71); and that of Henry, Earl of Derby made to six minstrels of the duke of Burgundy in 1393/4 (PRO, DL 41/10/43 (18)). For what follows see A. Wathey, 'The Peace of 1360–1369 and Anglo-French Musical Relations', *Early Music History*, 9 (1990), pp. 129–74, at 133–7.

18  For the chapel of the duke of Burgundy, see C. Wright, *Music at the Court of Burgundy: A Documentary Study*, Musicological Studies and Documents (Henryville, Ottawa and Binningen, 1979), pp. 55–84; Dijon, A. D. Côte-d'Or, B 234. See also the account of the duke of Berry's chapel, closely related to a narrative of conversation with Gaunt at Amiens, in I. Arnold, ed., *L'Apparicion maistre Jehan de Meung et le somnium super materia scismatis d'Honoré Bonet*, Publications de la Faculté des Lettres de l'Université de Strasbourg, 28 (Paris, 1926), pp. 91–2, 95 ff.

19  See PRO, DL 28/3/2, fol. 11v, DL 28/3/5, fol. 8; Lewes, East Sussex Record Office, Glynde Place MS 3469, Nos. 6–8, 11, 13. On Gaunt's chapel in general see Wathey, *Music in the Royal and Noble Households*, pp. 179–82, and Goodman, *John of Gaunt*, pp. 248–9. For the household in this period, see Walker, *The Lancastrian Affinity*, pp. 10–14.

20  For what follows, see Walker, *Lancastrian Affinity* pp. 12–13, 34–8.

21  ESRO, Glynde Place MS 3469, Nos. 6–8, 11, 13, covering the periods 1 November 1391–23 February 1392 (immediately preceding their departure for Amiens) and 1 December 1393–8 January 1394. For the dating of rolls 6 and 8 see R.F. Dell, *The Glynde Place Archives: A Catalogue* (Lewes, 1964), p. 261. The presence of the stable of Henry, Earl of Derby, who was abroad July 1390–May 1391 and July 1392–June 1393, allows a closer dating than that advanced by Dell (pp. 261–2) for rolls 7, 11 and 13, respectively for 1–31 January 1392, 1–31 December 1391 and 1 December 1393–8 January 1394. The month of roll 11 is also identified in a note concerning daily wages due to William Hagh. Other rolls in this series, between February 1392 and March 1394, from which the names have been cut off, may also record the clerks' presence.

22    This problem was experienced by the singers of Louis of Luxembourg's chapel during
      their master's visit to London in 1443; see A. Leroy, 'Catalogue des Prévosts du
      monastère de Watten, sur la rivière d'Aa, diocèse de Saint-Omer, 1072–1577', *Archives
      historiques et littéraires du nord de la France et du midi de la Belgique*, new ser., 6 (1847),
      p. 282.
23    For which see Goodman, *John of Gaunt*, pp. 302–3.
24    See PRO, DL 28/1/3, fol. 3v.
25    The clerks received a fee of 10 marks p.a. in both 1392/3 and 1396/7 (DL 28/3/2,
      fol. 11v; DL 28/3/5, fol. 8). For wages see Glynde Place, MS 3469.
26    For details see Wathey, *Music in the Royal and Noble Households in Late Medieval
      England*, p. 181, note 97.
27    For the seven pieces in the Old Hall manuscript (BL, Add. MS 57950) see A. Hughes
      and M. Bent, eds., *The Old Hall Manuscript*, 3 vols., Corpus Mensurabilis Musicae, 46
      (1969–73), Nos. 26–28, 35, 76, 78 and 123 (i, pp. 65, 70, 78, 115, 210, 373); for two
      others possibly by Pycard, see *NG*, xiv, p. 721. For Stratford, Shakespeare Birthplace
      Trust, DR 98/1744/1a (formerly Willoughby de Broke 1744), see K. von Fischer and
      M. Lütolf, *Handschriften mit mehrstimmiger Musik des 14., 15. und 16. Jahrhunderts*, 2
      vols., Répertoire International des Sources Musicales, BIV³⁻⁴ (Munich, 1972),
      pp. 726–8.
28    'Pycard's Double Canon: Evidence of Revision', *Sundry Sorts of Music Books: Essays on
      the British Library Collections, presented to O.W. Neighbour on his 70th Birthday*, ed.
      C. Banks, A. Searle and M. Turner (London, 1993), pp. 10–26.
29    A number of possible candidates for identification with the composer were advanced
      by Andrew Hughes, none of whom, however, was obviously a musician or closely
      connected with royal circles (A. Hughes and M. Bent, 'The Old Hall Manuscript: A
      Reappraisal and Inventory', *Musica Disciplina*, 21 (1967), pp. 113–14). More
      promisingly, a Thomas Pycharde appears alongside Thomas Damett (in all probability
      the composer whose works appear in Old Hall), in the witness list of a conveyance of
      1420, enrolled on the Close Roll, of lands in Walsoken from Sir John Colvyle to a
      group including several of the feoffees of Henry V's will (*CCR 1419–1422*, p. 107;
      see also Margaret Bent in *The New Grove Dictionary of Music and Musicians*, 20 vols.,
      ed. S. Sadie (London, 1981), xiv, pp. 720–1). The grantees were Thomas Langley,
      Bishop of Durham and Chancellor of England, Sir Thomas Erpingham, Treasurer of
      the Household, Sir Henry Rocheford, Sir Robert Hakebeche, John Wodehous esq.,
      Thomas Deerham, Henry Merston, Robert Wetheryngsete, William Derby and
      Thomas Blewycke, clerks, and William Fulbourne). It seems probable that the
      juxtaposition of names here is accidental: the terms of the conveyance make specific
      reference to the rights of the Chapel of St Mary in the Sea, Walsoken, of which
      Thomas Pycharde was rector. He appeared among the witnesses as the representative
      of the chapel's interests, and can thus be distinguished from the royal servants present.
      The absence of an initial in the ascription in the Old Hall manuscript, as Margaret
      Bent has pointed out, makes certain identification impossible (*New Grove*, xiv, p.
      721).
30    A book (now fragmentary) copied in part from the Old Hall manuscript, probably for
      the household chapel of Henry VI, may perhaps have included works by Pycard; for
      this later manuscript see M. Bent, 'A Lost English Choirbook of the Fifteenth
      Century', *International Musicological Society: Report of the Eleventh Congress, Copenhagen
      1972*, 2 vols., ed. H. Glahn, S. Sørensen, and P. Ryom (Copenhagen, 1974), i,
      pp. 257–62; M. Bent, 'The Progeny of Old Hall: More Leaves from an English Royal
      Choirbook', *Gordon Athol Anderson (1929–81) in Memoriam*, 2 vols., Musicological
      Studies 49 (Henryville, Ottawa and Binningen, 1984), i, pp. 1–54.
31    See R. Bowers, 'Some Observations on the Life and Career of Lionel Power',

*Proceedings of the Royal Musical Association*, 102 (1975–6), pp. 109–10; Bent, 'The Progeny of Old Hall', pp. 26–7; Wathey, *Music in the Royal and Noble Households*, pp. 35–45.

32  Wathey *op. cit.,* p. 44; for Gerveys, see PRO, E 101/398/9, fol. 31; E 101/397/20, m. 20; E 101/400/4, m. 21.

33  See Wathey, 'The Peace of 1360–1369', pp. 144–50.

# 2
# Tapestries from the Low Countries in England during the Fifteenth Century

Scot McKendrick
*British Library, London*

Probably the best surviving example of Netherlandish tapestry produced in the fifteenth century for an Englishman is a heraldic millefleurs tapestry, formerly at Appleby Castle and now at the Cloisters, New York.[1] Bearing the full achievement of arms and personal devices of John, Lord Dinham (d. 1501), together with the arms of his father and mother, this work was almost certainly made to order for Dinham. Given also that the three arms are encircled by a Garter, it was definitely produced for him after he became a Knight of the Garter in 1487. Comparison with surviving tapestries not only confirms such a dating, but also establishes Dinham's tapestry as a high quality work of Netherlandish weavers.

The aim of the present paper is to set out clearly the context in which this work came to be produced and brought to England. This I wish to do in two stages. In part I I hope to determine what survives and is acceptable as secure evidence for the presence of Netherlandish tapestry in England during the fifteenth century. In part II I exploit that evidence to give an overview of the different types of English owners and their collections, their means of collecting, their likely reasons or intentions in collecting, and the use to which they put Continental tapestry.

# I

What then can be accepted as secure evidence? Of surviving pieces another heraldic millefleurs tapestry, this time bearing the royal arms of England and still in the possession of the duke of Rutland at Haddon Hall, has in the past been considered of an earlier date than, but of similar origins to Lord Dinham's tapestry.[2] The basic heraldic structure was very probably the same. Moreover the weaving of both the heraldic elements and the millefleurs, although executed with less skill and lower quality materials than the Cloisters piece, is still of good quality. The so-called *Union of the Roses* fragments at Winchester College, on the other hand, are simple in design and weave, and, like similar fragments in the Musée des Arts

Décoratifs, Paris, are much more difficult to localize.[3] Any perceived Englishness of design is of course irrelevant to the issue of where the tapestries were woven, as is the question of whether they were woven for the baptism of Prince Arthur at Winchester in 1486.

A more straightforward example is the very large tapestry in St Mary's Hall, Coventry, in the lower tier of which the *Assumption of the Virgin* is contemplated to left and right by a young royal couple attended by many courtiers.[4] Comparison with Netherlandish tapestries clearly shows the Continental origins of this piece and, together with an examination of the costume, also suggests a date of production in *c.* 1500–10, a dating which could agree with the traditional story of its having been woven to celebrate the visit to the Hall by Henry VII in 1500 and the identification of the royal couple as Henry and Elizabeth of York. Its iconography and measurements certainly suggest that this tapestry was specially made for its present situation. A detailed modern study of this work, however, is needed to settle this issue and resolve the many questions it continues to pose.

Within a clearer historical context is the small tapestry of *Saints Martin of Tours and Dunstan* which belongs to the London Company of Vintners.[5] Dated 1466 this piece bears an inscription requesting prayers for the souls of John Bate of Ware and his wife Joan, and for their son Walter Hertford 'monk of this church'. Since in 1466 Hertford was 'custos maneriorum et bertonarius' of Christ Church, Canterbury,[6] it was presumably there that Bate's tapestry was intended to be hung. Although arras still at Canterbury in 1563 was described as 'made by' Hertford,[7] the style and quality of the surviving piece which includes precious metal thread and Hertford's own status suggest that all these pieces were both made for him and made across the Channel.

Other definite products of professional Netherlandish weavers which have early English provenances are the four famous Devonshire *Hunting* tapestries, now in the V. & A., which may well have been at Hardwick since the Hall was built in the 1590s,[8] the two fragments of a *David* tapestry at Winchester College which were there as early as 1580,[9] and the *Roman de la Rose* tapestries formerly at Skipton Castle which may have been there since 1572.[10] All, however, lack a precise medieval English context.[11] And that is the sum of the extant evidence for the fifteenth century – altogether very scanty and miscellaneous.[12]

Little further evidence is added by the records of English antiquarians, almost all of which relate to the few surviving pieces already mentioned.[13] Rare and invaluable exceptions are John Carter's drawings of five tapestries of the *Trojan War* then in the Painted Chamber of the Old Palace of Westminster, which almost certainly preserve the appearance of a set of eleven large pieces purchased by Henry VII in 1488 from Jean Grenier of Tournai.[14] Without these drawings it could have been argued that Henry's set was of similar appearance to several surviving tapestries. With them the issue is as good as settled, and they now constitute the most important link between surviving pieces and known sales by the Grenier family in the 1470s and 1480s.

By far the greatest part of the evidence lies in contemporary documents. And some of these are clear and unambiguous on the subject. Gifts from the duke of Burgundy, for example, often took the form of tapestries, and for these we still have his payments to known tapestry merchants of Arras, Paris, Tournai, Brussels and so on. Between 1390 and 1396, for example, in the course of cross-Channel diplomatic negotiations and meetings Richard II, together with his uncles, Lancaster, Gloucester and York, were sent no fewer than eleven tapestries, several of which contained gold thread and measured up to 14m in length.[15] The most costly piece, one of the *Trinity* with gold thread bought for 675 fr., was presented to Richard II during a visit to Calais in 1396 around the time of his marriage to the Princess Isabel.[16] Further gifts to English ambassadors include those to Francis de Courte, Henry Chichele and John Cadryk during dynastic marriage negotiations in 1411[17] and that to the earl of Warwick during diplomatic negotiations with Burgundy in 1416.[18] Less open gifts include the 'chambre' of verdure tapestry depicting 'enfans alans a lescolle', which was bought by Philip the Good from an Arras merchant for around 600 fr. and sent in 1447 from Brussels to London via Calais to an unspecified Englishman.[19] In 1478 five tapestries bought by Maximilian and Mary of Burgundy from a Bruges merchant for over 1,000 li. were also secretly sent across the Channel, this time to William, Lord Hastings.[20]

Further unambiguous documents are those recording the purchase on the Continent of Netherlandish tapestry intended for Englishmen and its importation across the Channel. From these it clearly emerges that there were several different ways by which tapestries could be purchased and come to England. In the retail trade Continental documents suggest that a special commission was the rarest way of buying a tapestry; it was certainly the most expensive. Yet at Bergen-op-Zoom in 1479 two English skinners ordered from a Brussels tapestry merchant two tapestries to be made from cartoons supplied by the skinners themselves.[21] The exact appearance of the work could also be negotiated, as when in 1477 one of the same skinners ordered from the same Brussels merchant a tapestry which was to have its central subject altered from the *Last Supper* to the *Mass of St Gregory*.[22] More commonly tapestries were bought both singly and in batches from existing stocks or to a design proffered by a Continental merchant. Sometimes this took the form of a direct purchase by an English collector from a Continental merchant. As I have argued elsewhere, Edward IV's very large purchase in 1467–8, which included three sets of tapestry, almost certainly derived from the capacious stockrooms of Pasquier Grenier of Tournai, or at least from designs employed by him for other clients.[23] Tapestries were also bought on the Continent and then imported in bulk for specific individuals by English merchants, as in 1440 and 1442 when Robert Worsely, an English merchant based at Bruges, imported tapestries for William de la Pole and Lord Say and Sele.[24] In 1441 Worsely was granted the rare privilege of importing as much arras as he bought on the Continent for English lords without payment of customs.[25] As in the case of the 1477 and 1479 purchases mentioned earlier and that of a *History of Thebes* bought for Edward IV through the English mercer John Pickering at the Easter market for 1482,[26] many purchases were probably made from Continental tapestry merchants at the cycle of fairs in the Low Countries.

Another option appears to have been that of buying second-hand. In 1480, for instance, Edward IV may well have acquired seven tapestries of the *Story of Rome* which had previously been sold at Antwerp in 1478 at the auction of the goods of Charles the Bold's chancellor Guillaume Hugonet.[27] A more desperate measure was theft, as in the case of several tapestries which in 1459 were specially commissioned for the Medici from a tapestry master at Lille, but went missing in London the following year and still could not be found in 1463.[28]

Among more legitimate methods there was also the wholesale trade in importing tapestry across the Channel. Customs accounts, particularly those of the second half of the fifteenth century, suggest that this trade was vigorously engaged upon by many merchants, both foreign and English.[29] The boarding point, when stated, is almost without fail Flanders. The declared values of these pieces, often described as tapestry coverlets, are relatively small, between £1 and £5 a piece. Such pieces appear to have formed the lower end of the trade in tapestry across the Channel, but also a growing part in which merchants imported on the speculation of a sale in England. Steady importation suggests that such speculation was not miscalculated and that there was a healthy market for such goods.

So much for the unambiguous evidence for the collection of tapestry in England. What it has yielded is a suggestive picture, one of several significant gifts from the duke of Burgundy, a variety of purchasing routes on the retail market and a growing wholesale trade in goods at the lower end of the quality scale. Yet such a picture is unlikely to convince the sceptic of the importance of tapestry as a factor in cultural exchange between the Continent and England. So far collecting appears circumstantial, patchy and erratic, wholesale trade merely on a scale with many other goods crossing the Channel.

What needs to be attempted, therefore, is a clarification of the much larger group of references to tapestries found in English inventories, wills and accounts. In these the origin of the works is rarely given and the central problem with them is how to distinguish Continental works from home-produced ones and how to be sure that they were produced in France or the Low Countries. Superficially this problem is easily resolved: the term 'arras' frequently met with in these documents denotes an origin in Arras, a known and important centre of production of high quality tapestries. Yet, as has been shown for the many Continental equivalents of 'arras', such as 'arazzi' and 'draps de ras', such literalism cannot be upheld on account of the many examples where such named pieces are demonstrably not the products of Arras. Also, what is to be made of the other frequently used English terms, 'tapestry' and 'counterfeit arras'?[30]

In the light of all the documents that I have so far consulted, there appears to be much truth in the general observation that in formal documents, especially those drawn up by experts in valuation, 'arras' (and its Continental equivalents for that matter) is applied to tapestries that are woven with high quality materials, including fine wool and silk thread and sometimes also gold and silver coated silk thread; they are also often large, figurative or historiated.[31] As such these works are almost certainly the products of large-scale professional production of the highest standards. For England during the fourteenth and fifteenth centuries there is a complete lack of evidence for such production.[32] 'Tapicers' were not the equivalent of Continental tapestry weavers; the king's tapicer, keeper of the king's cloths of arras and tapestry or royal arras-maker was employed principally to repair tapestries and only occasionally produced small-scale heraldic works for the king and his family.[33] There is also a complete lack of evidence for purchases of high quality tapestry being made in England from English workers or their agents. It is, therefore, probable that 'arras' used in a formal context to distinguish works by quality or value also suggests the Continent as their origin.

The most important Continental centres for the professional production of tapestry from the middle of the fourteenth century and throughout the fifteenth were undoubtedly those in the north of France and the Low Countries.[34] The documented scale of their production outstrips that of all other contemporary centres and the many surviving pieces attributable to them merely confirm such dominance. Moreover, unlike the only major centres of production in Switzerland and Germany which provided almost solely for local needs, French and Netherlandish centres exported their works all over Europe.[35] Close similarities between pieces of arras recorded in English documents and those recorded in French and Netherlandish ones in terms of subject, size, materials and cost further strengthen arguments for such origins of arras. Thus, although, for example, we know for certain of the Netherlandish origins of four of Richard II's pieces of arras, each being a gift from Philip the Bold, comparison of Richard's other arras collected by 1399 with documented Continental works very soon suggests that almost all were of similar origins.

Of course any general statement about 'arras' can only be a rule of thumb. Each case requires some consideration, since use of the word is not consistent either between individuals or over time.[36] Moreover, even if 'arras' is generally a sufficient term for French or Netherlandish tapestry, it is not a necessary one. Other English words are certainly used for Continental works.

Take 'tapestry', for example. In the same formal context as before the word was used to denote works which were perceived to have been woven with less costly materials than arras and require less intensive skill and labour in their production. They were therefore not only sold at a lower price per square yard, but also valued in a similar manner. Guidelines for such a judgement must have depended on the expertise of the individual, but probably included such considerations as the density of the weave, the proportion of silk used, the quality of wool, and the level of complexity of the design. On such grounds solely decorative or heraldic works were more likely to be classed as tapestries, but not necessarily so. Origin, therefore, is again not the principle of distinction. Also no specific origin can be deduced from the particular characteristics of tapestry as defined in the fifteenth century. Although several tapestries were definitely English products, such as those produced by the royal arras maker,[37] many others were of Continental origin. Several of the textiles bought in Flanders and imported across the Channel by Robert Worsely in the middle of the century were described as tapestries and so too many imported wholesale from the same parts.[38]

'Counterfeit arras', on the other hand, is like 'arras' in that it points by implication and not directly to a work's likely origin. Although as early as 1374 a woman was accused of making a sort of fake arras using linen thread for the warp,[39] such faking is not, I think, the force of 'counterfeit' in the expression 'counterfeit arras', since it seems to have been commonly applied to works made of high quality materials and requiring much intensive skill and labour, and also to those imported from the Continent.[40] In 1478, for example, Edward IV paid the London draper, Edmund Rigon, for counterfeit arras which was almost certainly imported across the Channel.[41]

# II

Of all English collections the king's was undoubtedly the most important throughout the fifteenth century. It was he who owned the largest number of pieces and the most of great value. The monarch was of course in a very advantageous position. He was the one person who over the century had sufficient wealth to acquire works of the highest quality; and, given the surprising continuity and stability of the royal collection of tapestries, he had the best opportunity of building up a very large collection.[42] His favour being of much importance to many, gifts to him were commonplace. Among the most luxurious offered during diplomacy with Burgundy and France were tapestries produced in their own lands.[43] The king could also select and retain the choicest tapestries from the goods forfeited to the Crown, such as Thomas, earl of Warwick's *Alexander* tapestries,[44] Thomas, duke of Gloucester's *St George* tapestry,[45] and Henry, Lord Scrope's chamber of *Hunting*.[46]

The first most substantial additions to the royal collection were made during the reign of Richard II. When Edward III died in 1377, the collection appears to have included only seven miscellaneous pieces of arras, only one of which included gold thread.[47] By 1399 there were no fewer than fifty pieces, many of which included gold and some measured over 30 yards in length.[48] Although four were gifts from Burgundy and three forfeited by Warwick,[49] no fewer than twenty-four pieces of arras with gold were purchased between 1394 and 1398.[50] By Henry IV's death in 1411 few additions seem to have been made,[51] but by the time of his son's death in 1422 the collection had grown again to comprise just under 100 pieces of arras, with the addition of such substantial pieces as two of the *Credo* with gold thread, which even then were valued at over £200.[52] A large part of this collection passed to Henry VI, most having been bought from his father's executors at the artificially low price of just under £1,500,[53] and it was to this collection that Henry made such additions as the two rich pieces of *St George* and the *Virtues and Vices* bought from Robert Worsely in 1444 for £413.[54] While retaining the core of this collection, Edward IV and Henry VII made their own contributions, the most impressive of which is the expenditure by Edward in 1467 of £1,400 on arras supplied by Pasquier Grenier of Tournai, a figure which may have risen in 1468 to £2,500.[55] Not all royal purchases were of new goods. Henry VI bought tapestries from the executors of William Ayscough bishop of Salisbury in 1450 for 40 marks,[56] Edward from those of Walter Lyhert bishop of Norwich in 1476 for 100 marks,[57] and Henry VII from those of Thomas Savage, archbishop of York in 1507 for over £200.[58] Plunder from the Continent also supplied the royal collection, as in the case of a piece of blue arras with the motto of Charles VI[59] and the *Clovis* tapestry which sixteenth-century visitors to Windsor Castle were told was captured from the French in the previous century.[60]

Of all the works thus acquired the subjects were very much in line with those in comparable Continental collections. Particularly prominent were secular subjects, especially romances and scenes of courtly love and hunting. Allegory, particularly on the subject of love, was also popular. A few had a specific relevance to their English royal owners, such as the two pieces depicting the English royal saints Oswald and Lucius[61] or the five including portraits of Henry V, Henry VI, and the dukes of Clarence, Bedford and Gloucester.[62] These were almost certainly specially commissioned. Others which might seem particularly appropriate, such as that of *King Richard*,[63] appear also in Continental collections and were not unique to the English royal collection.[64]

Although several pieces were allocated at an early date to particular royal residences,[65] much of the collection was kept in repositories, such as the Prince's Wardrobe in the Old Jewry or the Wardrobe of Beds in the Tower.[66] There necessary maintenance was carried out and the pieces kept secure. From there they were moved as instructed for specific ceremonial occasions, such as the Garter ceremonies, coronations and diplomatic meetings. Such moves sometimes took important pieces back across the Channel, on which occasions arras served a prominent role in the king's general projection of his great personal wealth and power, and, particularly at events involving Continental rivals, ensured that he was not outshone by their magnificent trappings.[67]

As for other members of the royal family, the magnates and nobility, although the relevant documentation is patchy, there is evidence of considerable interest in Netherlandish tapestry. As early as 1397 the duke of Gloucester left at Pleshy no fewer than eighteen pieces of arras, five of which were over 15 yards in length and five contained gold thread.[68] His brothers who, like him, had received several gifts of tapestry from Philip the Bold,[69] most probably owned similar collections. Contemporary collections of prominent nobles, although far from negligible, appear to have been smaller. The earl of Warwick, for example, apparently owned only four sets of arras[70] and the earl of Arundel also only four.[71] Such collections were generally allowed little time to grow and mature in the same way as that of the king. Yet, as early as 1415 Lord Scrope owned no less than thirty-nine pieces of arras, eleven of which included gold,[72] and, as the century progressed and more arras came to England, so the opportunities for acquiring pieces cheaply increased. Those in favour with the king could have tapestries forfeited to the Crown reassigned to them, or be allowed to avoid import duties, or extract pieces from the royal collection. Thus in 1401 the king's son Thomas of Lancaster and his half-brother Thomas Beaufort were each granted three pieces of arras formerly belonging to the earl of Salisbury,[73] in 1440 and 1442 the earl of Suffolk and Lord Say and Sele were exempted from duties at Sandwich and Dover,[74] and in 1423 Thomas Beaufort was allocated a fine set of *Hawking and Hunting*,[75] part of which had in 1415 been forfeited by Lord Scrope.[76] Arras could also be bought from executors. The earl of Northumberland bought arras worth 200 marks from the executors of George Nevil, archbishop of York,[77] and Maud, countess of Cambridge bought one piece from one of the executors of Henry V.[78] By such means there could develop by the middle of the century such larger collections as that of John Holland, duke of Exeter[79] and that recorded at Ewelme in 1466 and associated with William de la Pole, duke of Suffolk.[80]

The subjects were very similar to those pieces owned by the king. Some, such as the *Siege of Falaise* in Fastolf's collection[81] and the set of *Guy of Warwick* owned by the earl of Warwick,[82] may have been specially made. Most, however, bear close resemblance to pieces cited in Continental documents and were probably not unique. The most important large pieces or sets of pieces owned by such members of the nobility were those intended to line the great hall and the great bed of state with attendant chamber pieces. Repeatedly it is these works that are specifically cited in wills.

Apart from such references as that to Richard, Lord Scrope's bed for the principal chamber at Bolton Castle,[83] the duke of Norfolk's hanging of the *Story of Hercules* specially commissioned for the great hall at Framlingham[84] and the 1st earl of Westmorland's bed for the great hall at Sheriff Hutton,[85] there is very little evidence for the type of 'hang' likely to have been encountered in an English noble household of the fifteenth century. The little further evidence that does survive, however, such as the room by room listing for the manor house at Ewelme[86] and the room references given in Fastolf's inventories,[87] suggests that arras constituted both one of the principal features of household decorations and one of the most precious treasures to be kept in reserve for special occasions.[88] The walls and beds must have been an impressive sight, deliberately calculated to convey the wealth, power and family pride of the noble owner. As with the royal collection several pieces were kept in a central reserve or wardrobe, and in some households, such as that of the earl of Northumberland, there was an officer called the mender of arras.[89]

As I have already shown,[90] several English merchants were much involved in the importation of tapestry. It is therefore not surprising to find that from an early date they corporately emulated the nobility in the furnishings for their guild halls. In 1431 the drapers at London spent over £10 on arras for their new hall,[91] and by 1441 the Trinity Guild at Coventry had hanging in their hall a dorser of arras of *Hawking* as the precursor of the present St Mary's Hall tapestry already mentioned.[92] The ironmongers at London also had some arras by 1489 and around 1495 the mercers had their hall measured up for the same.[93] Most impressive of all was the set of nine pieces of arras of the *Life of St John the Baptist* which was bought for the Merchant Taylors' hall at the end of the century at the cost of £343.[94]

Finally, what of the many great religious establishments of England? Here the surviving documentation suggests a striking contrast with both the royal and noble households in England and comparable Continental collections. For example, in the early sixteenth-century inventories of the secular cathedrals of Exeter, Lincoln and Salisbury, there is to be found only one piece of arras.[95] Among the many Dissolution inventories hardly any tapestries at all are recorded[96] and even the very few that are, such as those at Winchester, may, like those given to Canterbury in 1511, date from the sixteenth century.[97] Such a dearth of tapestry is of course particularly striking in contrast to the rich personal collections of several English archbishops and bishops[98] and to the collections of the nobility, many of whose pieces of arras were of religious subjects and probably adorned their chapels. Yet, almost without exception bequests of tapestry in England were made by one individual to another and not to an institution.[99] Alternatively, tapestries, such as those of William Ayscough, bishop of Salisbury,[100] and George Nevil, archbishop of York, were sold off by their executors.[101]

Since the practice was very different on the Continent some explanation needs to be sought. An explanation appears even more pressing, when comparison is made with contemporary Scottish practice. Glasgow Cathedral, for example, had by 1433 a large piece of arras depicting the life of St Mungo,[102] which was presumably specially made for that church. Aberdeen Cathedral had by 1436 fifteen pieces of arras, nine of which were gifts from individuals,[103] and St Salvator's College at St Andrews had by the middle of the century several pieces including some for hanging at the altars there.[104]

One possible explanation is that English establishments were already well supplied with other textiles, particularly home-produced embroidery. Moreover such textiles may have completely filled the necessary roles and established themselves as proper and fitting works for, say, hanging before and behind an altar. Repletion and tradition may, therefore, have been two of the factors that worked against the introduction of tapestry. Only exceptional cases, such as the effigy of Henry VI at York Minster,[105] appear to have allowed arras a place in cathedrals otherwise almost totally empty of tapestry. Yet I cannot pretend to have fully explained this peculiar situation in England which requires further and separate consideration.

In conclusion, from late in the fourteenth century until the end of the fifteenth century Netherlandish tapestries performed a tangible and visible role in secular English life. For many at the highest levels of society they appear to have supplanted home-produced wall paintings and historiated textiles, such as worsted, and consequently projected much that was fashionable on the Continent in terms of both literature and art into the heart of English court life. As such, tapestries are worthy of close consideration. For when English wool returned from the Continent woven into tapestries, very much more occurred than an economic exchange.

# Notes

1   See *Chefs-d'oeuvre de la tapisserie du xiv$^e$ au xvi$^e$ siècle*, Grand Palais exhibition catalogue compiled by F. Salet and G. Souchal (Paris, 1973), pp. 124–6 No. 45 and H. Nickel, 'Some Remarks on the Armorial Tapestry of John Dynham at the Cloisters', *Metropolitan Museum Journal*, XIX/XX (1984/5), pp. 25–30.

2   B. Young, 'John Dynham and his Tapestry', *Metropolitan Museum of Art Bulletin*, XX (1962), p. 315.

3   For the Winchester tapestries see A.F. Kendrick, 'Tapestry at Winchester College', *Burlington Magazine*, VI (1904–5), pp. 490, 495 and W.G. Thomson, *Tapestry Weaving in England* (London, 1915), pp. 20–22. A further study by Michael K. Jones is to appear in the proceedings of the 1993 Harlaxton Symposium.

4   See A.F. Kendrick, 'The Coventry Tapestry', *Burlington Magazine*, XLIV (1924), pp. 83–9.

5   N. Ramsay and M. Sparks, *The Image of Saint Dunstan* (Canterbury, 1988), pp. 32, 35 (fig.) and 'The Cult of St Dunstan at Christ Church, Canterbury', in *St Dunstan: His Life, Times and Cult*, N. Ramsay, M. Sparks and T. Tatton-Brown (eds) (Woodbridge, 1992), p. 321.

6   *Christ Church, Canterbury, I, The Chronicle of John Stone . . .* , W.G. Searle (ed.) (Cambridge, 1902), p. 115 No. 34.

7   'Item iiij pendauntes of arras wroghte withe golde and ij frountes for the same of the gifte of S$^r$ Anthonie Sentlygr knyghte sometime made by one herteforde a monck of this house' (J.W. Legg and W.H. St. John Hope, *Inventories of Christ Church Canterbury with Historical and Topographical Introductions and Illustrative Documents* (Westminster, 1902), p. 222). The replacement of 'by' for 'for' after 'made' could easily have arisen through the misunderstanding or mistranslation of an earlier text.

8   G. Wingfield Digby and W. Hefford, *The Devonshire Hunting Tapestries* (London, 1971), pp. 2–4.

9   H. Chitty, *Mediaeval Sculptures at Winchester College* (Oxford, 1932), p. 15. For a double now at Baltimore of the tapestry of which these pieces once formed a part see J.-P. Asselberghs, *Tapisseries flamandes aux États-Unis d'Amérique* (Brussels, 1974), p. 46, fig. 33.

10  For the 1572 inventory see T.D. Whitaker, *The History and Antiquities of the Deanery of Craven, in the County of York*, A.W. Morant (ed.) (3rd edn, Leeds, 1878), p. 401. For all the pieces as they survived at Skipton until early this century see H.A. Tipping, *English Homes*, per. II, vol. 1, *Early Tudor, 1485–1558* (London, 1924), pls 84, 85, 87. The principal piece subsequently passed to the American dealers French and Co. (see *Catalogue of the Retrospective Loan Exhibition of European Tapestries . . .* (San Francisco, 1922), No. 4) and then in part to an Argentinian collection (see *Arte Flamenco en las Colecciones Argentinas*, Museo Nacional de Arte Decorativo exhibition catalogue (Buenos Aires, 1965), No. 67). A further small fragment is now in the Philadelphia Museum of Art (George Grey Barnard Coll. 45–25–241). I most grateful to Tom Campbell of the S. Franses Tapestry Research Archive for information on the whereabouts of these pieces.

11  For over-optimistic and unconvincing speculations on their fifteenth-century owners see A. Claxton, 'The Sign of the Dog: An Examination of the Devonshire Hunting Tapestries', *Journal of Mediaeval History*, XIV (1988), pp. 127–79 and several previous contributions evaluated in Wingfield Digby and Hefford, *Devonshire Tapestries*, pp. 32–4, 80–81.

12  Many more tapestries dating from the early sixteenth century survive, several of which retain their original very large dimensions. Among these are four of the *Triumphs* bought by Cardinal Wolsey from the executors of the Bishop of Durham, which

remain at Hampton Court (H.C. Marillier, *The Tapestries at Hampton Court* (London, 1962), pp. 19–23), and the pieces of the *Life of the Virgin* and *Life of Christ*, recently stolen from Aix, which can be identified with works given to Christ Church, Canterbury, in 1511 (*Chefs-d'oeuvre de la tapisserie*, pp. 185–90 Nos. 78, 79). A tapestry of *Judith* now at Sens and another of *Tobias* at the Musée Lécuyer, St Quentin, both retain Wolsey's arms (Marillier, *Tapestries*, p. 12 and J. Duverger, 'Bijdragen tot de Inventaris van Vlaamse Tapijten in Franse, I, Vlaamse Legwerk te Saint-Quentin', *Artes Textiles*, IV (1957–8), pp. 9–15, pl. 2).

13   A rare example is a description of a tapestry of *Haman and Mordecai*, which includes an attempted transcription of its panels of French inscriptions (*The Gentleman's Magazine*, LIV (1784), pp. 268–9). This work was said to have come from Old Somerset House. Another may be the so far untraced drawing of a tapestry of *St George* said to date from the reign of Henry VII, which was sold at John Carter's sale (Sotheby's, London, 23–25 Feb. 1818, lot 345). This tapestry was once owned by Adair Hawkins, but is now also untraced.

14   S. McKendrick, 'The Great History of Troy: A Reassessment of the Development of a Secular Theme in Late Medieval Art', *Journal of the Warburg and Courtauld Institutes*, LIV (1991), pp. 59–61.

15   For the Duke of York in 1390 were sent 'j tapis à l'histoire de Octavien de Romme, contenant 5 aunes de large et 17 aunes de long' and 'un tapis ouvré à l'histoire de Percheval le Galoix, contenant 6 aunes un quartier de large et 17 aunes de long', both of which were purchased from tapestry merchants of Arras, the first for 148 fr. and the second for 150 fr. (B. and H. Prost, *Inventaires mobiliers et extraits des comptes des ducs de Bourgogne de la maison de Valois (1363–1477), Philippe le Hardi (1363–90)*, II (Paris, 1913), Nos. 3570, 3590). For Richard II in 1394 were sent 'trois tapiz de hauteliche ouvrez à or de Chippre, l'un du Cruxefiement de Nostre Seigneur, l'autre a un mont de Calvaire et l'autre du Trespassement Nostre Dame, contenant ensemble ix$^{xx}$xv aunes quarrées à l'aune d'Arras', bought from Jacques Dourdin of Paris for 900 fr. (C. Dehaisnes, *Documents et extraits divers concernant l'histoire de l'art dans la Flandre, l'Artois, et le Hainaut avant le XV$^e$ siècle* (Lille, 1886), p. 709). For the dukes of Lancaster and Gloucester in 1394 were respectively 'un [drap de hauteliche] ouvré de l'histoire du roy Clovys, contenant xxxij aunes de long et six aunes et demie de lez, l'autre ouvré à or de l'histoire de Nostre Dame, contenant xx aunes de long, v aunes et demie de lé . . . tout à l'aune . . . d'Arras', bought from another tapestry merchant of Arras (Dehaisnes, *Documents*, p. 710). For the dukes of Lancaster, Gloucester and York in the same year there was 'un drap de hauteliche senz or de l'ystoire du Roy Pharaon et de la nacion de Moyse, contenant à l'aune dudit Arras viij$^{xx}$v aunes quarrées', 'j drap à or de l'istoire d'Amis et d'Amie, contenant à la dite aune iiij$^{xx}$vij aunes quarrées', and 'un autre drap de l'istoire de Deduit et de la Plaisance, ainsi qu'il sont en gibier, contenant à la dite aune lij aunes quarrées', all bought from Arras merchants, the first for 247 fr. 10 s.t., the second for 207 fr. and the third for 125 fr. (*ibid.*, p. 710). Richard II was presented at Calais in 1396–7 'un tappis de hauteliche ouvré à or, de l'istoire de la Trinité', bought from an Arras merchant for 675 fr. (*ibid.*, p. 737). In his will of 3 Feb. 1398 John of Gaunt bequeathed to Richard II 'la piece d'arras la quelle le Duc de Burgoyn me donna a derrein qe jeo estoie a Calays devant la date du cestes' (S. Armitage-Smith, *John of Gaunt* (London, 1904), p. 426).

16   For Richard at Calais see J.J.N. Palmer, *England, France and Christendom, 1377–1399* (London, 1972), pp. 174–7. Despite its high value Richard's *Trinity* tapestry appears not to have been a very large piece, measuring only 7 verges in length and 5 in height (see *Rotuli Parliamentorum*, IV (1773), p. 234).

17   'A Jehan de Capelles, tapicier demourant à Arras, et autres la somme de 149 li. 2 s.p. pour . . . un tappis sans or, ung aultre tappiz de iiij$^{xx}$ et iiij aulnes et un tappiz ou il a

plusieurs ymaiges de belles filles au conte de Pennebroc, ung autre tappiz comme dessus à messire Jehan Cadric, deux tables d'autel et ung autre tappiz audit evesque de Saint-David' (C. Dehaisnes, *Inventaire sommaire des archives départementales antérieures à 1790, Nord, Archives civiles, série B*, IV (Lille, 1881), p. 63 (B 1894, f. 234)). On the negotiations see T. Rymer, *Foedera*, VIII, p. 699 and *Proceedings and Ordinances of the Privy Council of England*, Sir N.H. Nicolas (ed.), II (London, 1833), p. 20.

18  A. Pinchart, *Histoire de la tapisserie dans les Flandres* (Histoire générale de la tapisserie, III, 1885), p. 19.

19  M.-R. Thielemans, *Bourgogne et Angleterre. Relations politiques et économiques entre les Pays-Bas bourguignons et l'Angleterre, 1435–1467* (Travaux de la Faculté de Philosophie et Lettres de l'Université Libre de Bruxelles, vol. XXX, 1966), pp. 153, 232, and Dehaisnes, *Inventaire*, p. 173 (B 1991, f. 220).

20  'deux pieces de tappisserie historiee de l'empereur Maximien . . . ung tapiz d'eglise historie des Troix Roix . . . une autre petite piece de tappiserye ouvree a or . . . une autre piece de tappisserie historiee de l'istoire d'Absalon' (A. Pinchart, *Archives des arts, des sciences et des lettres. Documents inédits*, I (Ghent, 1860), pp. 20–1). See also E. Duverger, 'Les tappisseries, le commerce et la fabrication de tapisseries à Bruges de la fin du moyen âge au début du XVIII<sup>e</sup> siècle', in *Bruges et la Tapisserie*, G. Delmarcel and E. Duverger (eds) (Bruges, 1987), pp. 44–6.

21  S. McKendrick, 'Edward IV: An English Royal Collector of Netherlandish Tapestry', *Burlington Magazine*, CXXIX (1987), p. 522 n. 20.

22  *Ibid.*, p. 522 n. 20.

23  *Ibid.*, pp. 521–2.

24  *Ibid.*, p. 521 n. 5.

25  *Ibid.*, p. 521 n. 5.

26  For the 1482 purchase see *ibid.*, p. 523.

27  *Ibid.*, pp. 522–3.

28  A. Grünzweig, *Correspondance de la filiale de Bruges des Medici* (Brussels, 1931), Nos. 35, 37, 39.

29  See, for example, *The Port Books or Local Customs Accounts of Southampton for the Reign of Edward IV*, D.B. Quinn and A.A. Ruddock (eds.) (Southampton Record Society Publications, Nos. 37, 38, 1937), I, pp. 48, 49, 51, 97; II, pp. 106–8, 114, 118, 167, 183–4, 197; also *The Overseas Trade of London Exchequer Accounts 1480–1*, H.S. Cobb (ed.) (London Record Society Publications, vol. 27, 1990), Nos. 28, 30, 56, 83, 139, 159, 175, 567.

30  Another term which requires further attention is 'verdure'. By 1475 when Edward IV made his will this term was being used to designate a category distinct from both arras and tapestry (see *Excerpta Historica*, S. Bentley (ed.) (London, 1831), p. 378).

31  Thielemans, *Bourgogne et Angleterre*, p. 232 recognises 'arras' and 'tapestry' as designating works of higher and lower quality.

32  Despite the claims of Thomson, *Tapestry Weaving*, pp. 9–22 and J. Lestocquoy, *Deux siècles de l'histoire de la tapisserie, 1300–1500* (Mémoires de la Commission départementale des monuments historiques du Pas-de-Calais, XIX, 1979), p. 55 the only works explicitly said to have been produced in England are much simpler and smaller than arras, e.g. Richard, earl of Arundel's 'grand sale q'estoit darreynement fait a Loundres del overaigne de tapeterye blewm ove roses rouges en ycell, et mes armes et les armes de mes filz' (J.G. Nichols, *A Collection of all the Wills Known to be Extant of the Kings and Queens of England . . .* (London, 1780), p. 128.

33  Typical products of a 'tapicer' are the five 'tapets' of tapestry, each bearing two escutcheons with the arms of Margaret of Anjou, made in 1444 by John Bonauntre with the aid of a pattern supplied by the king's painter John Stratford (London, P(ublic) R(ecord) O(ffice), E.101/409/12 ff. 21v, 35). Typical of the work of the royal

officeholder is the production in 1425 of tapestry cushions and bench covers for the Star Chamber by John Stout, 'tapicer' and keeper of the king's arras and tapestries (see F. Devon, *Issues of the Exchequer, Henry III to Henry VI, from the Pell Records* (London, 1837), p. 393) and the repair of royal tapestries in 1502–3 by Cornelius van Descrete, royal arrasmaker (P.R.O. E.101/415/7 Nos. 5, 91, 98, 111). Those responsible for the king's arras and tapestry were successively John Bullock (*C(alendar of) P(atent) R(olls)*, 1364–67, p. 421), John Lettreford (*C.P.R. 1388–92*, p. 262), John Stout (*C.P.R. 1413–16*, p. 69), William Jeynkyns (*C(alendar of) C(lose) R(olls)*, 1435–41, p. 404), John Wylde (*C.P.R. 1461–66*, p. 152), John Bakes (*C.P.R. 1485–94*, p. 69) and Cornelius van Descrete (*C.P.R. 1494–1509*, p. 278).

34   See Lestocquoy, *Histoire de la tapisserie, passim.*

35   See R.-A. d'Hulst, *Tapisseries flamandes du XIV<sup>e</sup> au XVIII<sup>e</sup> siècle* (Brussels, 1960), p. xvi.

36   Henry VII's *Trojan War* tapestries, for example, were described in 1488 and 1539 as arras (P.R.O. P.S.O.2/3/s.n.; E.315/456, ff. 47, 47v) and in 1547 as tapestry (B(ritish) L(ibrary), Harley MS. 1419, f. 299).

37   See note 33 above.

38   For Worsely's imports in 1440 see P.R.O. Customs Accounts, E.122/208/1 f. 29v and *C.C.R. 1435–41*, pp. 396, 399. For the wholesale trade see Quinn and Ruddock, *Port Books, passim.*

39   H.T. Riley, *Memorials of London and London Life in the XIIIth, XIVth and XVth Centuries* (London, 1868), pp. 375–6.

40   Tom Campbell kindly informs me that by the sixteenth century arras was formally distinguished from counterfeit arras on the basis of the former's inclusion of silk thread. He will discuss this distinction in his Ph.D. thesis on the tapestry collection of Henry VIII.

41   McKendrick, 'Edward IV', p. 524.

42   Richard II's tapestries can easily be seen as forming the greatest part of the collection that passed to Henry V (compare P.R.O. E.101/403/19 No. 67 and E.361/6/8). Most of Henry's own collection passed to his son, although this time by purchase (compare *Rotuli Parliamentorum*, IV, pp. 229–41 and P.R.O. E.101/408/2). The foundations on which was built the huge collection of Henry VIII, as recorded in 1547, were the collections of previous monarchs.

43   See p. 45 above.

44   Of the five pieces originally owned by Warwick (see P.R.O. C.145/266/12) Richard II secured in 1398 'j dozour et ij costres dovereign de aras del estory de Roy alisandre contenants cxvj verg.' (P.R.O. E.153/1826/16), which were listed together with his other arras in 1399 (P.R.O. E.101/403/19 No. 67).

45   'j pece d'arras d'or de Seint George, que comence en l'escriptur' des lettres d'or *Geaus est Agles*, ovec les armes de monseigneur de Gloucestre . . .' (*Rotuli Parliamentorum*, IV, p. 238). This piece appears to be the same as that found at Pleshy in 1397 (W.H. St. John Hope, 'Inventory of the Goods and Chattels Belonging to Thomas, Duke of Gloucester, and Seized in his Castle at Pleshy, co. Essex, 21 Richard II (1397), with their Values, as Shown in the Escheator's Accounts', *Archaeological Journal*, LIV (1897), p. 288 No. 6. Henry V also possessed armorial tapestries of the duke of Gloucester (*Rotuli Parliamentorum*, IV, p. 241), which were first recorded in his father's collection in 1405–6 (P.R.O. E.361/6/2 m.1).

46   'j lite d'arras d'or de Chessis qui jadis estoit a Seigneur d'Escrop qui forfist a Roy' (*ibid.*, p. 235).

47   'vij dorsaria de opere de aras unde j textum in diversis locis cum auro de Cipro, j de fama mundi, j de regibus exulatis, et ij de diversis historiis' (P.R.O. E.361/5/1). The earliest documented pieces of arras owned by a member of the royal family, namely

those listed among the goods of Queen Isabel in 1358–9 (F. Palgrave, *The Antient Kalendars and Inventories of the Treasury of His Majesty's Exchequer*, III (London, 1836), pp. 239, 240, 246) appear great rarities.

48  P.R.O. E.101/403/19 No. 67.

49  See notes 15, 44 above.

50  'xxiiij dorsaria d'arras operata cum auro de Cipre' (P.R.O. E.361/5/7).

51  P.R.O. E.361/6/8. Most of the pieces listed here can be identified in Richard II's list (P.R.O. E.101/403/19 No. 67).

52  *Rotuli Parliamentorum*, IV, pp. 229–41 (p. 232 for the *Credo* tapestries).

53  See P.R.O. E.101/408/2.

54  McKendrick, 'Edward IV', p. 521 n. 5.

55  *Ibid.*, pp. 521–22.

56  'divers tapetts of Aras and tapestre werk' (P.R.O. E.404/67/34). The bishop himself had bought 'certein beddes of silk and arras and costeres of arras to the same and other tapestrie' costing £100 from the executors of John Holland (d. 1447), duke of Exeter (W(estminster) A(bbey) M(uniments), 6643 m. 4).

57  'clothes of tapestry werk otherwise called verdours' (P.R.O. E.404/76/1 No. 84).

58  'all the arras, as well as the fyne arras as counterfait arras, with silloures, testours, and counterpoyntes of arras, amountyng to the some of ccxxxij li. xx d.' *Testamenta Eboracensia, or Wills Registered at York,* J. Raine (ed.) IV (Surtees Society, vol. LIII, 1868), p. 311.

59  'blew clothe of arras with flordeluce perssis, and written in golde "Jamais"' (*The Chronicle of Calais,* J.G. Nichols (ed.) (Camden Society, 1846), p. 50). This piece was then prominently displayed at the meeting of Henry VII and Philip the Fair at Calais in June 1500. For similar pieces in the collection of Charles VI see J.J. Guiffrey, 'Inventaire des tapisseries du roi Charles VI vendues ou dispersées par les Anglais de 1422 à 1435', *Bibliothèque de l'Ecole des Chartes*, XLVIII (1887), pp. 74, 77, 87, 401, 410.

60  T. Platter, *Beschriebung der Reisen durch Frankreich, Spanien, England und die Niederlande, 1595–1600,* R. Keiser (ed.) (Basel/Stuttgart, 1968), II, p. 847. This piece is recorded, without reference to its origin, in royal documents from 1543 until its sale in 1649 (B(ritish) L(ibrary), Add. MS. 30367, f. 6 and Harley MS. 1419, f. 300v; O. Millar, 'The Inventories and Valuations of the King's Goods, 1649–51', *Walpole Society,* XLIII (1970–72), p. 292 No. 198). It is possibly to be identified with the 'petit dosseret d'or et de soye, de tapisserie, de l'ystoire du Roy Cloviz brodé autour de fleurs de lys' which was listed in the 1422 inventory of Charles and acquired by John, duke of Bedford in 1423 (see Guiffrey, 'Inventaire', p. 86 No. 135, pp. 401–2). On Bedford's collection see J. Stratford, *The Bedford Inventories: the Worldly Goods of John, Duke of Bedford, Regent of France (1389–1435),* (London, 1993).

61  'j autre pece d'arras d'or, d'estorie de Royes, qui commence *Sanctus Lucius* . . . j autre pece de mesme la suite, qui commence *Sanctus Oswaldus* (P.R.O. E.101/408/2). *Rotuli Parliamentorum,* IV, p. 232 incorrectly give 'Edwardus' for the second piece.

62  'fyve pecys of Arrays made with imagery of King Henry the Vth, Henry the VIth, the Duke of Clarence, the Duke of Bedford, the Duke of Gloucester, with diverse other great men' recorded in the will of Sir David Owen, the natural son of Owen Tudor (W.H. Blaauw, 'On the Effigy of Sir David Owen in Easeborne Church, near Midhurst', *Sussex Archaeological Collections,* VII (1854), pp. 38–9).

63  'una pecia consimilis [i.e. de opere d'arras] de rege Ricardo' (P.R.O. E.101/408/19 No. 67).

64  See, for example, J.J. Guiffrey, *Inventaires de Jean duc de Berry (1401–1416),* II (Paris, 1896), p. 209 No. 20.

65  At his death, part of Henry V's collection was at Westminster in the charge of Robert

Rolleston, keeper of the Great Wardrobe (*Rotuli Parliamentorum*, IV, pp. 233–34) and another part at Windsor in the charge of Roger Assent, keeper of the king's beds at Windsor (*ibid.*, IV, pp. 237–38). Several pieces then at Windsor remained there until the death of Henry VIII (see B.L. Harl. MS. 1419, ff. 298–300v), some still after the death of Charles I (Millar, 'Inventories', p. 290 No. 182) and one, that of *Charlemagne*, as late as 1695/6 (P.R.O., L.C.5/87, s.p.).

66   On the Prince's Wardrobe see R.A. Brown, H.M. Colvin and A.J. Taylor, *The History of the King's Works. The Middle Ages*, II (London, 1963), pp. 981–2. On the Wardrobe of Beds see *The Household of Edward IV. The Black Book and Ordinances of 1478*, A.R. Myers (ed.) (Manchester, 1959), pp. 119–20.

67   Henry VII, for example, had specially transported to Calais and back much rich arras for his meeting with Philip the Fair in 1500 (P.R.O. E.101/415/3 f. 24; *Chronicle of Calais*, pp. 4, 49–50).

68   St. John Hope, 'Thomas, Duke of Gloucester', pp. 288–9. In the great hall at Castle Philip in 1396 there was a doser of arras with a lion carrying a 'giant', which came from Gloucester's wife, Eleanor Bohun (*C(alendar of) I(nquisitions) M(iscellaneous) 1392–99*, p. 116) and in London two 'tablementz' of arras for an altar (*ibid.*, p. 225).

69   See note 15 above.

70   Among his goods forfeited to the Crown in 1397 were two pieces of arras of 'Ferumbras' (*C.I.M. 1392–99*, p. 168); one coster of arras with the story of St John the Baptist (*ibid.*, pp. 171, 172), one doser and four costers of arras with the story of Guy of Warwick (*ibid.*, p. 171) and one doser and four costers of arras with the story of Alexander (*ibid.*, p. 171).

71   Among his goods forfeited to the Crown in 1397 were 'A bed of arras, namely a coverlet and a tester, marked with a castle on each piece' and a doser of arras (L.F. Salzman, 'The Property of the Earl of Arundel, 1397', *Sussex Archaeological Collections*, XCI (1953), p. 50). In his will of 4 March 1393 he bequeathed to his son Richard 'un dorcer d'arras qu'est acustume d'estre pur la chambre pane a Arondell', to his son Thomas 'un petit doser de arras embroudez d'or en certeins lieux d'icell, quele Monsieur William Brian moy donna' and to his daughter Elizabeth 'mon lit de arras, ove touts les tapits que j'avoie a la fesaunce d'icestes fait en mesme la pais except les trois dossers de arras que j'ay devise en autre lieu' (Nichols, *Royal Wills*, pp. 131, 132, 133).

72   C.L. Kingsford, 'Two Forfeitures in the Year of Agincourt', *Archaeologia*, LXX (1920), pp. 80, 91. Unfortunately only two are described in any detail, viz. 'uno alio coster de Aras sine auro cum uno castro albo' and 'j selour de novo Aras dupplicato et operato cum auro, cum sole levante in eodem'.

73   *C.C.R. 1399–1402*, p. 344 and *C.P.R. 1399–1401*, p. 423.

74   *C.C.R. 1435–41*, p. 399 and *C.C.R. 1441–47*, pp. 15–16, 25, 101.

75   *Proceedings and Ordinances of the Privy Council of England*, Sir N.H. Nicolas (ed.) III (London, 1834), pp. 57–9, 60.

76   See note 46 above.

77   *Testamenta Eboracensia*, III (Surtees Society, vol. XL, 1864), p. 306.

78   *Testamenta Eborancensia*, II (Surtees Society, vol. XXX, 1855), p. 121.

79   See W.A.M. 6643, mm. 1, 3.

80   Oxford, Bodleian Library, MS DD Ewelme A.7. Calendared in Thomson, *Tapestry Weaving*, p. 28 and Hist. Mss. Comm., *8th Report* (1881), Appendix I, pp. 628–9.

81   *The Paston Letters*, J. Gairdner (ed.) III (London, 1904), p. 178; *Paston Letters and Papers of the Fifteenth Century*, N. Davis (ed.) I (Oxford, 1971), p. 109.

82   *C.I.M. 1392–99*, p. 171. In 1396, however, Charles VI had repaired a large 'tappiz du duc de Warvic' (Guiffrey, 'Inventaire', p. 94 n. 1).

83   *Testamenta Eboracensia*, I (Surtees Society, vol. IV, 1836), p. 275.

84 'Our hanging of the storye of Hercules made for our great Chamber at Fframynham' (P.R.O., P.R.O.B. 11/21).

85 'unum lectum de arras, cum costers paled de colore rubeo et albo, qui solebant pendere in magna camera infra castrum de Sherifhoton' (*Wills and Inventories Illustrative of the History, Manners, Language, Statistics, etc., of the Northern Counties of England from the Eleventh Century Downwards*, I (Surtees Society, vol. II, 1835), p. 70).

86 See note 80 above.

87 Gairdner, *Paston Letters*, III, pp. 178–86.

88 Later inventories arranged by room include those of Sir Gilbert Talbot taken in 1517 (B.L. Add. Roll 74187) and Sir Reginald Bray in 1503 (P.R.O. E.154/2/10).

89 Thomson, *Tapestry Weaving*, p. 17.

90 See pp. 45–6 above.

91 A.H. Johnson, *The History of the Worshipful Company of the Drapers of London*, I (London, 1914), p. 321.

92 *The Records of the Guild of the Holy Trinity, St. Mary, St. John the Baptist and St. Katherine of Coventry*, II, G. Templeman (ed.) (Dugdale Society, vol. XIX, 1944), p. 143.

93 S.L. Thrupp, *The Merchant Class of Medieval London* (Michigan, 1989), p. 141 n. 122; *Acts of the Court of the Mercers' Company*, L. Lyell and F.D. Watney (eds.) (Cambridge, 1936), p. 239. For further references to the Mercers' arras see *ibid.*, pp. 176, 237, 240, 310, 470.

94 C.M. Clode, *The Early History of the Guild of Merchant Taylors of the Fraternity of St. John the Baptist, with Notices of the Lives*, I (London, 1888), pp. 88–90.

95 For the one piece at Exeter in 1506 see G. Oliver, *Lives of the Bishops of Exeter and a History of the Cathedral* (Exeter, 1861), p. 328. No arras or tapestry is listed at either Lincoln in 1536–57 (see Sir W. Dugdale, *Monasticon Anglicanum*, J. Caley, H. Ellis and B. Bandinel (eds.) VI (London, 1830), pp. 1278–92) or Salisbury in 1536 (see W. Dodsworth, *A Historical Account of the Episcopal See . . . of Sarum, or Salisbury* (Salisbury, 1814), pp. 229–32).

96 See M.E.C. Walcott, 'Inventories and Valuations of Religious Houses at the Time of the Dissolution from the Public Record Office', *Archaeologia*, XLIII (1871), pp. 201–49. Apart from 'a great old arres at the hye dease' in the Hall and a few pieces of the *Planets*, partly in the Jerusalem Chamber, almost nothing was recorded at Westminster (see M.E.C. Walcott, 'The Inventories of Westminster Abbey at the Dissolution', *Transactions of the London and Middlesex Archaeological Society*, IV (1874), pp. 313–64 (esp. pp. 359–60).

97 For the Winchester pieces see Walcott, 'Inventories and Valuations', p. 237; for that given to Canterbury see note 12 above.

98 Owners of tapestry included the archbishops of York Alexander Nevill (*C.I.M. 1387–93*, pp. 19–20, 61), George Nevill and Thomas Savage (*Testamenta Eboracensia*, III, p. 306; IV p. 311), Walter Skirlaw, bishop of Durham (*ibid.*, pp. 316, 320, 324–25) and William Ayscough, bishop of Salisbury (see note 56 above; also *C.C.R. 1441–47*, p. 15).

99 Even the 'pannus de Arys de historia Ducis Burgundie' given to Exeter Cathedral is said to have been a gift not of the bishop, Edmund Lacy, but his executors (Oliver, *Lives of the Bishops of Exeter*, p. 328).

100 P.R.O. E.404/67/34.

101 See *Testamenta Eboracensia*, III, p. 306.

102 'magnus pannus de arrace de vita sancti Kentigerni' (*Registrum Episcopatus Glasguensis*, C. Innes (ed.) (Maitland Club, Edinburgh, 1843), II, p. 334.

103 *Registrum Episcopatus Aberdonensis. Ecclesie Cathedralis Aberdonensis Regesta que extant in unam collecta*, C. Innes (ed.) (Maitland Club, Edinburgh, 1845), II, pp. 141–2. Of these

pieces of arras one of the *Epiphany* was given by Bishop Gilbert Greenshaw (d. 1424), five for the choir of the *Salutation* by Bishop Alexander de Kinnimund (d. 1382) and one 'cum duabus ymaginibus' by Thomas, Earl of Mar and Lord of Garioch (*c.* 1330–?74). In 1403 Greenshaw had himself been given by King Robert 'unum . . . laneum de arras de historia oblationis trium regum de Colonia ad beatam Virginem' which had previously belonged to Bishop Walter Trail (d. 1401) (*ibid.*, I, p. 208).

104    'Register of Vestments, Jewels, and Books for the Choir, etc., Belonging to the College of St. Salvator in the University of St. Andrews, circa A.D. MCCCCL', in *Maitland Miscellany*, III (Edinburgh, 1843), pp. 198–9.

105    'unus pannus operis le arras pendendum pone altare nuper Regis Henrici vj' (*Dugdale, Monasticon Angliae*, VI, p. 1207).

# 3
# Choosing a Book in Late Fifteenth-century England and Burgundy

Anne F. Sutton
*Mercers' Company, London*
Livia Visser-Fuchs
*Baarn, The Netherlands*

'The galeye of myn engyn floting not long syn in the depnes of the sees of diverce auncient histories . . . Sodaynly apperid by me a ship conduited by one man only. This man . . . behelde my regarde . . . and sayde . . . "Man of rude engyn what mervailest thou? Ancre thy galeye here and take thy penne for to write and put in memoire my faites and deeds . . . I am Iason that conquerd the Flees of Golde in the Yle of Colchos . . . I pray the that thou do make a boke unto them that daily speke and inpugne my gloire maye knowe their indiscrete Iugement. And for taccomplisshe the same I have chosen the to thende that thou presente this present writing unto the fader of writars of histories, wiche ys unto Phelip, fader and lover of all vertues in his time Duc of Bourgoygne and of Brabant etc. The whiche hath ben in all his time enclined and of grete affeccion to here and see red the auncient histories . . . for his singuler passetemps." '[1]

As a result of his surprise encounter with his dictatorial hero, Jason, Raoul le Fèvre's search for a book ended successfully: 'I ancred my galeye and put in wrytyng hys faytes.' Le Fèvre's rather laboured metaphor dramatises the difficulties of finding in the late fifteenth century the book that you wanted, whether just to buy and read, to translate, copy, or even rewrite and present to someone who might reward you. In practical terms how did you find a desirable book, discover what was available or locate a copy of a particular text you had heard of? What variety was available to the Yorkist royal family, to William Caxton, Louis of Gruuthuse or Philip of Cleves, or any of their contemporaries with an interest in books and the money to indulge that interest?

Any study of books and their owners is dependent on the vagaries and misleading emphases of survival. It is obvious that inventories are an essential starting point for such a study, to show which were the standard books 'everyone' needed, which were popular and which unusual; but even a long inventory may be selective or only reflect the range of a library accurately for a very short space of time. The simple selection of four 'libraries', two on each side of the Channel poses considerable problems. There are no significant inventories of books belonging to any English secular person of rank in the second half of the fifteenth-century.[2] The brief lists of books known for Sir John Paston (17 volumes),[3] John Howard (14),[4] or Thomas Charleton (9),[5] cannot be dignified by the title of library inventories. In contrast across the Channel, there are substantial records that even permit discussion of the building-up of a single collection over the years, like the fine sequence of twelve inventories with supporting accounts of the dukes of Savoy covering most of the fifteenth century.[6] The dukes of Burgundy in 1467 owned about 900 books;[7] aristocrats like Philip de Croy 88 books;[8] of the Grand Bastard Anthony's books 33 survive;[9] Rafael de Mercatellis, another bastard of Duke Philip, had about 300 books;[10] and about a dozen survive for Jean de Wavrin, the historian of England.[11] From these riches two libraries have been selected to provide a basis for this enquiry: that of Philip of Cleves, lord of Ravenstein and a close relative of the dukes of Burgundy (1456–1528) for which an inventory of about 127 books exists and 49 books survive;[12] and secondly that of Louis of Gruuthuse, governor of Holland when Edward IV was exiled there and well known to the Yorkist court, of which about 175 volumes survive containing more than 150 titles.[13]

As stated, there are neither inventories nor comparable survivals of books for late-fifteenth-century England. There is, however, the ready-made list of William Caxton's publications, a total of 99 books and 72 titles.[14] As a professional chooser of books Caxton can act as a touchstone for the popularity of a text, far more telling than the regular recurrence of a title in the inventories of aristocrats.

The second English 'library list' has to be a compilation – put together from all the books associated with members of the Yorkist royal family.[15] Richard, Duke of York, four books;[16] Cecily, Duchess of York, seven English devotional works, 39 service books, a total of 46.[17] Of their children who survived into the reign of Edward IV, nothing is known for George of Clarence or Elizabeth of Suffolk. Edward IV had at least 40 books, not including any service books. His queen, Elizabeth Woodville, can be associated with six texts including the London poem celebrating Barnet and Edward IV's return which was dedicated to her.[18] Of their children, Edward, Prince of Wales, can be linked with two books and one poem, a total of three;[19] Elizabeth of York as princess and then queen can be associated with about eight texts.[20] To return to the older generation, Anne of Exeter owned two books that survive, and possibly received the dedication of another.[21] Margaret of York, Duchess of Burgundy, is in a class by herself: she both commissioned and gave away many books. Twenty-eight can be associated with her, of which 22 survive.[22] Richard III can be linked to twelve volumes (18 texts), including two dedications.[23] His queen can only be allotted one text in which her name occurs with his.[24] The total number of known books for these members of the Yorkist royal family including all dedications is 149, obviously a very low figure; the requisite 30–40 service books each of them must have owned bring the number up to about 400.[25]

In order to answer the original questions – what books were available and how did one get them – using these four 'inventories' as the basic tools of reference and comparison, five topics will be discussed: the book-trade around 1480, especially from Caxton's point of view; the business of translation; the popularity of romances; the popularity of books about or by the ancients; and lastly some aspects of Edward IV's library.

As a mercer and merchant adventurer, Caxton had learnt the European trade in small-wares, including books, at first hand; as governor of the Merchant Adventurers in the Low Countries he had got to know most people worth knowing in trade and diplomacy between Calais and Utrecht, London and Cologne. In 1470–1, when he was in his early fifties, Caxton changed the direction of his life and set out to become a printer. After printing a few books in both French and English in Bruges he decided to settle in the sanctuary of Westminster Abbey, the sanctuary location being almost certainly the key to his choice.[26] Caxton must have been well aware of the hostility shown in European towns to the first printers who opened for business and his remarkable business acumen would not have allowed him to take avoidable risks.[27] In the sanctuary he was protected from the prejudices and laws of the city of London: its aversion to the employment of aliens who made up the workforce of his press; the possible jealousy of its book-traders, the company of Stationers.[28]

In order to form conclusions about all Caxton's options when he decided to print a work in English at his own risk – and it usually was at his own risk[29] – the ideal starting point would be a study of each of his books, taking in the availability of each in manuscript and print and the likely source of his copy, its subject matter and potential readership, its size and therefore its cost to print and hold in stock.[30] Caxton knew, for example, that a wealthy MP who could afford the 432 folios of the *Morte Darthur* might demand a coherent, well-planned and clean text for his money (and this Caxton laboured to produce[31]), and he knew that a chantry priest on 6–8 marks a year would not be able to afford more than a few pence for the text now usually known as the *Quattuor Sermones*, translated and cobbled together at high speed by Caxton.[32] Of necessity, however, this study has to rely on a few individual studies so far completed and some simple arithmetic.

Not only did each text that he printed for himself rather than on commission force Caxton to make choices, but his fellow book traders also limited his freedom. Although protected to a large extent by his sanctuary location he had to pay them careful attention, and his options are only fully understandable in the context of the varied activities of the few English book dealers about whom more than the minimum is known, such as the so-called 'Lydgate scribe' of Bury St Edmunds, John Multon, stationer of London (and possible part-inheritor of the John Shirley interest), quite apart from the several aliens handling extensive imports of foreign books and operating presses, however briefly, in the city of London, like Henry Frankenberg, John Lettou and William de Machlinia.[33] Native entrepreneurs like Caxton's fellow merchant adventurer, William Wylcocks, had joined him in making money from printed books by 1480–1, and the prominent alien booksellers, Henry Frankenberg, John of Westphalia and his associate, Peter Actors of Savoy, were between them importing nearly 1,500 volumes into London in 1480–81 alone.[34] All these were Caxton's competitors but also his potential allies as suppliers of new texts and as distributors. It is now generally agreed that Caxton dealt in books of all kinds and not just his own: he probably sold the books of Veldener who had taught him printing and made his type-faces;[35] it is equally possible he sold the up-market productions of his former Bruges colleague, Colard Mansion;[36] it has been suggested he collaborated with or employed Machlinia as well as the Oxford and St Albans printers;[37] he certainly commissioned books from William Maynal, a Paris printer in 1487 and he was apparently well aware of what was being printed in France.[38] Caxton's understanding of his market proved to be better than that of any of the early printers in England, all of whom had failed by 1486: like the equally successful Günther Zainer of Augsburg he specialised in vernacular books, made his own translations, and was not therefore overwhelmed by the flood of Latin texts printed abroad, especially in Italy.[39]

During the 1470s the printed book had become a familiar object in England and by 1480 the trade was well established,[40] indeed, the London book-trade's cosmopolitan, European nature can hardly be over-emphasised for this date. By the 1480s a large number of classical authors had been printed on the continent, and from the 1470s the French were busy printing French translations of classical texts. By 1480 it is estimated that any enthusiastic scholar could get any printed text from anywhere; it just took time and persistence. A shop in late fifteenth-century Tours had over 250 titles all in French and mostly history and literature.[41] Caxton, with all his merchant adventurer contacts at the fairs of the Low Countries, his mercery contacts with Italian merchants, his bespoke printing done for eager Italian authors like Lorenzo Traversagni and Pietro Carmeliano, was quite as able to keep his shop well stocked.[42] All he had to do was to select what to translate for his customers who wanted books in English: Ovid's

*Metamorphoses* in 1481, *Aesop* in 1484 from a Lyons edition of 1480, *Eneydos*, about 1490, probably from a 1488 French edition.[43]

Caxton's own description of his study full of books and pamphlets from which to choose his next project must contain a general truth,[44] but as a publisher he had particular requirements that a private reader did not necessarily share: he needed a complete text, one in 'modern' English,[45] and preferably a short one, long texts being tedious to translate and expensive to print. He was certainly on constant look-out for good English texts but he only tells one real story of his search for them: he went through Westminster Abbey's old books and gave up in the face of Old English and probably Anglo-Saxon as well.[46] In theory he could have bought any hopeful text from any stationer or scrivener, printed it, perhaps depriving the scribe of a regular income from a precious exemplar – he lived in a sanctuary, was not a member of the Stationers and owned no fraternal obligations to them, and he had powerful friends. There is, however, no evidence that Caxton ever operated in this way, and indeed open piracy would have been unprofitable as he needed to trade in manuscripts and needed the networks of the London Stationers – as well as his fellow Mercers – to sell the multiple copies of his books wherever he could; nor did he want his advertisements torn down as soon as he posted them up. It seems likely that the intruder's choice of texts was governed not merely by availability but by certain informal, well-understood and powerful controls within the book-trade over the reproduction of certain texts, even though this corpus of texts constantly changed as recognised owners of exemplars died or sold them on to others, as the texts were superseded or became so old and so well known that no one could claim any personal stake in them.[47] It was both the owners of exemplars and the increasing number of book producers who speculated in multiple copies of manuscripts in an increasingly 'managed' craft – whether Stationers, Mercers or Painters – who needed to have some security for their investment.[48] The most important controls were part of the city of London's own civic structure and second-nature to Caxton: the fraternal cooperation expected among citizens and more especially among those of one trade; the arbitration of wardens and above them the mayor and aldermen to whom all members of a company could refer.[49] Caxton's decision to live in Westminster may have been a tribute to the coercive powers of a London company, even such a comparatively lowly one as the Stationers.[50]

Support for this idea that Caxton's freedom of choice (among English texts) was limited by such informal controls is provided by his publication of the poet Lydgate. Out of a canon of about 150 works he printed only six texts, all early works of the poet, and only three of them of any size.[51] Four of these appeared in 1477 (the *Churl and the Bird, c.* 1398; the *Debate of the Sheep and the Goose*, 1398?; *Stans Puer*; and the *Temple of Glass*, 1400–20), all very popular and running to more than one edition. He printed no more until the *Pilgrimage of the Soul* (begun 1426) in 1483, and the *Life of the Virgin Mary* (1409–11) in 1484 which may have run into a second edition. Excellent sales would surely have spurred him to look for Lydgate's other works. As it is unlikely that he simply could not find any manuscripts, given the poet's popularity and the high survival rate of copies of his works,[52] the reasons for Caxton's limited publication of Lydgate must lie elsewhere. Lydgate had only died in 1451 and during his last years at least seems to have exercised authorial control over the dissemination of his compositions.[53] It may be significant that all Caxton's publications were of early works, the latest being *The Pilgrimage* begun in 1426. Some people who had known Lydgate were still alive and knew they owned copies endorsed by his friendship and approval: an unnamed scribe or stationer appears to have held an exemplar of the *Fall of Princes* (finished *c.* 1438) and produced a series of copies[54] and the so-called 'Lydgate scribe' of Bury St Edmunds retained exemplars of the *Life of St. Edmund* (1433–4) and the *Fall of Princes*.[55] John Shirley had been a friend of Lydgate and over a long life had collected a large number of his works, often poor copies from the point of view of modern scholars, but important, then and now, because of his personal acquaintance with the poet.[56] Some of Shirley's texts passed to a professional stationer, John Multon, whose career was flourishing by 1456, the year of Shirley's death. Copies of Lydgate's works deriving from Shirley's exemplars survive in Multon's handwriting.[57] Multon died in 1475 but two Robert Multons, who were his relatives, continued in the trade until 1495. If a personality like the 'Lydgate scribe' or publisher of Bury St Edmunds, for example, or a Multon, stationer of London, had a recognised corner in certain texts – however informally controlled – Caxton may have had to tread warily: he might be able to come to an arrangement of mutual profit or he might have to decide to choose another text. It would surely not have appealed to the ex-diplomat to antagonise established interests. It is possible to suggest that several, perhaps many, Lydgate texts were actually barred to Caxton and that prosperous London stationers like the Multons were well able to protect themselves.

This limitation of Caxton's freedom of choice to print did not of course apply to ordinary readers in London who were only checked by their purse and the text's availability. An examination of John Multon's shop before his death in 1475 shows that it was quite as exciting a place to visit as Caxton's after 1476. Texts that survive in Multon's hand include minor works by Lydgate and Chaucer (many of the Shirley/Lydgate pieces were no doubt recommended to customers as copies by a personal friend of the poet), as well as the *Canterbury Tales* and extracts from Lydgate's *Fall of Princes*; he copied the *Court of Sapience*, the *Assembly of Ladies*, Hoccleve's *Regiment of*

*Princes*, poems by the Earl of Suffolk, *Pierce the Plowman's Creed*, and the *Secret of Secrets* in verse and prose. He produced many English translations: Aesop's *Fables*, a prose *Merlin*,[58] the *Petyt Job*, Bacon's *Treatises*, the *Statutes* of England,[59] the *Gospel of Nicodemus*, Rolle's *Emendatio Vitae*, the *Acts of the Apostles*, the *Dicts of the Philosophers*, Alexander's Letter to Aristotle, the *Jesus Psalter*. He provided copies of London ordinances and civic texts, recipes, almanacs and nativities in English as well as Fortescue's *Governance of England*. It can be suggested he sold copies of the *Somnium Vigilantis*, the London poem on Barnet, dedicated to the Queen, the *Book of Nurture* and Fortescue's *Declaration* disavowing his anti-Yorkist writings. It is also fairly certain that he had access to most of the broadsides and accounts of political events that were circulating in London 1420–75, the kind of material London citizens put into their chronicles. Multon seems to have recognised that a good bookseller aims to hold in stock the greatest variety of texts possible and, like Caxton, he seems to have catered to the increasing demand for translations from Londoners who read only English with facility. Multon had no prescriptive right over any of these texts – only the means that every established citizen and stationer of London had to secure his livelihood and his pre-eminence as a supplier of particular texts.

At first glance the activities of Caxton or Multon appear very different from the more orderly and aristocratic world of David Aubert, scribe, translator and editor of the dukes of Burgundy, but the full range of commercial enterprises of a stationer like Multon is not known and there has been no study of Aubert.[60] Only the known surviving work of these men can be compared: Multon produced cheap, often textually careless, copies for the average Londoner who was certainly a lively customer but not always discriminating; Aubert produced elegantly planned, textually correct works on vellum, often beautifully illuminated and commissioned by aristocrats. Even Charles the Bold might wander into Aubert's shop and be greeted by the furious barking of the scribe's elderly dog, and prince and scribe were on such terms that the incident was recorded by the painter Loyset Liedet.[61] Such a scene was not necessarily impossible in Multon's shop: the city was packed with the town-houses of England's aristocracy and some of them bought books. The personal commissioning of a particular text remained one important way of choosing a book in the Yorkist period, even as buying ready-made, speculative productions was becoming increasingly common, first in manuscript and then in print.[62] Caxton, Multon and Aubert were all professional suppliers of books, however different: Caxton was as capable of arranging for magnificent manuscripts to be made as was Aubert; Caxton and Aubert included translation as a natural part of their activities; and some of the translations copied by Multon may possibly have been his own or commissioned by him.

The increasing demand for reading matter by those who only read their native language with facility made the supply of translation, from Latin into French and from both Latin and French into English, one of the most important aspects of the book-trade by the end of the fifteenth century. The conclusions of John Trevisa and Lord Berkeley at the beginning of the century about the merits of translation need little improvement: it enables knowledge to be transferred from the more learned to the less learned and facilitates communication between people otherwise barred from mutual understanding; it is beneficial and should be encouraged; it should be in prose because prose is 'more clear'.[63]

Fifteenth-century translators varied a lot in their backgrounds, careers and freedom of choice.[64] Some were religious like Osbern Bokenham, some held positions in a household like John Shirley, Stephen Scrope, Benedict Burgh, William Worcester, Gilbert Banaster or Nicholas Harpisfeld; some worked only on request, some were part of a literary circle like Shirley and Bokenham, others were professionals and doubled as scribes, printers, ambassadors or merchants like de Lucena, Aubert, Multon and Caxton. Others are virtually unknown like Raoul le Fèvre and John Kay.[65] The list of those who worked directly under the aegis of the Burgundian dukes is a long one; in contrast the Yorkist royal family seem to have had no in-house translators.

Vasco de Lucena worked ostensibly for Charles the Bold, perhaps at the instigation of the dowager duchess, a Portuguese like himself. He acted as an ambassador and moved later into the service of Margaret of York translating several religious treatises for her. He himself was a book-collector and a substantial art-patron. His first major work was an ambitious translation and expansion of Quintus Curtius' *History of Alexander*. It took seven years (1461–8) and the encouragement of both John of Calabria, brother of Margaret of Anjou, and Isabella of Portugal to complete, he tells us, in terms that are reminiscent of Caxton's own description of his first venture in translation.[66]

Few English translators were probably as well rewarded as de Lucena, but like him, few translated as a full-time occupation. Osbern Bokenham was a friar of Clare (active *c.* 1438–56) and was never dependent on his patrons. He was always on the look-out for new books: on a rain-drenched visit to the monastery of Montefiascone he made a copy of a life of St Margaret to take home to Clare. He is best known for his verse lives of female saints composed for, among others, Isabel, Countess of Essex and sister of Richard, Duke of York. He may be the translator of the *Golden Legend* used – or abused, depending on your point of view – by Caxton for his edition of 1481. Osbern wore his classical education lightly, he liked to show off with parallel texts in English and Latin, he composed in Latin and he liked explanatory addenda. In short, he was a scholar, like de Lucena, even a budding 'humanist', who had been to Italy at least twice.[67]

Far better known are the translations of Anthony Woodville, Earl Rivers, brother of Edward IV's queen. He described in detail how he was given the *Dicts and Sayings of the Philosophers* to read by a fellow passenger and pilgrim on board ship bound for Compostella. If the work was indeed the revelation to him that he claimed he was singularly behind the times: it had been a standard text for many years and was in most aristocratic libraries; it had been in print in French since 1473 and had certainly been translated into English before. In fact the point of Rivers' disingenuous story is that he was reading an improving book while on pilgrimage.[68] His other translations are of the same moralising and improving kind: Christine de Pisan's *Moral Proverbs* (1478) and the *Cordial* (1479). Translation was certainly never more than a hobby for Woodville and it can be unkindly wondered whether the secretary deputed to oversee the printing of the last two works was not more than a proof-reader and censor of any Caxtonian embellishments in the form of comments on the earl's love-life.[69]

William Worcester was another part-time, and in his case, under-rated translator. He too was published by Caxton, but unlike Woodville he had no secretary to protect his work, and unlike Sir Thomas Malory the manuscript of his translations does not survive to show how Caxton tampered with it.[70] He produced Cicero's *Old Age* for Sir John Fastolf,[71] Cicero's *Friendship* and Montemagno's *Declamation of Noblesse*. Caxton printed all three together in 1481: it is likely he somehow got hold of the only manuscript copy. Probably Worcester himself never knew that his work had been published 'under the umbre and shadow of [Edward IV's] noble protection'.[72]

Caxton himself was the most prolific of English fifteenth-century translators. Out of the 72 titles he published, 26 were his translations and three were his adaptations or editions. With these 29 books he can be said to have been most personally involved: he had to immerse himself in them and be convinced he was spending his time profitably. Eight were romances, eleven were books of moral guidance, four were histories, two were pagan and two were Christian collections of stories; there was one life of an earl, one life of a saint, and lastly one satire of chivalric romance, *Reynard the Fox*. The subject matter of his translations is as well balanced as it is for his overall output of 72 titles: 41 religious and didactic texts to 31 literature and history.

The romances in particular have usually been singled out as examples of the 'courtly' works which Caxton is supposed to have personally wanted to publish.[73] Was there, however, in fact a taste in England for 'courtly' romances in prose, and were any of the Yorkist royal family, Louis of Gruuthuse, Philip of Cleves, or Caxton himself, really interested in romance-reading? Romances are taken to include all tales of adventure, magical worlds, and the great 'matters' of France, Britain and Rome (entertaining narratives in a 'chivalric' setting).

Most English prose romances were produced between 1460 and 1520 and Caxton's translations form a significant proportion of these.[74] Across the Channel it is estimated that well over one hundred French poems alone were turned into prose romances from the fourteenth century onwards.[75] Caxton, therefore, had plenty of material in French to choose from and printing only made more of them accessible. Romances already in English prose, however, were almost certainly more difficult for anyone to find, including Caxton, if survival rates are anything to go by. There was an English prose *Alexander* (*c.* 1430), an *Ipomedon* (*c.* 1460), two prose *Merlins* (*c.* 1450–60), a *Melusine* (*c.* 1480), *King Pontus* (*c.* 1465), and the *Three Kings' Sons* (*c.* 1480–5) composed originally to flatter Philip of Burgundy's dreams of leading a crusade.[76] All survive in only one copy; none was printed by Caxton and some were certainly not good enough.

In fact Caxton published very few romances: eight out of his seventy-two titles. Nevertheless all of these were books he translated or edited and in the production of which he was personally involved. His first two English translations were the *Histories of Troy* (in fact the story of Hercules) and *Jason*, both printed 1473–6; presumably his French editions of both had done well. Over the following nine to ten years he printed no romances – he did print the satire of chivalric romance, *Reynard the Fox* in 1481 – and only in the middle of 1485 did he bring out the *Morte Darthur*, with his five other romances following 1485–90. Either he had found such books did not do as well in England as he had hoped – or as they did across the Channel – or he simply could not find suitable texts.[77] Three of the romances printed in and after 1485 were in fact suggested to him: *Charles the Great* (96ff.) by his friend, William Daubeney, *Blanchardyn and Eglantine* (51ff.) by Margaret Beaufort and the *Four Sons of Aymon* (278ff.) by the Earl of Oxford. Only the last was a large book and in his epilogue Caxton complains both of its length and his lack of reward from the earl. It is debatable whether this tale ever appealed to the average English reader as much as it did to the dukes of Burgundy who identified their opposition to the king of France with the rebellion of Aymon's sons against Charlemagne.[78]

Caxton's own choice among the romances he printed boils down to the *Histories of Troy, Jason, Paris and Vienne* and *Eneydos*. It can be suggested that the first two had little success and that this led to his failure to print any more romances for nearly a decade. Their lack of success could have been caused by the poor quality of his first efforts at translation, but also because the heroes of these stories, Hercules and Jason, were not the natural favourites in England that they were in Burgundy.[79] Caxton's other 'choices' were the short and lively *Paris and Vienne* (*c.* 1485; 36ff.), one of his best translations and one that also appealed to John Howard, and the *Eneydos* (*c.* 1490; 86ff.), also reasonably short and, as the story of the Trojan ancestors of the founder of Britain, fairly certain to appeal to an English readership. Caxton's greatest find and probably his only real success among his romances, and certainly the only one to become enduringly popular, was the *Morte Darthur*:[80] he only had to adapt Malory's translations, the subject was one of intense English interest, and the author was conveniently dead.

There is little hard evidence that Caxton particularly wanted to print, or had any preference for, what are called 'courtly' romances; he certainly steered well clear of verse romances and no romance is known to have been reprinted by him.[81] Nor is there any real evidence that romances were preferred reading in 'courtly' circles. Caxton's modest output of eight accords well with the overall profile of romances in the literature of his day: romances, tales and *facetiae* made up 3.81 per cent of early printed books;[82] the dukes of Savoy had 13 per cent romances, the dukes of Burgundy had no more, Philip of Cleves 6 per cent and the Croy family less than 20 per cent.[83] The Yorkist royal family had ten romances between them, but only when each Canterbury Tale is counted as a separate item. Edward IV *chose* none.[84] These figures, such as they are, all reflect the choice of readers of French who had a far better range of romances to choose from, both in quantity and quality.[85]

The prime function of a romance was to entertain and pass the time as Caxton, the true bookseller, admitted in his prologue to the *Morte Darthur*, but he also knew only too well that this admission had to be followed swiftly by reference to the same work's lessons of etiquette and social behaviour.[86] It is difficult to avoid the conclusion that by the second half of the fifteenth century many readers of the English language would have agreed that most romances in English were, or had become, 'bolde bawdrye';[87] they were hard to justify even in prose. Only if they overlapped with what was thought of as history – *Troy*,[88] *Charles the Great, Eneydos*, some of the *Morte Darthur* – were they acceptable reading matter for the young or serious minded adult; otherwise they were a frivolous alternative to *real* battles and *real* history. Caxton's careful and small selection of romances shows that he came to understand a risky branch of the English book market.

Printers, scribes and translators had practical reasons to select or reject a text and their options might be better described as limitations. 'Consumers' or private readers were, however, theoretically free in their choice. The *embarras de choix* that faced them in the shop of a scribe like Multon has been described. To look at the problem from another angle, one category of texts grouped by their contents has been selected to study

'our' owners' choice within a limited field: to what extent did they show
an interest in books by the 'ancients' and texts about classical history and
literature. It is obvious that there was such an interest, but what shape did it
take? Which texts did the Yorkist princes and their Burgundian
counterparts choose to own? What books did they have in Latin – always
excluding liturgical and school books – and what is the evidence of their
knowledge of Latin? Is it justifiable even to mention the word 'humanism'
in relation to them – humanism in the sense of an 'academic' interest in
antiquity and in classical texts for their own sake?[89]

They did have a choice. As implied earlier, a persistent scholar, any
'person with initiative, patience and the necessary cash' could obtain any
published book.[90] This applied principally to printed books, but, to a lesser
extent, it is true of manuscripts as well and probably more so of 'classical'
books than of any other category. This becomes clear when the collections
of men like Shirwood and Russell are examined, for example. They were
able to acquire very diverse books, printed and manuscript, in very diverse
places, in England and on the continent;[91] they seem to have obtained
more or less what they wished.

There was, of course, a difference between the collections of such
scholars and clerics and those of laymen: the quality and quantity of the
books owned by George Neville[92] are very different from the one surviving
manuscript of his brother, the Earl of Warwick,[93] two men from the same
background and presumably of similar intelligence. It is also remarkable that,
as far as it can now be concluded from such evidence as survives, the
general attitude to books of Edward IV and his two brothers should have
been so different: quite a few survive of Edward's, but very few were signed,
a number survive of Gloucester's and nearly all have been signed, and none
at all are known to be extant of Clarence's, signed or unsigned.

Personal inclination then as now played a large part in the choice of
texts, and this, combined with the general availability *and* the undoubted
reputation of the 'ancients' as the accepted authorities[94] on everything –
philosophy, history, literature – may perhaps justify the assumption that if
our owners did *not* have an existing book from or about antiquity they did
not *wish* to own it, though all evidence, of course, remains subject to the
arbitrariness of survival.

Books concerned with antiquity available in the late fifteenth century
were widely disparate in contents, date and origin. They were 'pagan' and
Christian and – for lack of a better word – humanist. Apart from the 'real'
classics, there were medieval compilations and redactions of the originals,
as well as apocryphal works, all equally popular. They were in Latin and in
the vernaculars; there was something for everybody.

In the period discussed here the Burgundian ducal library contained all
the standard classical texts and their vernacular versions, but the dukes'

collection can hardly be taken as representative. It had not been shaped by individual choice: it was, to put it crudely, a catch-all for everything that was produced at the time; it had been enlarged by successive dukes at great cost, it had absorbed part of the magnificent French old royal library and it had survived for three generations.[95] The last Valois duke, Charles the Bold, was less of a collector than his predecessors, but he may have been a better scholar and linguist. As he is the only prince resembling 'our' owners about whose scholarship some evidence other than from book-ownership is available, he can be used as a touchstone. He was educated by Antoine Haneron, an authority on the correct writing of Latin, and as a result – though Charles himself said he knew only 'soldiers' Latin' – people claimed he knew it as well as French, and had an *agu entendement latiniste*. He was able to use Latin quotations, and it is known that he – or perhaps his mother – stimulated the making of several new translations that can be called humanist in their conscientious faithfulness to the original.[96]

Among Gruuthuse's *circa* 175 extant volumes and the few he is known to have had but which have disappeared, there are only five in Latin; except for Ptolemy none of them is 'classical', one is a cleverly organised, glossed, parallel Dutch and Latin text of Boethius *De consolatione*.[97] We have to assume that this small number reflects his lack of interest, as there seems to be no particular reason why *Latin* books of his should not survive.[98] At the end of his career Gruuthuse had what amounts to every translation made in and before his time: St Augustine, Josephus, Justinian and other law books, Aristotle, Curtius, Livy, Caesar, Ovid and the inevitable Valerius Maximus; also the standard collections on Troy and the history of Rome. As far as we know he had no printed books at all.

Philip of Cleves had as many as fifteen items in Latin according to his inventory of 127 items,[99] several of them containing a number of separate works. They range from Terence and Virgil, to a five-volume printed version of works by Leonardo Bruni and various pieces by Petrarch. Philip, too, had a large array of translations, as many as Gruuthuse. His *compendia* included Jean Mansel's *Fleur des histoires*, which was virtually a history of the world and a standard text in every library.[100]

The comparable libraries of the Croy family,[101] Anthony of Burgundy – *le Grand Bâtard*[102] – and the historian Jean de Wavrin[103] appear to have contained no Latin texts at all, except another *De consolatione* with translation owned by Anthony. Wavrin had the histories of Troy in French, as well as the translation of the *Romuléon*,[104] which has most of ancient history up to Constantine the Great, and a French version of Aristotle's *Ethics*. Anthony, too, owned the Troy book, the *Romuléon*, several works by St Augustine, Caesar's *Commentaries*, Curtius' *Alexander* and Valerius Maximus, all in translation. The Croys had all these, and a *Fleur des histoires*, translations of Vegetius, Ovid and the *Punic Wars*.

Our other touchstone, Caxton's press, reveals a very limited selection, but one that resembles the collections of many of 'our' owners. He printed very few texts in Latin and in each case acted as jobbing printer rather than as publisher.[105] His Boethius – Chaucer's good and popular translation was available – his *Histories of Troy, Jason,* Ovid and Virgil, all fit the pattern found in private libraries: apart from the *De consolatione* they were all story-books. All these were moreover ready to hand in French for easy and rapid translation. The two dialogues by Cicero, *Old Age* and *Friendship,* and the *Declamacion of Noblesse* were popular in Burgundy, as Caxton must have known, but it was probably the accident of his coming across William Worcester's translations in manuscript that made him decide to publish these short, readable texts.

By comparison with the Burgundians the Yorkist princes do not do badly as potential scholars. Two of the very few, non-religious texts that can be linked to Richard, Duke of York, are in Latin, with a parallel English translation. Both can probably be ascribed to Osbern Bokenham, and they may, of course, reflect the nascent humanism of the author rather than York.[106] The longer of the two is a translation *cum* edition made in 1445 of part of a poem called the *Consulate of Stilicho* by the Roman author Claudian, who wrote *c.* 400.[107] Bokenham's translation has been called pedantic, but he knew what he was doing: he added a prologue and an epilogue, and some of his so-called errors appear to be omissions and changes by which he cleverly turned the text into a personal 'mirror' for the protector York, reminding him of the rewards of 'virtue', and stressing the importance of the 'common good'. The shorter text that can perhaps be connected with York is the so-called Clare Roll, a history of the Austin Friars at Clare celebrating their patrons, the Lords and Ladies of Clare, written in 1456 when York was its Lord. It is an original work, a dialogue between a layman – a visitor – questioning and a resident cleric answering. It is illustrated with a picture of the speakers and the coats of arms of the Lords of Clare. As in the Claudian a Latin and an English version are placed side by side.[108]

It can be objected that neither manuscript suggests that Richard of York *chose* it, and that they were composed wholly at the author's initiative. This problem, however, is raised by every dedicated work. The question remains why these bi-lingual texts – which were generally rare – were made for him. Why leave in the full Latin text, or compose one, if the recipient was not expected to take an interest? Why make a translation if the future owner knew Latin really well? Why have a display of knowledge if the patron's own knowledge was insufficient to allow him to be impressed? Perhaps one can take into consideration the remarks made by John Hardyng in the re-dedication of his *Chronicle of England* to Richard of York – assuming they are not mere flattery or commonplaces – where he claims that the duke had 'good inspeccion'[109] in Latin. Hardyng nonetheless wrote the book in English because Duchess Cecily, whom he also wanted to please, 'hath litell intellect' in Latin.[110]

Cecily Neville apparently did not own any Latin books except her numerous liturgical ones. She seems to have left nothing behind but material for the study of her piety, unlike Charles the Bold's mother, Isabel of Portugal. Of almost equal social status – though not of equal political influence – both women lived the latter parts of their lives in semi-religious retirement. Both were religiously 'active' and shared, for instance, an interest in the revelations of St Bridget. There is some evidence that Isabel of Portugal also actively supported and stimulated the translating work of a humanist like Vasco de Lucena: though officially his translations of Curtius' *Alexander* and Xenophon's *Cyropaedia* were done for Charles, there are some indications that they were commissioned by his mother, who hoped that they might instruct him in temperance and statemanship.[111]

Among the surviving books associated with the other Yorkist ladies there is hardly any non-liturgical text in Latin; there is just one among the manuscripts of Margaret of York. The latter's surviving texts give little indication of an interest in antiquity, but she did have – or at least gave away – Justinus' epitome of the work of Trogus Pompeius, de Lucena's *Alexander*, and his translations of treatises by the pseudo-St Augustine and (pseudo)-St Bernard were made for her.[112] She had, of course, a Boethius and the ubiquitous *Fleur des histoires*. One may assume that she owned Caxton's *Recueil of the Histories of Troy*, but otherwise she is not known to have had any English text, on classical subjects or otherwise.

Edward IV himself owned several volumes in Latin, none of them light reading. Two he had before he became king. One is a small composite fourteenth-century volume, consisting of medical treatises and a glossed version of the pseudo-Aristotelian *Secret of Secrets*. One has to assume Edward was either genuinely interested, or was happy, as a young man, to have any book he could lay hands on.[113] The other Latin book that has his name in it, is a collection of very useful but unexciting formulas for legal documents. Its most remarkable feature is a full-page *ex libris* with much penwork, stating the ownership of Edward, Duke of York. The I of *Iste constat* contains a tiny falcon perching on a closed fetterlock. The dating is almost too pat, but the ownership note must have been written after his father's death and before his coronation.[114] At least two theological books were given by Edward to the library of St George's, Windsor, but he was probably not even aware that they contained Gregory's *Homilies* and early medieval commentaries on the gospels.[115]

More remarkable and less remarked upon are three books given to Edward by foreigners. The first is a text that stressed the necessity of a new crusade. Cardinal Bessarion, the Greek book-collector, humanist, theologian and papal legate composed a plea to the leaders of western Europe, the princes of Italy in particular, to settle their differences and join forces against the Turks. He explained the dangers and exhorted the princes directly; he added the speech of Demosthenes impressing the Athenians with the need to help other city states of Greece against the Macedonian imperialist threat, thus cleverly and aptly using classical history and literature in a contemporary context.[116] The book was printed in Paris 1471/2 and copies were sent, each with a rather impersonal letter of dedication, to the Emperor, the Kings of France and England, the Dukes of Burgundy and Savoy, to prelates and abbots, and others whose copies do not survive. Edward's copy was printed on vellum, has a hand-painted presentation page and survives in the Vatican.[117]

Lorenzo Traversagni, Italian humanist and Franciscan friar, taught at the universities of Cambridge and Paris and frequently stayed in London. Caxton printed his *Pearl of Sacred Eloquence* and its *Epitome*. While in London Traversagni started writing a sequence of theological treatises called 'triumphs'. His *Triumph of the Chastity of the Blessed Virgin Mary* was written in 1477; his *Triumph of the Love of Christ* was presented to William Waynflete in April 1485. In between he dedicated to Edward IV the *Triumph of the Justice of Christ*, which urges king and princes to imitate the justice of their biblical predecessors and Christ himself. These unpublished tracts are elaborate flights of humanist and rhetorical fancy in which classical learning is called in to support Christian ideals.[118]

Pietro Carmeliano, recently called one of 'that series of free-lance Italian intellectuals', arrived in England after 'some years of itinerant humanism'.[119] He is better known for his dedications to Henry VII, but at some time after 1481 he presented a book to Edward IV: a printed copy of Cicero's *De oratore*, the long dialogue that claims that the real orator should have knowledge of everything. It was probably a copy from the edition printed at Venice in 1478 and Carmeliano prefaced it with a Latin poem and covered its margins with his own commentary.[120]

There is a relatively high proportion of Latin texts among the non-liturgical books of Richard III, comparable to the number owned by Philip of Cleves. The long, heavily abbreviated *De regimine principum*, the large compilation of English history, the companion volumes containing Guido delle Colonna's *Historia Destructionis Troiae*, Geoffrey of Monmouth's *Historia Regum Britanniae* and the *Prophecy of the Eagle* and Carmeliano's verse *Life of St Katherine*: none of these would have been of any use to him without a good working knowledge of Latin. The English translations that Richard owned were few: Vegetius' *De re militari* and Mechtild of Hackeborn's *Book of Special Grace*; the one may have been his son's, the other his wife's.

On the whole one gets the impression from our limited circle of owners that the Yorkist princes chose to own at least as many, and perhaps even more, Latin texts than their Burgundian counterparts. In the 1470s they, too, started to acquire copies of the French translations of classical and Christian-Latin texts that were popular on the continent, but these never made up so large a proportion of their collections as is sometimes thought.

As far as we know, no one has ever bothered to say that the Yorkist kings 'held back' the arrival of the new learning, and the word 'humanism' has never been mentioned in the context of their patronage and book ownership. On the evidence of their books, however, their occasional encouragement of public displays of learning and their patronage of scholars, it can be said that the Yorkist princes were as interested in the progress of learning as could be expected of any fifteenth-century prince.

The English kings may have been a little 'behind' because they lived at the edge of the civilised world: as Osbern Bokenham wrote, their island was 'clepyd Anglia or *angulus*, the which is "a corner", for England . . . stant in a corner of the world'.[121] They still took the practical, 'immediate' kind of interest in antiquity that had prevailed all through the middle ages – and was also still the prevalent attitude at the Burgundian court. They still had the wish to use its potential in real life, to better themselves with its assistance. This is an attractive, personal kind of interest; it leaves the impression that the literate 'lived' with the ancient past as much as they 'lived' with the stories of the Bible. The attention of the humanists to the text for the text's sake and the illusion that they, at last, understood the mind of the Romans is not necessarily to be preferred. The borderline between the 'practical' ('medieval') and the 'academic' ('humanist') attitudes is also difficult to draw. There were many transitional figures, exponents of the 'middle way', such as Lydgate, Bokenham, Whethamstede, William Worcester, Russell. Some of these men were no doubt forced by their position in life to express themselves more traditionally than they actually may have wanted. Edward IV did not personally 'choose' the three humanist books just mentioned, but they were available to him and he may have benefited from them. Is it too much to assume that when Carmeliano presented Cicero's *De oratore* to the king there ensued at least some discussion about the book and its contents and the use of commentaries? Did Bessarion's propaganda for a crusade provoke not only some argument about the political and strategic difficulties of such undertaking, but perhaps also some curiosity about the historical background of Demosthenes' speech? Because of the break represented by the year 1485 we tend to forget that the coming of humanism was a gradual process and merely a matter of time. Men like Traversagni and Carmeliano had been in England and trying to bring themselves to the notice of Edward IV and Richard III from the 1470s.

Much of the knowledge for which they are celebrated was already available in England: it should be remembered that though in Henry VII's time Carmeliano was honoured with the title 'Latin secretary' of the king, it is likely that before that it was silently assumed that the king's secretary knew Latin. Three successive generations of one family may serve as another example of the gradual change: Nicholas Harpisfeld, who served Richard of York, Edward IV and Richard III, was a clerk of the signet with a knowledge of French; his son studied at Oxford and Bologna; his grandsons were, the one a professor of theology, the other Regius professor of Greek.

It is no longer necessary to labour the point that English kings and queens were book owners before 1461 and that some of their books were available to Edward IV when he came to the throne.[122] Individual kings, queens and princes had always had their own collections, they gave their books away, were given others, inherited them from their parents and relatives and at their deaths their collection was rifled for bequests and by the opportunist courtier and collector. In 1461 Edward would have inevitably become the owner of a royal collection, however disordered and depleted by greedy courtiers and civil war.

It is worth repeating that an officer with the status of yeoman of the crown was in charge of the king's books; the office is described in Edward IV's Black Book of the 1470s — the library has been tentatively located as part of the inner chamber of the king's household.[123] The actual word 'librarian' is not used, but if Henry IV had a *custos librorum* why should this office have disappeared by Edward IV's time?[124] There is no evidence one way or the other whether this yeoman was a well educated man, interested in the books he managed, but if Gilbert Banaster, master of the chapel royal 1478–86, translated Boccaccio's tale of *Guiscardo and Ghismonda*, and Stephen Hawes, a groom of Henry VIII's chamber could recite many poets by heart, especially Lydgate, why should not this unknown 'yeoman' have been as erudite?[125]

The Yorkist court was a cultivated one: surviving books are associated with many men around the kings: John Donne, William Hastings, Anthony Woodville, Thomas Thwaytes, William Hopton, Robert Brackenbury. Their clergy and officials included several with European educations: William Hatclyf, John Gunthorpe, William Grey, George Neville, Thomas Penketh, John Shirwood, Thomas Langton, John Russell and Robert Stillington. Officials of the English court were at home in the court of the dukes of Burgundy on embassies and visits and lesser mortals like English heralds had no problem fitting in and speaking the language of their hosts. In his turn Louis of Gruuthuse did not complain of his treatment or surroundings when he was fêted by Edward in 1472; nor had

Olivier de La Marche found fault with the organisation and splendours of the Smithfield tournament in 1468. There was probably very little difference in the level of sophistication between the English and Burgundian courts, and a great similarity can be assumed in intellectual interests and book ownership.

In the fifteenth century it was expected that a king, duke or any leading aristocrat would have a library – and any wealthy person followed suit. All the evidence shows that the upper classes of Europe were increasing their stock of vernacular literature, encouraging translation, and that they expected to own the standard texts themselves. The evidence is more difficult to collect in England but the examples of Lord Berkeley, Sir John Fastolf and Thomas Thwaytes spring to mind.

It is also now recognised that the book trade was responding to this demand. High quality, accurate copies in legible hands could be produced quickly and in large quantities for those literate in French and able to afford them.[126] Aimed at a lower level of the market from the early fifteenth century, the ateliers of Ghent and Bruges had a profitable line in comparatively cheap books of hours for foreign markets – including, and perhaps especially, England.[127]

Production of both text and illustration was standardised and regularised both for the richer and the less well-off customer.[128] Those books that were certainly bought by Edward IV all fall into the category of standard texts. A study of the three Low Countries artists most closely connected with Edward IV *and* closely related to each other – the Master of Edward IV, the Master of the White Inscriptions and the Master of 1482 – is needed and might help to clear up the confusion about who ordered and owned which Flemish manuscript at the Yorkist court.

It can be suggested that Edward IV – or perhaps his maligned yeoman – was remarkably well informed about what was available. Someone was probably sent over to investigate the ateliers and bookshops of Flanders – let alone those of London – someone who knew the king's taste and had been to Burgundy before, like Piers Courteys, acting keeper of the Great Wardrobe from 1478, who was commissioned to buy jewels abroad in 1480. The sophisticated level of standardisation reached in book production in the Low Countries meant that Edward and his agent just had to compile a list of titles and what they needed the texts for, as that affected size and execution: reading at a lectern, or private study, gift or display.

In this context, with all its possibilities for actually choosing a book or being given one from the large number of titles available, it is interesting to look at the range of Edward IV's collection in more detail, particularly as too much emphasis has often been placed on one category: the enormous volumes made in Flanders. It has often been implied that these were virtually his first books and that his exile in Burgundy suddenly opened his eyes to illuminated manuscripts and the attractions of Low Countries book production. The volumes have also been thought of as magnificent and mainly for display. There has been a general tendency to draw all such books, with or without the royal arms, into the orbit of Edward IV, as well as to stress the great similarity between these manuscripts and those once owned by Louis of Gruuthuse.[129] All these ideas have already been modified by recent research,[130] but they can be toned down still further and the image of Edward IV lolling among his superb coffee-table books dispelled.

If all the titles associated with Edward IV are considered in the same prosaic way that other fifteenth-century libraries and their owners are studied, and his library reconstructed by *including* dedications to him and texts owned by him in his youth and *excluding* purely speculative links, his collection turns out to be as miscellaneous in quality and contents as, for instance, his brother, Gloucester's. It ranges from the small Latin formulary mentioned above to the English translation of the *Siege of Rhodes*, and from St Augustine's *City of God* to tracts on alchemy[131] and Traversagni's *Triumphus justitiae.*

As far as Edward's sudden Flemish bibliophilia is concerned, it has to be remembered that communication in all fields, at every level of society between England and the Low Countries, was constant and intensive both before and after the exile. He stayed only a month at Gruuthuse's townhouse in Bruges in the winter of 1471 and had many more vital matters on his mind at the time. He may have been pleased with what he saw at the Gruuthuse palace, but it is unlikely that he was surprised. In additon, his host's collection was by no means fully formed: he had another twenty years of bibliophile activity ahead of him and it is not known which books he could have shown to his guests at that time. If Edward was so much struck by the items in Gruuthuse's library, he took a long time to make up his mind: most of his datable Flemish books belong to the years 1479–82. Lastly it is as well to remember that the survival of the big Flemish books must be partly due to the awe that they inspired in *later* generations by their size alone (which also made them difficult to walk off with!).

In terms of content Edward's books largely overlap with Gruuthuse's, but then Gruuthuse was an avid collector and eventually owned almost every title available except classical and professional texts. Exactly the same range of titles can be found in other libraries such as that of the dukes of Savoy.[132] In size there is a decided difference: on average the Flemish manuscripts of the king are considerably bigger than those owned by Louis of Bruges.[133] The quality, but especially the quantity, of the illumination of the king's selection is not impressive, particularly when one realises that he could afford whatever he wanted. To give one example: in Royal 16 G ix, the French *Education of Cyrus*, which has the royal arms and Yorkist badges, the presentation miniature is by the same artist – so presumably from a workshop with the same potential – as the illumination of the chronicles of Froissart produced for the historian Philip of Commines,[134] but the latter are infinitely more magnificent and lavishly illustrated than the king's book.

Several of Edward's manuscripts are very scantily illustrated indeed, and the amount of text is daunting: the *Education of Cyrus* has six pictures to 406 pages of text; the *City of God*, now bound in two volumes, eleven pictures to 1,154 pages of text,[135] and a Valerius Maximus, in two volumes, nine pictures to 1,342 pages.[136] No modern coffee-table book produced like some of Edward's Flemish manuscripts would have any chance of selling. These books were bought for reading, not for showing off. As has been suggested recently[137] they were used for reading aloud: their contents – essentially all stories – as well as their lectern size suggest it. A number, if not all, were perhaps intended for the young Prince of Wales' household and the date of their production – as far as it can be known – accords with that: Edward would hardly have ordered books for him when his son was four months old; eight or ten years is much more acceptable. Unfortunately there is no obvious difference in contents between those manuscripts containing only the royal arms and those having the arms of one or two princes as well.

Of the Flemish manuscripts that can be linked with some certainty to Edward IV or at least to *a* king of England, there are six volumes of stories from classical times, three books of religious narrative, two containing more practical knowledge, four historical titles and seven didactic ones. There is only one that can be called a romance: the *Recueil des Histoires de Troie*. This choice of books argues for possible use in a young man's household, though the inclusion of Boccaccio's *Decameron*, however 'moralised' by its translator, rather weakens the argument. None of the Flemish manuscripts was signed by Edward IV; he may have thought they were sufficiently marked as his by the illuminator, but there is no extant book signed by him as king.

It is important to remember that twelve of these books have only the royal arms and any of them could have been ordered by or finished for Richard III or Henry VII and the arms painted in at any time; the royal arms are also the only arms that could have been added by others, as homage or as mere decoration. There are, for instance, two copies of Valerius Maximus' *Memorabilia*, one with the king's arms and those of the two princes, one, less splendid, with only the royal arms very simply painted on top of the border decoration.[138] Nine of the 'Flemish' volumes have only empty spaces for arms; two have neither marks of ownership nor space for them. Six or seven have the coats of others: Thomas Thwaytes, John Donne and William Hastings. An intriguing example – and one that shows how confusing these manuscripts and their ownership are – is the four-volume edition of Froissart's *Chronicles*: they clearly go together, but volume 1 is lost; volume 2 has a sketch of Hastings' arms; volume 3 has an empty space for arms; volume 4 bears the royal arms.[139] They were made in the early 1480s and their date and marks of ownership clearly allow of endless speculation about who chose this series and ordered it and who eventually lived to enjoy it.[140]

To sort out this and similar problems, not only is more research necessary on the various workshops, it would also be useful to study what could be called the 'Calais group'[141] of book-owners, which included Lord Hastings, Sir John Donne his brother-in-law,[142] Sir James Tyrell[143] and the man who may have been the only true book-collector among them, Thomas Thwaytes. Such a study might tie in many more Calais officials, diplomats, mercers, merchant adventurers and merchants of the Staple. Many of them were acquaintances of Caxton from his pre-printing days. Books made for both Thwaytes (d. 1503) and Donne (d. 1503), and some of Tyrell's books (d. 1502) had found their way into the royal library certainly before the end of Henry VII's reign.[144] It has been suggested that Sir Thomas Thwaytes planned to give books to Edward IV and Henry VII, but neither project came off.[145]

In the case of Thwaytes' books – and indeed in the case of the two known books of James Tyrell – it is most likely that they passed into the royal library on the respective arrests for treason of their owners, 1494 and 1502. Thwaytes' books are by far the most important, all made for him in the 1480s.[146] He was an official at Calais from 1468, meeting and escorting Gruuthuse as well as Margaret of York while there, but in 1494 he was arrested on suspicion of supporting Warbeck. He survived but paid a heavy fine to the king. He died in 1503; his will mentions a collection of books but none in detail.[147]

The social, military and mercantile milieu of Calais has scarcely been studied, but its potential for cultural contacts between England and the territories of the dukes of Burgundy does not need explaining.[148] It was a cosmopolitan commercial centre, where leading officials would have constantly entertained diplomats, clerics and merchants, any of whom might introduce the subject of books or have new books in their luggage, and any of whom may have decided to buy one, have a copy made or illustrated, either for their own use or as a present for a friend or relative, or indeed the king himself – or his queen.

One particular group of books still in the royal collection is a reminder of how unknown is the role of the queen in Yorkist book collecting. This group can be tentatively linked to Edward himself but seems to be separate from the texts concerned with antiquity, the big manuscripts acquired from the Low Countries and the translations and dedications mentioned above.

Using the early inventory numbers in royal library manuscripts[149] some suggestions can be made. A group of three surviving books all bear the same type of distinguishing inventory number, the highest number of the three being 93.[150] All three texts are fine manuscripts; two were made in the late 1470s or early 1480s before 1485; the third dates from the 1430s–50s and bears Yorkist emblems. The three books contain four texts, mostly didactic literature, and one volume of lives of saints. All are comparatively small, slim volumes and one has exceptionally fine illumination: they were books for private study, not for reading aloud. It is therefore likely that a different type of book was being acquired while Edward bought his lectern books in the Low Countries: these could have been the purchases and acquisitions of women of the House of York.

What is to be concluded about choice, availability and ownership? The evidence, such as it is, shows that the Yorkist court was a cultivated one. No one gave him or herself up to a 'passion' for acquiring books, as had Richard of Bury, and as, one suspects, Louis of Gruuthuse did, but the accumulated evidence for the book ownership of the Yorkist family is not unimpressive.

The physical proximity of the Low Countries and the fact that they inevitably were the threshold for whatever *translatio studii* went on between England the rest of Europe, sufficiently explain the close similarity in the interests and life-style of the educated on both sides of the sea; it did not need the unexpected exile of Edward IV or the sudden intervention of William Caxton to bring it into existence. On both sides of the sea, scribes, printers and translators had similar attitudes to the acquisition of texts; their choice was not decided by their own preference alone. They not only chose from what was available, they were also the means by which texts became available to others, whose choice in its turn decided theirs. Scribes, printers *and* translators worked speculatively as well as 'on request'. Caxton's choice, like Multon's, was decided by physical availability, some form of 'copyright' and the preference of their customers. Many Burgundian scribes and translators, as well as men like William Worcester, were servants of their patrons and worked as required, but there is also evidence of personal inclination, scholarly interest and a simple 'itch to write'.

It was the individual customer and book 'lover', particularly the wealthy one, who benefited in an unprecedented way from the wide range of available books at the end of the fifteenth century, enjoying both the Indian summer of manuscript production and the early spring of printing.

## Edward IV's Books

This list of books probably owned by Edward IV, whether extant or not, is based on the evidence of dedications, the presence of his arms as well as those of his sons, actual *ex libris* and/or mention of titles in the great wardrobe accounts. Those with only the royal arms have been entered provisionally and indicated by a question mark.

### BOOKS FROM OR ABOUT ANTIQUITY INCLUDING ANCIENT HISTORY

Livy, mentioned in the great wardrobe accounts, all other particulars unknown but presumably a French translation.

Cicero, *Old Age*, English, translated by William Worcester, printed and dedicated by Caxton in 1481.

———, *Friendship, idem.*

———, *De oratore*, Latin, with a commentary by Pietro Carmeliano, printed in Venice, 1478, presented to Edward by Carmeliano 1481–3.

Valerius Maximus, *Memorabilia*, French, translated by Simon de Hesdin and Nicholas de Gonesse 1375–1401, MS. with arms of Edward IV and his sons (Royal 18 E iii, iv).

Josephus, *Antiquités judaiques*, French, anonymous translation, end 14th c.(?), MS. with royal arms only (Sir John Soane Museum MS.1) but Edward's ownership is corroborated by mention in the great wardrobe accounts.

*La Grande Histoire Cesar*, French, MS. with arms of Edward and his sons (Royal 17 F ii).

Roberto della Porta, *Romuléon*, French, translation by Jean Miélot, 1465, MS. with arms of Edward and his sons (Royal 19 E v) and dated 1480.

? Jean Mansel, *Fleur des histoires*, French, MS. with royal arms only (Royal 18 E vi).

? Xenophon, *Cyropédie*, French, translated by Vasco de Lucena, 1470, MS. with royal arms only (Royal 16 G ix).

? Raoul le Fèvre, *Recueil des histoires de Troye*, French, MS. with royal arms only (Royal 17 E ii).

? Valerius Maximus, *Memorabilia*, French, translated by Simon de Hesdin and Nicholas de Gonesse, MS. with the royal arms only (Royal 17 F iv).

### BOOKS OF CONTEMPORARY AND NEAR-CONTEMPORARY HISTORY

Vincent de Beauvais, *Miroir historial*, French, translated by Jean de Vignay *c.* 1350, MS. with arms of Edward and his sons (Royal 14 E i).

Jean Froissart, *Chroniques* vol. 4, French, MS. with royal arms only (Royal 18 E ii; Royal 18 E i has Froissart vol. 2 and contains the sketched arms of William Hastings), but Edward's ownership is corroborated by mention in the great wardrobe accounts.

Jean de Wavrin, *Chroniques* vols. i, iii, French, MSS. have the royal arms only (Royal 15 E iv, 14 E iv), but Edward's ownership is corroborated by the dedication to him of the work as a whole, after 1471.

John Hardyng, *Chronicle*, English, dedicated 1463 (?).

John Capgrave, *Abbreviation of Chronicles*, English, dedicated 1462–3.

Guillaume Caoursin, *Siege of Rhodes*, English, translated and dedicated by John Kay, printed 1480–83.

William of Tyre, *Geoffrey of Boulogne*, English, translated, printed and dedicated by Caxton 1481.

? William of Tyre, *History of the Crusades*, French, anonymous translation, MS. with royal arms only (Royal 15 E i).

## RELIGIOUS AND DIDACTIC BOOKS

St Augustine, *City of God*, bks. 1–10, French, anonymous translation, MS. with arms of Edward and his sons (Royal 17 F iii).

Guyard des Moulins, *Bible historiale,* vols. 1 and 2, French, MSS. with arms of Edward and his sons (Royal 18 D ix, x; vol. 4, in Royal 15 D i, has the royal arms only, dated 1470; ownership is perhaps corroborated by mention in the great wardrobe accounts); the MSS. are dated 1479.

*Holy Trinitee*, other particulars unknown, mentioned in the great wardrobe accounts.

Jean de Courcy, *Chemin de vaillance*, French, MS. with arms of Edward and his sons (Royal 14 E ii).

Christine de Pisan, *Epistre d'Othea*, French, same MS. as above.

Alain Chartier, *Bréviaire des nobles*, French, same MS. as above.

*Des ix malheureux et des ix malheureuses*, French, same MS. as above.

Ramon Lull, *Ordre de chevalerie*, French, same MS. as above.

Boccaccio, *Des cas des nobles hommes*, French, translated by Laurent de Premierfait 1404/9, MS. with arms of Edward and his son (Royal 14 E v).

——, *Décaméron*, French, translated by Laurent de Premierfait 1414, MS. with arms of Edward and his sons (Royal 19 E i).

Pierre Richart, *Forteresse de la foi*, French, MS. with empty space for arms (Royal 17 F vi, vii), but Edward's ownership is corroborated by mention in the wardrobe accounts.

*Gouvernement of Kinges and Princes*, other particulars unknown but mentioned in the great wardrobe accounts.

A version of the *Secreta secretorum*, Latin, MS. with hand-written *ex libris* (Royal 12 E xv).

Basil Bessarion, *Orationes*, Latin, printed by Guillaume Fichet in Paris, 1471/2, and dedicated to Edward by the printer and author (Vat. lat. 3586).

Lorenzo Traversagni, *Triumphus iustitiae domini Jhesu Christi*, Latin, dedicated to Edward between 1477 and 1483.

Buonaccorso da Montemagno, *Declamacion of Noblesse*, English, translated by William Worcester, printed and dedicated by Caxton, 1481.

? *Court of Sapience*, perhaps written at Edward's command, *c.* 1475.

? Gregory the Great, *Homilies*, French, anonymous translation, MS. with royal arms only (Royal 15 D v).

## SCIENTIFIC/PRACTICAL/INFORMATIVE BOOKS

A book of legal formulas, Latin, MS. with hand-written ornamental *ex libris* (Harl. 3352), datable to 1460–1.

Medical treatises, Latin, MS. with hand-written *ex libris* (Royal 12 E xv), datable to before 1461.

Petrus de Crescentiis, *Profitz ruraulx*, French, anonymous translation, MS. with arms of Edward and his sons (Royal 14 E vi).

George Ripley, *Compound of Alchemy*, dedicated to Edward, 1471.

Thomas Norton, *Ordinal of Alchemy*, dedicated to Edward, before 1477.

William Worcester, *Boke of Noblesse*, dedicated to Edward, 1475.

? Bartholomaeus Anglicus, *Des propriétés des choses*, French, translated by Jean Corbechon in 1372, MS. with royal arms only (Royal 15 E ii, iii), dated 1482.

## Notes

1   *The History of Jason translated from the French of Raoul le Fèvre by William Caxton, c. 1477*, J. Munro (ed.), (E.E.T.S. E.S.111 (1913)), p. 3. Ampersands have been extended and the usage of *u* and *v* modernised by the present authors.

2   For salutary remarks on survival rates, see e.g. R. Hirsch, *Printing, Selling and Reading 1450–1550* (Wiesbaden, 1967), pp. 148–50, B. Guenée, *Histoire et culture historique dans l'Occident médiéval* (Paris, 1980), ch. 6, 'Le succès de l'oeuvre', and P. Needham, *The Printer and the Pardoner. An Unrecorded Indulgence printed by William Caxton . . .* (Washington D.C., 1986), pp. 30–31. K. Harris, 'Patrons, buyers and owners: the evidence for ownership, and the role of book owners in book production and the book trade', in *Book Production and Publishing in Britain, 1375–1475*, D. Pearsall and J. Griffiths (eds.), (Cambridge, 1989), pp. 163–7, on paucity of English sources. The second half of the century has received no survey comparable to S.H. Cavanaugh, 'A Study in Books privately owned in England 1300–1450' (unpub. PhD thesis, University of Pennsylvania, 1980). See also P. Kibre, 'The intellectual interests reflected in libraries of the 14th and 15th centuries', *Journal of the History of Ideas*, VII (1946), pp. 257–97; and nn. 7–11 below.

3   Over forty main texts, see *The Paston Letters*, J. Gairdner (ed.), (3 vols., London, 1875), 3, pp. 300–1, and G.A. Lester, *Sir John Paston's 'Grete Boke'. A Descriptive Catalogue . . . of British Library MS Lansdowne 285* (Woodbridge, 1984), pp. 34–43.

4   *The Household Books of John Duke of Norfolk and Thomas Earl of Surrey*, J. Payne Collier (ed.), (Roxburghe Club 1844), pp. xxvii–viii, 277.

5   Two lists exist for Charleton (d. 1465), K.B. McFarlane, *The Nobility of Later Medieval England* (Oxford, 1973), pp. 237–8.

6   This comprised 298 volumes in 1498, S. Edmunds, 'The medieval library of Savoy', *Scriptorium*, XXIV (1970), pp. 318–27; *ibid.*, XXV (1971), pp. 253–84; *ibid.*, XXVI (1972), pp. 269–93.

7   For the various inventories of the dukes and their problems, G. Doutrepont, *La littérature française à la cour des ducs de Bourgogne . . .* (Paris 1909, repr. Geneva 1970), pp. xxxiii–l; he concludes that Philip the Good left more than 876 books to his son. P. Cockshaw, in *Karel de Stoute*, catalogue of the exhibition at the Royal Library Brussels, 1977, p. 4, has 'more than 900'. A definite number will be very difficult to reach for any period.

8   A. Bayot, *Martin le Franc, l'Estrif de Fortune et de Vertu* (Brussels, 1928), pp. 52–5.

9   A. Boinet, 'Un Bibliophile du xve siècle. Le Grand Bâtard de Bourgogne', *Bibliothèque de l'Ecole des Chartes*, LXVII (1906), pp. 255–69.

10  A. Derolez, *The Library of Raphael de Mercatellis, Abbot of St. Bavon's, Ghent (1437–1508)* (Ghent, 1979), *passim* and references given there.

11  Antoinette Naber, 'Les manuscrits d'un bibliophile bourguignon du xve siècle, Jean de Wavrin', *Revue du Nord*, LXXII (1990), pp. 23–48.

12  *Inventaire sommaire des Archives Départementales antérieures à 1790*, M.J. Finot (ed.), vol. 8, Archives Civiles. *Série B, Chambres des Comptes de Lille, nos. 3390–3665* (Lille, 1895), pp. 433–4; *Boeken van en rond Willem van Oranje . . .*, catalogue of the exhibition at the Royal Library, The Hague, 1984, pp. 26–7.

13  On Gruuthuse's library see also the article by Malcolm Vale elsewhere in this volume. The main sources are still J.B.B. van Praet, *Recherches sur Louis de Bruges* (Paris, 1831), and the chapter on his library by C. Lemaire in *Vlaamse Kunst op Perkament*, catalogue of the exhibition at the Gruuthuse-museum, Bruges, 1981, pp. 207–72.

14  One hundred and seven, including indulgences and the advertisement in the list in N.F. Blake, *Caxton's World* (London, 1969), pp. 224–39. And see S. de Ricci, *A Census of Caxtons* (London, 1909). Caxton's second editions can be treated as a 'comparable' to the second copies of texts in a private library.

15  The list is hampered by the problems of counting texts or volumes. Where possible we have counted texts: we have not distinguished between print and ms., between short and long texts, or between languages; all dedications have been included however short. For the books of the house of York see also the present authors' *Richard III's Books*, (Stroud, 1997), ch. 2.

16  Hardyng's Chronicle, BL. Harl. MS. 661; Clare Roll, London, College of Arms, Box 21, no. 16; Claudian, *De consulatu Stiliconis*, BL. Add. MS. 11814; book of hours, Ushaw College MS. 43.

17  Of the 39 service books three were personal and in her closet. The source is her will, *Wills from Doctors' Commons*, J.G. Nichols and J. Bruce (eds.), (Camden Society 1863), pp. 4–5, and see C.A.J. Armstrong, 'The piety of Cecily, Duchess of York . . .' in his *England, France and Burgundy in the Fifteenth Century* (London, 1983), pp. 144–52.

18  Three Arthurian romances, BL. MS. Royal 14 E iii; (?)Caxton's *Recueil of the Historyes of Troye*, San Marino, Huntington Library MS. R. B. 62222; poem on Barnet dedicated to her, BL. MS. Royal D xv; fragments of Lessons and Collects, Toronto, Bergendal MS. 60; book of hours, Liverpool Cathedral Radcliffe MS.6. Counted as seven. See also the present authors' 'The cult of angels in fifteenth-century England: a

book of hours of the Guardian Angel presented to Queen Elizabeth Woodville', in *Women and the Book*, (ed.) J. Taylor and L. Smith (London, 1997), and the same, '"A most benevolent queen": Queen Elizabeth Woodville's reputation, her piety and her books', *The Ricardian*, X (1994–96).

19  *Jason* translated by Caxton; *The Testament of Mahomet*, Princeton University Library MS. Garret 168; poem *De vere* dedicated to him by Pietro Carmeliano, BL. MS. Royal 12 A xxix; and perhaps the *Dicts and Sayings of the Philosophers*, translated by Anthony Woodville, see the present authors' article in *The Ricardian*, IX, 118 (Sept. 1992).

20  A *Prose Tristan* previously owned by her uncle Richard (and counted here as his), BL. Harl. MS. 49; she also claimed her brother's *Testament of Mahomet*; and signed her mother's book of Arthurian romances; a Boethius, BL. MS. Royal 20 A xix; 3/4 books of hours, Stoneyhurst College MS. 37, BL. MSS. Add. 17012 and 50001, and possibly Vienna, Austrian National Library, Cod.1840; lectionary, Berlin Kupferstichkabinett MS.929; with Margaret Beaufort she suggested Caxton print the *Fifteen Oes*; bequeathed a psalter by Cecily Neville. Her sisters have not been counted here.

21  Book of hours, Sidney Sussex College, Cambridge, MS.37; a magnificent psalter now in two parts, Rennes MS.22 and BL. MS. Royal 2 A xviii; (?)dedication of *Epistle to Othea*, Pierpont Morgan Library MS.775.

22  The latest, most detailed and best study of Margaret's books is the collection of essays in Thomas Kren, (ed.), *Margaret of York, Simon Marmion and The Visions of Tondal. Papers Delivered at a Symposium Organized by the Department of Manuscripts of the J. Paul Getty Museum in collaboration with the Huntington Library and Art Collections, June 21–24, 1990* (Malibu, 1992).

23  Including two rolls of arms. The present authors' articles, 'Richard III's Books,' *The Ricardian*, VIII–X (1986–93); the same, *Richard III's Books*, passim.

24  This is the Mechtild of Hackeborn's *Book of Special Grace*. Their son can be linked to his father's *De re militari* and the *Beauchamp Pageant*; he is not incuded in this count.

25  We have compared Cecily Neville's will (39 service books) to the inventory of Thomas, Duke of Gloucester's books of about a hundred years earlier (42 service books), and on this basis estimate that 30–40 service books would be usual for a leading English aristocrat. See above n. 17 for Cecily; Thomas's inventory is in Cavanaugh (see n. 2), pp. 849–50. It is also worth comparing the service books owned by some of the Savoy princes (Edmunds, 'The medieval library of Savoy', p. 324) and those of Philip the Bold, see M.J. Hughes, 'The Library of Philip the Bold and Margaret of Flanders, first Valois duke and duchess of Burgundy', *Journal of Medieval History*, IV (1975), pp. 145–88.

26  G. Rosser, *Medieval Westminster* (Oxford, 1989), pp. 209–15, for the many advantages of Westminster to a bookseller. G. Pollard, *The English Market for Printed Books* (Sandars Lectures, London 1959), pp. 16–17, emphasises the importance of a protected location for the early printers.

27  Hirsch, *Printing, Selling and Reading*, pp. 27–9: Augsburg in the early 1470s, Genoa 1472, Toulouse 1477–8.

28  The Stationers included all the book-artisan trades by the 1480s, see especially G. Pollard, 'The Company of Stationers before 1577', *The Library*, 4th ser., XVIII (1937), pp. 2–15. Recent research has found little evidence of hostility to the new craft, C.P. Christianson, *A Directory of London Stationers and Book Artisans 1300–1500* (Bibliographical Society of America, New York, 1990), p. 43 (compare Pollard, 'Stationers', pp. 19–20).

29  For his 99 books Caxton only *names* 13 'patrons', and only 4 of these actually paid or rewarded him in any way; see the present authors' 'Ramon Lull's *Order of Chivalry* translated by William Caxton,' *The Ricardian*, IX (1991), pp. 112–17, for this tally of

his 'patrons'. All his Latin works were bespoke, and he is known to have bought in at least a good proportion of standard religious texts such as the missals he commissioned from a Paris printer.

30      Compare A.S.G. Edwards' plea for a detailed study of the Lydgate mss., a potential database as valuable as Caxton's output, 'Lydgate manuscripts: some directions for future research', *Manuscripts and Readers in Fifteenth-Century England*, D. Pearsall (ed.), (Woodbridge, 1983), pp. 15–26.

31      W.F. Oakshott, 'Caxton and Malory's *Morte Darthur*', *Gutenberg Jahrbuch* 1935, pp. 112–16. N.F. Blake, 'Caxton prepares his edition of the *Morte Darthur*', *Journal of Librarianship*, VIII (1976), pp. 272–85.

32      In fact the 'Poor Folks' Catechism', S. Powell, 'Why *Quattuor Sermones?*' Talk at the Early Book Society Conference, Trinity College, Dublin, 11–14 July 1990. It was a printing success, going into two editions in 1483; in 1491 he was happy to pirate the superior Oxford edition for his third edition.

33      For the evidence that Frankenberg was also a printer, see A.F. Sutton, 'Caxton was a mercer', *England in the Fifteenth Century*, (ed.) N. Rogers, Proceedings of the 1992 Harlaxton Symposium, Stamford 1994, pp. 136–8.

34      E. Armstrong, 'English purchases of printed books from the continent 1465–1526', *English Historical Review*, LXXXXIV (1979), pp. 268–90. It may also be worth emphasising that MSS. production went up *before* the real impact of printing, see e.g. R. Watson, review of *Book Production*, in *The Ricardian*, IX (1991), p. 83.

35      E.g. it is likely it was Veldener's edition of the *Fasciculus Temporum* (1475) which he knew when he dismissed its potential as a possible conclusion to the *Polychronicon* (1482).

36      C. Lemaire, *Le Cinquième centenaire de l'imprimerie dans les anciens Pays-Bas* (Brussels, 1973), pp. 219–38. P. Saenger, 'Colard Mansion and the evolution of the printed book', *The Library Quarterly*, XLV (1975), pp. 415–6.

37      W.J. Partridge, 'The use of Caxton's Type 3 by John Lettou and William de Machlinia . . .', *The British Library Journal*, IX (1983), pp. 56–65. L. Hellinga, *Caxton in Focus* (London, 1982), pp. 72–6. N.F. Blake, 'Wynkyn de Worde's early years', *Gutenberg Jahrbuch*, 1971, p. 65, and his 'The spread of printing in England', *Gutenberg Jahrbuch*, 1987, pp. 26, 28–9.

38      H.R. Plomer, *Wynkyn de Worde and his Contemporaries* (London, 1925), pp. 28–9. Armstrong, 'English purchases', p. 274. His *Chronicles of England* followed hard upon the printing of the *Grandes Chroniques de France*.

39      Hirsch, *Printing, Selling and Reading*, p. 50. For the unwisdom of printing Latin books in England, Armstrong, 'English purchases', pp. 286–9. And see M. Lowry, *The World of Aldus Manutius* (Oxford, 1979), ch. 1.

40      Armstrong, 'English purchases', pp. 289–90. N.J.M. Kerling, 'Caxton and the trade in printed books', *The Book Collector*, IV (1955), pp. 190–5.

41      Hirsch, *Printing, Selling and Reading*, pp. 31, 72–3, 144. E.g. James Goldwell's collection given to All Souls in 1499, mostly printed before 1475, and John Russell's gift to New College in 1482, Armstrong, 'English purchases', pp. 282–3.

42      Caxton printed Traversagni's *Nova Rhetorica* and its *Epitome*; and the *Sex Epistolae*, proof-read by Carmeliano. William Tose, an Englishman, sold books for Jensen and other Venetian presses north of the Alps in 1478, Hirsch, *Printing, Selling and Reading*, p. 74. The Venetians were particularly aggressive booksellers, Armstrong, 'English purchases', p. 275, and see Lowry, *The World of Aldus Manutius*, ch. 1.

43      The relationship between Caxton's text of the Ovid and the printed text of his colleague Mansion (1484), remains a mystery, Lemaire, *Cinquième centenaire*, pp. 227–38. Jeanne Veyrin-Forrer, 'Caxton and France', *Journal of the Printing Historical Society*, XI (1976–7), pp. 40–44 on the printed French texts used by Caxton; he was

first in the field with several texts. Armstrong, 'English purchases', p. 277, suggests that access to French printed texts increased after Henry VII's succession, but trade was good after the 1475 treaty apart from troubles with Louis XI, 1482–3, and in any event French books required in England could travel easily via the Low Countries.

44   *Eneydos* (prologue), N.F. Blake, *Caxton's Own Prose* (London, 1973), p. 78.

45   He came to the conclusion that he was not going to find a complete text of Chaucer's *House of Fame* and finished it off himself; he explains that he could not find a suitable chronicle to act as a continuation for the *Polychronicon* and had put one together himself; he had also modernised its English. Blake, *Caxton's Own Prose*, pp. 102–3, 132–3.

46   *Eneydos*, prologue, Blake, *Caxton's Own Prose*, p. 79. And see preceding note.

47   One of the main objectives of any London company was to control competition, and the Stationers were no exception, Pollard, 'Stationers', *passim*, Christianson, *Directory*, pp. 25–7, and see Hirsch, *Printing, Selling and Reading*, p. 81. We do not intend to suggest any master-exemplars or ultimate controls; only groups of copies derived from one or several exemplars in accordance with the research of A.I. Doyle and M. Parkes, 'The production of copies of the *Canterbury Tales* and *Confessio Amantis* in the early fifteenth century' in *Medieval Scribes, Manuscripts and Libraries. Essays presented to N.R. Ker*, M.B. Parkes and A.G. Watson (eds.), (London, 1978), esp. p. 201. The control of exemplars had been made into a fine art by the *pecia* system from the twelfth century onwards in university towns; speculative production of large numbers of copies by stationers and booksellers is known on the continent in the fifteenth century and this increases in volume until the advent of printing (D. Pearsall, Introd. to *Book Production*, pp. 3–6); certain stationers are known to have maintained exemplars: John Pye *c.* 1430s–60s and Peter Bylton 1404–54, Christianson, *Directory*, pp. 79–82, 145–8, and his 'Evidence for the study of London's late medieval book trade' in *Book Production*, pp. 100–1.

48   It is now generally agreed that speculative production of multiple copies of MSS. took place in London as well as across the Channel: Saenger, 'Colard Mansion', pp. 405–18; Pearsall, Intro. to *Book Production*, pp. 3–7; K.L. Scott, *The Mirroure of the Worlde: MS Bodley 283* (Roxburghe Club, Oxford, 1980), pp. 45–50 (illuminated copies of the English statutes *c.* 1460–90); A. De La Mare, *Lyell Manuscripts*, pp. 81–5 (genealogies of the kings of England); highly professional and routine production of books of hours is known for Bruges, Ghent, and London; London standardised dialect, spelling, script and format, D. Pearsall and A.S.G. Edwards, 'The manuscripts of the major English poetic texts' in *Book Production, passim*. R. Watson urges further consideration of manuscript speculation in London at this date – printing merely accelerated this process, review of *Book Production* (see n. 34), pp. 81–4.

49   The book-trade depended particularly upon cooperative working, Christianson, *Directory*, pp. 25–7, 29–37 (production and control), 40–2 (limits of control). Doyle and Parkes, *passim*, on cooperative working methods.

50   Pollard, 'Stationers', p. 10 on lowly status; but compare his pp. 24–38 on their absorption and regulation of printers, a control unmatched in the rest of Europe.

51   *A Manual of the Writings in Middle English 1050–1500*, J.B. Severs and A.E. Hartung (gen. eds.), (8 vols., New Haven, Conn., 1962–89) VI, pp. 1809–920, 2071–175.

52   Edwards, 'Lydgate manuscripts', p. 15, for high survival rate.

53   For authorial control, Pearsall, Intro., *Book Production*, pp. 2, 5–6.

54   Doyle and Parkes, p. 201.

55   Edwards, 'Lydgate manuscripts', pp. 17–19. K.L. Scott, 'Lydgate's Lives of Saints Edmund and Fremund: a newly located manuscript in Arundel Castle', *Viator*, XIII (1982), pp. 341–3, 360–6.

56   A.I. Doyle, 'More light on John Shirley', *Medium Aevum*, XXX (1961), pp. 93–101.

J. Boffey and J.J. Thompson, 'Anthologies and miscellanies: production and choice of text', in *Book Production*, pp. 284–7, and R.J. Lyall, 'Materials: the paper revolution', *ibid.*, pp. 16–21.

57    BL Harl. MS. 2251, Add. MS. 34360. Multon can also be called the 'Hammond scribe': Christianson, *Directory*, pp. 136–7 and esp. the works by A.I. Doyle cited there; also Boffey and Thompson, 'Anthologies', pp. 287–9, and the present authors' chapter on the provenance of BL. Add. MS. 48031A, *The Politics of Fifteenth-Century England: John Vale's Book* (Stroud, 1995).

58    There exist two copies of the *Prose Merlin* closely related but probably not derived from each other; for Multon's, C.M. Meale, 'The manuscripts and early audience of the middle English *Prose Merlin*, in A. Adams *et al.* (eds.), *The Changing Face of Arthurian Romance. Essays on Arthurian Prose Romance in memory of Cedric E. Pickford*, Arthurian Studies, XXI (Woodbridge, 1986), pp. 95–7.

59    Up to 18 Henry VI, BL.MS.Harl.4999. We are most grateful to Dr. A.I. Doyle for this reference.

60    *Biographie nationale de Belgique*, XXXVIII (Brussels, 1971), p. 12; *Nationaal Biografisch Woordenboek*, I (Brussels, 1964), cols. 53–4.

61    Brussels, Bibliothèque Royale MS.8, f.7.

62    See n. 48 above.

63    A.W. Pollard, *Fifteenth Century Prose and Verse* (Westminster, 1903): 'Dialogue between a Lord and a Clerk upon Translation', from Trevisa's translation of Higden's *Polychronicon*, pp. 203–10, esp. p. 207.

64    P.J. Lucas, 'The growth and development of English literary patronage in the later middle ages and early renaissance', *The Library*, 6th ser., IV (1982), pp. 234–6, 240. And see S.K. Workman, *Fifteenth Century Translation as an Influence on English Prose* (Princeton, 1940).

65    *Raoul Lefèvre – Le Recoeil des Histoires de Troyes*, M. Aeschbach (ed.), (Bern, 1987), esp. pp. 7–23, and the review of this work by F. Vielliard, *Romania*, CVIII (1987), pp. 395–400. Guillaume Caoursin, *Obsidionis Rhodie urbis descriptio* (1480), translated by John Kay who described himself as Edward IV's 'humble poete lawreate and moste lowly servant'; facsimile with introd. by D. Gray, New York 1975, esp. pp. 1–3 and Kay's dedication. The translation was printed at an unknown date, perhaps by Lettou and Machlinia, see *A Manual* VIII, XXI [86] for all references. Colard Mansion printed the Latin text; French translations were owned by Gruuthuse (BN MS. fr.5646) and Philip of Cleves (not extant; Finot, no. 75).

66    D. Gallet-Guerne, *Vasque de Lucene et la Cyropédie à la cour de Bourgogne (1470)* . . . (Geneva, 1974), p. 12.

67    *Osbern Bokenham's Legenden*, C. Horstmann (ed.), (Heilbronn, 1883), pp. 3–4, lines 107–21 of the Prologue to the Life of St Margaret; Bokenham seems to have satisfied at least one of the three traditional requirements of 'true' humanism: the journey to Italy; we do not care to judge whether his Latin was good; and whether he collected books is not known.

68    Copies survive for the dukes of Burgundy and Savoy (Brussels, BR MSS.11108, 11109), Anthony the Grand Bastard (private collection), Croy family (Brussels, BR MS.11114), Gruuthuse (BN MS.fr.1105); Philip of Cleves (not extant; Finot 68); printed by Mansion at Bruges *c.* 1473. *The Dicts . . .*, C. Bühler (ed.), E.E.T.S. O.S.211 (1941 for 1939), pp. xiii–xix, lists many but not all French MSS.; *Caxton's Own Prose*, pp. 73–7.

69    Compare Caxton's intimacies in the epilogue to the *Dictes* to his obsequiousness in the *Moral Proverbs* and the *Cordial* (Blake, *Caxton's Own Prose*, pp. 73–6, 119, 70–72); and see the present authors' 'The *Order of Chivalry* translated by William Caxton', *The Ricardian*, IX (1991), p. 113.

70    Caxton's several prologues to Worcester's texts do not admit to any meddling, but they also omit to mention Jean Miélot's translation of the *Declamacion* (1449) printed by Mansion (before 1480) which he must have known. Blake, *Caxton's Own Prose*, pp. 120–5.

71    He also presented a copy to Bishop Waynflete in 1472 and got no reward, J.H. Harvey, ed., *William Worcestre: Itineraries* (Oxford, 1969), pp. 252–3.

72    For the argument that he was the translator of the *Declamacion* rather than John Tiptoft, see the present authors' 'William Worcester's *Boke of Noblesse* and his collection of documents on the war in Normandy', *The Ricardian*, IX (1991), pp. 160–61. There is no surviving MS.

73    E.g. H.B. Lathrop, 'The first English printers and their patrons', *The Library*, 4th ser., III (1922–3), pp. 71, 81–5, was especially concerned to answer the contemporary debate over whether Caxton followed or guided popular taste; N.F. Blake, 'William Caxton: his choice of text', *Anglia*, LXXXIII (1965), p. 307; M. Kekewich, 'Edward IV, William Caxton and literary patronage in Yorkist England', *Modern Language Review*, LXVI (1971), pp. 181–7; and D. Bornstein, 'William Caxton's chivalric romances and the Burgundian renaissance in England', *English Studies*, LVII (1976), pp. 1–10. On romances see also *Richard III's Books*, ch. 9.

74    For all this paragraph: D. Pearsall, 'The English romance in the fifteenth century', *Essays and Studies*, XXIX (1976); pp. 72–83. G.R. Keiser, 'The Romances', in *Middle English Prose. A Critical Guide to Major Authors and Genres*, A.S.G. Edwards (ed.), (New Brunswick, New Jersey, 1984), pp. 271, 273, 275–6, 278, and the list on p. 284; *A Manual*, I, *Romances*, *passim*.

75    This figure does not include those composed in prose like the vast texts of the *Prose Tristan* or *Perceforest*, G. Doutrepont, *Les Mises en prose des Epopées et des Romans chevaleresques du xive au xvie siècle* (Brussels, 1939), pp. 9–10.

76    Not 1500, as often stated, e.g. Pearsall, 'The English romance', p. 82; the sole MS., BL. Harl. 326, is clearly datable to the early 1480s by its illumination; H.R. Grinberg, '*The Three Kings' Sons*: Notes and Critical Commentary' (unpublished Ph.D. thesis, New York University, 1968), pp. 10–16.

77    *Guy of Warwick* may be an example of the lack of a suitable MS: it was very popular and should have appealed to Caxton's 'courtly/chivalric' tastes. Verse texts were presumably readily available but he never printed any verse romances unless they were contained in a larger poetic work, only prose translations. In fact it is unlikely he could get a copy of the French prose version (considered a better work than the poems) even if he knew of it. Three of the known MSS. belonged to the kings of England (BL. MS. Royal 15 E vi given to Margaret of Anjou by Lord Talbot), to Jean d'Orleans? (BN. MS. fr.1476), and to the dukes of Burgundy (lost); the fourth is the unknown parent of the first printed edition of 1525. *Le Rommant de Guy de Warwick et de Herolt d'Ardenne*, D.J. Conlon (ed.), (Chapel Hill, 1971), pp. 13–47. R. Crane, 'The vogue of *Guy of Warwick* from the close of the middle ages to the romantic revival', *PMLA*, XXX (1915), pp. 125–94.

78    Reprinted three times before 1550, A.W. Pollard and G.R. Redgrave, *A Short Title Catalogue of Books printed in England . . . 1475–1640* (rev. ed., London, 1986), 1007–10. *Charles the Great* was never reprinted, *ibid.*, 5013.

79    *Histories of Troy* reprinted once before 1550, Pollard and Redgrave, *Short Title Catalogue*, 15375–82; *Jason* has only been reprinted once, *ibid.*, 15383–4. And see L. Hellinga, 'Caxton and the bibliophiles', *Actes du XIe Congrès International de Bibliophile*, P. Culot (ed.), (Brussels, 1979/81), p. 31.

80    Reprinted at regular intervals 1498 onwards, Pollard and Redgrave, *Short Title Catalogue*, 800–6.

81    N.F. Blake, 'Caxton's reprints', in his *William Caxton and English Literary Culture* (London, 1992), pp. 109, 117, notes that no chivalric text was reprinted by Caxton,

but nevertheless asserts they were part of a printing policy which he may have made financial sacrifices to maintain.

82 The figures, compiled by Lenhart, are open to dispute, Hirsch, *Printing, Selling and Reading*, pp. 127–8; compare C. Pickford, 'Fiction and the reading public in the fifteenth century', *Bulletin of the John Rylands Library*, XLV (1963), pp. 430–1 and n. 1, 436–7.

83 Based on our analysis of the sources in nn. 6–13, above. The data on the ducal library are hard to interpret, but they appear to show a similar trend.

84 Except possibly Caxton's *Jason*. Even among the Flemish MSS. that do *not* have the royal arms, but are very similar to the ones that Edward probably *did* order, there is only Royal 20 C ii that contains *Cleriadus et Meliadice* and *Appolin de Tyr* which can both be called true romances. Compare Pearsall, 'The English romance', pp. 77–81, on Edward's desire for the original French texts in MS., and his assertion that Caxton transplanted Burgundian chivalry to England.

85 Compare: one lady's great interest in her *Prose Merlin*, C. Meale, *Prose Merlin*, pp. 98–104; Talbot's gift to Margaret of Anjou contained 10 French prose romances, among other more serious texts, BL. MS. Royal 15 E vi; Pickford, 'Fiction', pp. 434–6, sees printed editions of French romances building up a taste for romances.

86 Blake, *Caxton's Own Prose*, p. 109. Another author justified his romance as a pastime to combat melancholy and the fantasies of idleness, *Le Roman du Comte d'Artois*, J.-C. Seigneuret (ed.), (Geneva, 1966), p. 12. The printer, Vérard, like Caxton, said his romances taught the young, Pickford, 'Fiction', p. 436.

87 Roger Ascham, *The Schoolmaster*, E. Arber (ed.), (Birmingham, 1870), p. 80. The quality of verse romances declined (perhaps accounting for Caxton's avoidance of them); they were continuously adapted until well into the sixteenth century, but for an ever lower class of reader, Pearsall, 'The English romance', pp. 58–67.

88 Le Fèvre's introduction does not treat his material as a romance.

89 See e.g. Doutrepont, *La littérature*, ch. 2, *passim*; Gallet-Guerne, introduction and *passim*; R. Weiss, *Humanism in England During the Fifteenth Century* (Oxford, 1967); W.F. Schirmer, *Der Englische Frühhumanismus . . .* (Leipzig/London, 1931).

90 Hirsch, *Printing, Selling and Reading*, p. 147.

91 P.S. Allen, 'Bishop Shirwood of Durham and his Library', *EHR*, XXV (1910), pp. 445–56; Ron Kuil, 'John Russell en het vroege Engelse humanisme', in *Excursiones Medievales, opstellen aangeboden aan Prof. A.G. Jongkees door zijn leerlingen . . .*, preface by H. Schulte Nordholt (Groningen, 1979), pp. 151–73.

92 Weiss, *Humanism*, pp. 140–8; G.I. Keir, 'The Ecclesiastical Career of George Neville, 1432–76' (unpubl. B.Litt. thesis, Oxford, 1970), ch. 3, *passim*.

93 Geneva, Bibliothèque publique et universitaire Ms.fr.166, *L'enseignement de vraie noblesse*; see B. Gagnebin, 'L'enluminure de Charlemagne à François Ier', *Geneva*, n.s., XXIV (1976), pp. 155–6. Warwick's text was one of the standard chivalric/didactic ones of the period; see F. Hachez, 'Un manuscrit de *l'Enseignement de la vraie noblesse . . .*', *Annales de Cercle Archéologique de Mons*, XXIII (1892), pp. 94–104.

94 One example may be given of over-emphasis on the classics: in Antoine de La Sale's novel *Petit Jehan de Saintré* occurs one of the few contemporary lists of obligatory reading for a young man. It contains only classical titles, virtually all of them history. It is tempting to interpret this list as proof of the author's ironic exaggeration, or of his learnedness, but in fact it is neither. He was not satirising contemporary education, he wanted to be taken seriously and no doubt was. Many of his contemporaries, and at least one modern commentator, failed to realise that he took the list wholesale and at random from Simon de Hesdin's translation of Valerius Maximus and through ignorance confused and garbled it hopelessly, all because he wished to offer his readers

what they expected. See Antoine de La Sale, *Jehan de Saintré*, J. Mishari and C.A. Knudson (eds.) (Geneva, 1978), p. 76; A. Coville, *Le Petit Jehan de Saintré. Recherches complémentaires* (Paris, 1937), pp. 71–8; S. Anglo, 'Humanism and the Court Arts', in *The Impact of Humanism on Western Europe*, A. Goodman and A. MacKay (eds.), (London, 1990), p. 72, appears to be deceived by de La Sale.

95   Doutrepont, *La littérature*, ch. 2; Gallet-Guerne, introduction, *passim*.

96   R. Vaughan, *Charles the Bold* (London, 1973), p. 162 and references given there; R. Walsh, 'The Coming of Humanism to the Low Countries', *Humanistica Lovaniensia*, XXV (1976), pp. 18–2; Gallet-Guerne, p. xiii; BL. MS. Royal 16 G viii, *Les Commentaires de César*, f. 337v. H. Stein, 'Un diplomate bourguignon du xve siècle, Antoine Haneron', *Bibliothèque de l'Ecole des Chartes*, XCVIII (1937), pp. 283–348; Haneron's interests can certainly be called humanist. In this context one should remember the learned disputations that Edward IV – he is even said to have answered – and Richard III witnessed at Oxford in 1481 and 1484. These should not be too easily dismissed by assuming that neither king understood a word of what went on; after all they did not *have* to ask for them or sit through them, and the lowest one can put it is that they did not mind stimulating such a learned display or appearing interested in something so un-martial and un-chivalric.

97   The five books are: BN MSS. latin 6049, historical texts of English origin; latin 8733 a, Nicholas Oresme, *De origine . . . monetarum*; néerl. 1, Boethius, *De consolatione philosophiae*; latin 4804, Ptolemy, *Cosmographia*; latin 7321 a, *Introductorium Alcabitii*.

98   Since Gruuthuse's collection in its entirety was taken to France some time after his death, the survival pattern of his MSS owes as much to the taste of the French kings into whose library the Gruuthuse books were absorbed, as to the original owner's preference. It is remarkable that hardly any texts in Dutch/Flemish have survived, particularly as Flemish was Gruuthuse's mother tongue. Did he not acquire them or were they 'thrown out' by the French kings who could not read them?

99   See Finot, *Inventaire*, pp. 433–4; *Boeken van en rond Willem van Oranje*, pp. 26–7.

100  Mansel's *Fleur des histoires* starts at the Creation and ends at the reign of Charles VI of France. Philip of Cleves' (partial) copy is now BL. Royal MS. 16 F vi, vii.

101  Bayot, *Martin le Franc*, pp. 52–5.

102  Boinet, 'Un bibliophile', pp. 255–69.

103  Naber, 'Les manuscrits', pp. 23–48.

104  The *Romuléon* was composed in Latin by Roberto della Porta, and translated by Jean Miélot.

105  The *De proprietatibus rerum* is left out of the discussion and so are all liturgical books. John Russell's *Propositio* was made to order as were Traversagni's *Nova rhetorica* and its *Epitome*, and Carmeliano's *Sex epistolae*. These last three titles were meant for students and not for the general reader.

106  On Bokenham see *A Manual*, II, V; also above and the next note.

107  BL. Add. MS. 11814. On this MS. see E. Flügel, 'Eine mittelenglische Claudian-Übersetzung (1445) . . .', *Anglia*, XXVIII (1905), pp. 255–99, 421–38; W.J. Fahrenbach, 'Vernacular Translations of Classical Literature in Late-Medieval Britain: Eight Translations made directly from Latin between 1440 and 1526' (University of Toronto unpublished Ph.D. thesis 1975), pp. 150–82; John Watts, '*De Consulatu Stiliconis*: text and politics in the reign of Henry VI', *Journal of Medieval History*, XVI (1990), pp. 251–66.

108  On the Clare Roll see *A Manual*, III, VII, and references given there. Also a note by the present authors in *The Ricardian*, IX (1992), pp. 266–9.

109  Middle-English 'inspeccion' does not only mean 'careful scrutiny', but also 'knowledge or understanding gained by examining and considering', *Middle English Dictionary*.

110  *Chronicle . . .*, H. Ellis (ed.), (London 1812), p. 23. Hardyng had written much of the

book before he ever thought of dedicating it to the Duke and Duchess of York.

111 Armstrong, 'The Piety', pp. 135–6; C.C. Willard, 'Isabel of Portugal, patroness of humanism?', in *Miscellanea di studi e richerche sul quattrocento francese*, F. Simone (ed.), (Turin, 1967), pp. 519–44; C. Lemaire *et al.*, *Isabella van Portugal . . .*, catalogue of the exhibition at the Royal Library, Brussels, 1991, which gives the latest research on Isabel's life and interests, with a bibliography.

112 The *Alexander* is now BL. MS. Royal 15 D iv. The treatises were to be found in a MS. lost in Poland in 1944; it was described by A.L.J. de Laborde, *Les principaux manuscrits à peintures conservés dans l'ancienne bibliothèque impériale publique de Saint-Petersbourg*, (Société française de Reproductions de Manuscrits Peintures, 2 vols., Paris 1938), II, pp. 109–10, when it was in St Petersburg, MS. fr. O.v.I.2. It contained three translations possibly all by de Lucena: the first may have been the pseudo-Augustinian *Manuale,* but has not been identified with certainty: the second is the pseudo-St Bernard *Meditationes de cognitione humanae cognitionis,* the third St Bernard's *De diligendo deo.* We are grateful to Dom Eligius Dekkers for his assistance; see also Gallet-Guerne, pp. 19–20, nn. 129–30.

113 BL. MS. Royal 12 E xv.

114 BL. MS. Harl. 3352. Other fifteenth-century inscriptions refer to, among others, a grocer of London.

115 Oxford, Bodleian Library MSS. Bodl. 192 (2099) and 729 (2706); see M.R. James, 'The Manuscripts of St. George's Chapel, Windsor', *The Library*, 4th s., XIII (1932–3), pp. 55–76, esp. 58, 61, 65–6, 70.

116 The First Olynthiac (349 BC), in which the orator urged the Athenians to take action while Philip of Macedon was still far away. Bessarion in his running commentary continuously emphasises the similarity of the situation in Demosthenes' time and his readers'.

117 *Bessarionis Orationes,* printed by Guillaume Fichet, Paris 1471/2. See Jules Philippe, *Origine de l'Imprimerie à Paris d'après des documents inédits* (Paris, 1885), pp. 84–102; and e.g. Armstrong, 'English purchases', pp. 269–70. Edward's copy is now Rome, Vatican Apostolic Library, MS.[sic] lat. 3586; it has a presentation picture (ill. in Philippe, *Origine*) showing a cleric, kneeling and presenting the book, supported by a standing figure holding a crozier and wearing a cardinal's hat. The first is apparently Fichet, who was in orders, the other Bessarion himself. The seated king and his attendants should not in any way be regarded as portraits, nor does the picture betray any knowledge of England or the English court.

118 J. Ruysschaert, 'Lorenzo Guglielmo Traversagni de Saone (1425–1503), une humaniste franciscain oubli', *Archivum Franciscanum Historicum*, XLVI (1953), pp. 195–210; his, 'Les manuscrits autographes de deux oeuvres de Lorenzo Guglielmo Traversagni imprimées par Caxton', *BJRL*, XXXVI (1954), pp. 191–7. The text of the *Triumph of justice* survives in an autograph copy, Vatican Apostolic Library MS.Vat.lat.11608, ff.90–157v; we have not yet been able to see the text of the dedication. The *Pearl of Sacred Eloquence* according to its colophon was composed in Cambridge 'under the protection of' Edward IV (see Ruysschaert, 'Les mss.', p. 193). For Waynflete's *Triumph* see M.R. James, *A Descriptive Catalogue of the Manuscripts in the Library of Lambeth Palace: The Medieval Manuscripts* (Cambridge, 1932), MS.450.

119 D. Carlson, 'King Arthur and Court poems for the Birth of Arthur Tudor in 1486', *Humanistica Lovaniensia*, XXXVI (1987), pp. 147–83, esp. 153–5; and see references given there on Carmeliano generally. See also the present authors' 'Richard III's book: XIV. Pietro Carmeliano's early publications: his *Spring,* the *Letters of Phalaris,* and his *Life of St Katherine* dedicated to Richard III', *The Ricardian*, X (1994–96).

120 The book used to be in the library of Ely Cathedral but has disappeared, see Weiss, *Humanism,* p. 171, n. 2; Thomas Tanner, *Bibliotheca Britannico-Hibernica. . .* (repr.

1963), p. 155. On the edition see *Gesamtkatalog der Wiegendrucke . . .*, VI (Leipzig, 1934), p. 535. Carmeliano came to England in 1481 and before August 1485 he had presented this Cicero text to Edward IV; 'Spring', a Latin poem of his own making, to the Prince of Wales (BL MS. Royal 12 A xxix) and dedicated a life of St Katherine of Alexandria in verse to John Russell while he was chancellor (Cambridge, Gonville and Caius College MS.196) as well as, indirectly, to Richard III, asking Sir Robert Brackenbury, Constable of the Tower, to recommend him and his book to the King (Oxford, Bodleian Library MS. Laud. misc. 501).

121   See C. Horstmann (ed.), *Mappula Angliae, von Osbern Bokenham, Englische Studien*, X (1886), p. 7; Bokenham correctly gives Isidore of Sevilla as his source.

122   See e.g. the studies by J.W. Sherborne, V.J. Scattergood, J.J.G. Alexander and A.I. Doyle in *English Court Culture in the Later Middle Ages*, V.J. Scattergood and J.W. Sherborne (eds.), (London, 1983).

123   A.R. Myers, *The Household of Edward IV* (Manchester, 1959), p. 116; R.F. Green, *Poets and Princepleasers* (Toronto, 1980), pp. 64, 96; Harris, 'Patrons', *Book Production*, p. 179.

124   Meale, 'Patrons', *Book Production*, p. 203.

125   Green, *Poets and Princepleasers,* pp. 88, 68.

126   Saenger, 'Colard Mansion', p. 408, cites 40–50 texts of the *Fleur des histoires* produced 1450–70.

127   See Nicholas Rogers, *Books of Hours produced in the Low Countries for the English market in the Fifteenth Century* (unpubl. M. Litt. dissertation, Cambridge 1982).

128   Saenger, 'Colard Mansion', pp. 407–9.

129   For the conventional picture see e.g. Margaret Kekewich, 'Edward IV, William Caxton', pp. 481–7; Charles Ross, *Edward IV* (London, 1974), pp. 263–70; Gordon Kipling, *The Triumph of Honour* (The Hague, 1977), pp. 31–2; Hellinga, 'Caxton and the bibliophiles', pp. 11–14. This picture of Edward's 'conversion' is, of course, attractive as a literary conceit.

130   J. Backhouse, 'Founders of the Royal Library: Edward IV and Henry VII as Collectors of Illuminated Manuscripts', in *England in the Fifteenth Century. Proceedings of the 1986 Harlaxton Symposium*, D. Williams (ed.), (Woodbridge, 1987), pp. 23–41; for evidence from a specific MS. (Royal 17 F ii) Scot McKendrick, *'La Grande Histoire Cesar* and the Manuscripts of Edward IV', *English Manuscript Studies*, II (1990), pp. 109–38.

131   Edward IV may have been particularly interested in alchemy: Thomas Norton dedicated his *Ordinal of Alchemy* to him (see *Thomas Norton's Ordinal of Alchemy*, John Reidy (ed.), (E.E.T.S. O.S. 272, 1975), introduction), and George Ripley his *Compound of Alchemy* (see *DNB*, vol. 48, and the facsimile, Amsterdam 1977, of the edition of 1591). Norton is said to have accompanied Edward into exile; Ripley maintained in the dedicatory epistle that Edward had *asked* for the text and that he (the author) was willing to share his knowledge only with the King, who was sworn to secrecy!

132   Edmunds, *passim.*

133   We have compared the size of a dozen of the books of each. Edward's turned out to be on average as much as four inches taller and three inches wider than Gruuthuse's.

134   BL MS. Harl. 4379–80.

135   BL MS. Royal 17 F iii.

136   BL MS. Royal 18 E iii, iv.

137   By Janet Backhouse, 'Founders of the Royal Library', p. 24.

138   See the very useful list included by Backhouse, 'Founders of the Royal Library', pp. 39–41. These two MSS. are Royal 18 E iii, iv and 17 F iv; the second is listed as having no arms by Backhouse.

139   Vol. 2: BL MS. Royal 18 E i, with Hastings' arms; vol. 3: Malibu, J. Paul Getty

Museum MS. Ludwig XIII 7 (See A. von Euw and J.M. Plotzek, *Die Handschriften der Sammlung Ludwig* (4 vols., Cologne, 1979–85) IV, pp. 257–66) has no arms; vol. 4: BL MS.Royal 18 E ii, with the royal arms. These four volumes could presumably each have been part of separate series all made in the same workshop.

140    Not only is it very difficult, if not impossible, to establish which artists worked physically together in one 'workshop', it also has to be emphasised that many different patrons frequented one such shop or group of illuminators. If art historians are right, for example, in saying that Simon Marmion worked for Guillaume Fillastre, Philip of Cleves, members of the Croy family, Claudio Villa, David of Burgundy and Engelbert or Henry of Nassau, etc. confusion was and is inevitable. In view of the practical problems of standardised mass-production, it is very likely that badly-timed completion as well as confusion over the combining of gatherings, painting of initials, choice of miniatures, sketching or painting in the arms of several patrons, are enough to explain most of the errors and alterations that confront us. How can we be really sure, in fact, that any MS., however magnificent the arms and badges that were included, ever actually reached its intended owner if it has no signature or hand-written *ex libris*?

141    There is a danger in creating another literary 'circle' out of such evidence as survives, but a group of people regularly frequenting Calais could at least be said to have a physical advantage over some other circles, rather like the Kent gentry and their literary interests, favoured by their geographical position, described by P. Fleming in his 'The Hautes and their 'Circle' . . .', in *England in the Fifteenth Century*. Like the 'Haute Circle' a 'Calais group' would not necessarily consist of people who devoted all their life to the arts, but they would have been much more aware of the perfection of Low Countries art than many of their countrymen, and easily fall under its spell.

142    For Donne see K.B. McFarlane, *Hans Memling* (Oxford, 1971), pp. 5–11, 52–5; Backhouse, 'Founders of the Royal Library', pp. 30–1, 40–1.

143    James Carley is working on them.

144    It is difficult to establish with any certainty when any MS. entered the royal collection. The list published by H. Omont, 'Les manuscrits français des rois d'Angleterre au château de Richmond', in *Etudes romanes dédiées à Gaston Paris* (Paris, 1891), pp. 5–21, which is often called in to testify to the early presence of a MS. is tantalisingly vague and misleading.

145    Edward was to have a volume of the poems of Charles of Orleans, the letters of Heloise, the 'Demands and Answers of Love' and the 'Governance of a Prince', for which the texts and only two miniatures were completed (16 F ii), plus a magnificent five-volume Froissart (14 D ii-vi), Xenophon's *Cyropédie*, and Vegetius' *De re militari* (17 E v), see Backhouse, 'Founders of the Royal LIbrary' p. 30. For Henry a vast collection of French chronicles in six volumes was projected in 1487 (20 E i–vi). The evidence for these gifts is the uncertain one of the inclusion of royal arms and badges in the decoration, except for the gift to Henry VII which is actually recorded in the colophon, though only in one of the six volumes.

146    We would also tentatively link with Thwaytes Lambeth Palace MS.6, the lavishly illustrated *Brut* chronicle in English probably by a Flemish copyist; the 1st and 4th quarters of the owner's arms are identical with those occurring in the Royal MSS. usually ascribed to Thwaytes' ownership (14 D ii–vi, 17 E v, 20 E i–vi). The arms in Lambeth 6 have been connected with William Purches, mercer and mayor of London in 1498, but the evidence for this connection is uncertain. The arms might be those of Thwaytes, quartered with, for example, those of his wife, whose identity is unknown. See E.G. Millar, 'Les Principaux Manuscrits à peintures de Lambeth Palace à Londres', *Bulletin de la Société française de reproductions des manuscrits à peintures*, 9e

année (Paris, 1925), pp. 5–19, pl. xliv; Meale, 'Patrons', *Book Production*, pp. 266–7, n. 38.

147    Backhouse, 'Founders of the Royal Library', pp. 30, 34–8; *The Coronation of Richard III. The Extant Documents*, Anne F. Sutton and P.W. Hammond (eds.), (Gloucester, 1983), p. 405, and the *full* copy of his will: Dean and Chapter of Canterbury, Reg. F., ff. 185v–186v.

148    See e.g. G.A.C. Sandeman, *Calais under English Rule* (Oxford, 1908); A. Hanham, *The Celys and their World* (Cambridge, 1985).

149    A provisional list of these numbers was supplied to us by James Carley.

150    BL. MS. Royal 19 A vi, numbered 60: *Ung tractie de conseil extraict du second livre de la thoison d'or*, by Guillaume Fillastre, and *Tulle de veillesse*, before 1477; MS. Royal 20 B ii, numbered 62: lives of saints in French, with good quality illumination, 1480s, arms of John Donne; MS. Royal 19 A xix, numbered 93: *Cité des Dames*, unexciting illumination, *c.* 1430–50, Yorkist emblems.

# 4

# Traders and Playmakers: English Guildsmen and the Low Countries

Alexandra F. Johnston
*University of Toronto*

In recent years those working in late medieval English drama have become more and more aware of the close connection between the popular drama of England and the popular drama of the Low Countries. Gradually, English speaking scholars are coming to understand that the influences, in all probability, flowed from the continent to England. The primacy of the Dutch morality play, *Elckerlijc*, over its English counterpart, *Everyman*, has been established beyond any reasonable doubt for over a generation[1] and, as more and more Dutch and Flemish texts are made available in editions and translations, the similarities between this drama and that performed in England become ever more apparent. Themes and preoccupations echo across the 'Middle Sea' and staging and stage devices are similarly mirrored.

The main reason for this close connection is to be found in the trading links between the Low Countries and the east coast ports of England in the late Middle Ages. The drama of this period is, above all, drama of the towns and cities – quasi professional productions that combined religious piety with civic pride. It was quintessentially a bourgeois art-form produced and promoted by the town councils of England and the Low Counties. When they were not engaging in their annual playmaking activities at home, the burghers of England were loading their ships with cloth and lead and themselves heading out across the 'German Sea' to buy and sell in the markets of the Brabant, Zeeland, Holland and Flanders. Chaucer's Merchant, for example, sets out on his pilgrimage sporting a Flemish beaver hat wishing that 'the see were kept for any thyng/ Bitwixe Middelburgh and Orewelle'.[2] Middelburg was a great trading centre in Zeeland; the Orwell flows between Ipswich and Felixstowe in Suffolk. He was typical of his day and generation, taking his 'bargaynes' and his 'chevyssaunces' to the Low Countries.

The heavily indented coastline curving north from Calais, with its many sea ports and its many rivers navigable by the small ships that plied across the North Sea, had been a prime centre of commerce since the eleventh century.[3] By the fifteenth century English traders had become 'the mainstay of the Flemish, Brabantine and Dutch fairs'.[4] The fairs or marts were held four times a year at the changing of the seasons: the winter or cold mart, the spring or pase mart, the summer or synxon mart and the autumn or balms mart. These were the occasions of great commercial gatherings with all their attendant celebrations, entertainments and exchange of news and ideas.[5] Here English seamen trading with the Low Countries from Newcastle, Hull, Boston, Ipswich, Lynn, Grimsby and London and the merchants from the wool towns of York, Beverley, Norwich and, in the sixteenth century, Wakefield, rubbed shoulders with their counterparts from all over Europe. Maud Sellers gives us a vivid picture of these occasions in Antwerp, the centre of the English traders in the fifteenth and sixteenth centuries:

> Four times a year in the spring, summer, autumn and winter, those non-resident masters, who left their cloth in charge of factors or apprentices, hurried over from London, York, Newcastle, Norwich, Lynn or other sub-posts to supervise the sales that took place at these seasons. Their days would be full; as well as their bargainings they had to attend the courts, where new ordinances were promulgated, new officials elected and the general policy of the company discussed; . . . The streets and market place of Antwerp, the 'English House,' where the most important merchants lived, and the lodgings of the less important, were filled with the cloth sellers; the buyers, too, came from far and near to these fairs.[6]

It is no coincidence that the provincial towns and districts represented annually at the fairs in the Low Countries are just those towns and districts from which the great bulk of surviving English drama comes. Nor is it coincidence that many of these towns had processions that paralleled the 'ommegange' of the Low Countries.

Of these trading and playmaking towns, York has the greatest amount of surviving archival material. The archives of the city itself and of the Worshipful Company of Merchant Adventurers[7] together provide a unique opportunity to see the Mercers and Merchants of York as both traders and playmakers. During this period York was a mercantile oligarchy and the same men were traders, guildsmen and members of the city government. Of the eighty-eight mayors between 1399 and 1509, sixty-eight were Mercers.[8] In some years they dominated the city council; for example on 1420 twenty-two of the twenty-nine members of the council were Mercers.[9] Their influence declined in the sixteenth century, a decline which reflected the serious economic depression which affected the city, but even then the number of mayors who were merchants exceeded that of all other vocations combined.[10]

As both guildsmen and aldermen they were personally involved in

4a   Leuven, Stedelyk Museum Ms Boonen, fos. 457ᵛ–458. The Annunciation wagon.

playmaking. The Mercers Guild was responsible for the episode of the Last Judgment, the lavish finale of the town's great Biblical play now known as the York Cycle. The city council took collective responsibility for the entire sequence and often individual members of the guild appear in the civic records in connection with the play. By matching the names that appear at meetings of the guild that make key decisions about the European trade or that appear on bills of lading with the playmaking references, we can gain some idea of the exposure that the men actively engaged in drama during this period in York had to the culture of the Low Countries.

The York Cycle, performed annually on Corpus Christi day, remains one of the great works of English literature from the fifteenth century.[11] We do not know who wrote it or when the city and its guilds became involved with it, but we do know that it existed in some form in the last quarter of the fourteenth century. The play was produced by the city council, with each of the forty-eight separate episodes recounting salvation history the responsibility of one or more of the many craft guilds. Over the two centuries that the play was performed, the craft guilds came to define themselves in relation to their sister crafts by a complex pattern of donations to the pageants of other crafts so that when the plays were suppressed in the 1560s, the guilds were hard put to find new ways to define their inter-connectedness.

The cycle began early in the morning with the creation of the heaven and earth and ended near midnight with the Last Judgment. The central action of the sequence depicted the Passion of Christ in long and gruelling detail. Each episode was performed on a moving stage called a pageant wagon at an average of twelve separate playing places or 'stations' designated by the city along a pre-determined route within the city walls. The stations were rented by the city council to the highest bidder who, in turn, had the right to sell seats and provide refreshments for the audience gathered to see the play at that location. The income from the station rents is a regular item in the account rolls of the city chamberlains throughout the life of the play. The night before the production, the mayor processed along the route and placed the arms of the city at each authorized place.[12]

As the producer of the play, the city council held the ultimate control over the performing guilds. Any changes in the sponsorship of episodes had to be authorized by the city council. An official 'check-list' known as the 'ordo paginarum' was drawn up about 1415 listing the performing crafts and the episodes for which they were responsible. For the rest of the life of the cycle, the town clerk kept the list up to date. Any changes in the content of an episode or the sponsoring guild or guilds were noted as they occurred.[13] All the episodes were sponsored by craft guilds except the pageant of the Coronation of the Virgin for which the city council itself took responsibility, sometimes in conjunction with one or more guild over the history of the performance of that pageant.[14] The 'ordo gathering' also contains the official proclamation of the play to be read on the vigil of the Feast of Corpus Christi laying out the regulations for the performance:

> And yat all maner of craftmen þat bringeth furthe ther pageantez in order & course by good players well arayed & openly spekyng vpon payn of lesyng of C s to be paid to the chambre withoute any pardon And that euery player that shall play be redy in his pagiaunt at convenyant tyme that is to say at the mydhowre betwix iiijth & vth of the cloke in the mornyng & then all oyer pageantes fast folowyng ilkon after oyer as yer course is without Tarieng sub pena facienda camere vj s viij d[15]

The fines were levied as the council monitored the annual performances. A regular entry in the Chamberlains' Rolls lists the annual expenses incurred by the mayor and the council on the day of the performance when they

4b   Leuven, Stedelyk Museum Ms Boonen, fo. 478. The burghers carrying the statue of the Virgin Mary.

watched the performance from one of the designated stations.[16] The mayors, chamberlains and all the aldermen, therefore, were intimately involved in the annual production in their official capacity.

The aldermen who were Mercers were doubly involved since their craft was responsible for the finale of the day's event. The first significant document concerning the Mercers' pageant that survives is an indenture drawn up in 1433 between the company and the four men who in that year acted as pageant masters. The post of pageant master was normally filled by a junior member of the guild but, on this occasion, two of the four men were merchants of some standing. One, William Bedale, had been master of the company the year before and would be mayor three years later.[17] The other, Henry Market, was a Hanse merchant who had become a freeman of the city in 1412 but had become naturalized only three years before by an act of parliament.[18] The two constables of the company that year, Nicholas Useflete and William Yarom[19] both became freemen the same year as Market. In 1433, these two men and the master of the company Richard Louth engaged the town clerk, Roger Burton, to write to the Lord of Campveer, the port town of Veere near Middelburg in

Zeeland.[20] In this combination of people and events we can see the York Mercers concerned on the one hand for the pursuance of their trade with the Low Countries but on the other hand, anxious to put the production of their play on a businesslike footing.

The 1433 indenture is one of the most remarkable pageant documents that has survived from anywhere in England. It lists the costumes, including angel wings with iron in the ends, and masks for most of the characters including double-faced masks for the devils. The wagon itself, according to the property list, was elaborately hung with painted cloths and was decorated with twenty artificial angels, nine of which were small and red with a string attached to make them 'run about in the heavens'. The central feature of the design was a hoisting device that took Christ up to heaven after the judgment.[21] This indenture became the controlling document for the next few decades of the life of the play. In 1443, the day that Thomas Scauceby was first elected master, the company issued an ordinance regulating the election and activity of the pageant masters 'by Indentour'.[22] The pageant masters were expected to collect the annual levy or 'pageant silver' from all the members of the craft and, using this money, refurbish the wagon, hire the players and ensure that the episode was performed in a seemly fashion so as not to incur a civic fine. They were to account to the company for all the costumes and properties listed in the indenture.

Thomas Scauceby, who oversaw the adoption of the ordinance for the pageant masters, was five times master of the guild, bailiff of the city in 1447, mayor in 1463 and a regular patron of the entire play renting the second station on the pageant route in 1454,[23] 1462[24] and 1468.[25] Since only these three rolls survive from this period, he may have rented the station for the entire twelve years. The next account roll is for 1475, four years after his death.[26] His name appears frequently in the Mercers' rolls as a trader but our most vivid picture of him in this capacity is as the overseer of the loading of the ship *Kattryn* bound for Bruges in 1457. Most of the bill of lading speaks only of chests and containers but there is some detail in one section where cloth specified as whites and western whites, and melds are listed along with calf skin, lead, and breast plates, helmets and other pieces of 'harnes' or armour.[27]

A rather tattered document survives telling us of two meetings of the craft held between 1472 and 1475 that governed their trading activities. One decreed that no ship should sail 'newther of thissyde see or on tother syde of the see'[28] unless they were fully loaded. The other sets the fee for trading abroad:

> . . . Also it is enacted by the masteres, constables, and all the fellyshipp
> that everie brother of the said fellyshipp occupying as maistre in

Flanders, and Braband, and Seland shall pay at his hansynge (i.e. entry into the guild) at Bruges, Andwarpe, Barow (i.e. Bergen op Zoom) and Midilburg, ijs. at everie place aforesaid, and no more. And everie apprentice of the said fellysship shall pay at his hansynge in Bruges, Andwarpe, Barowe, and Midilburg, xvjd. at everie place aforesaid, and no more. . . .[29]

Of the twenty-eight members of the company (twenty-seven men and one woman) named in the second document, fourteen appear in the dramatic records of York because of their specific involvement in playmaking activities. Ten of the men were mayor at least once and three more held office as sheriff. As members of the city government, as we have seen, they would have been closely involved with the annual festivities at Corpus Christi – proclaiming the play, setting out the banners of the city at the stations, walking in the Corpus Christi procession and, of course, watching the play from their assigned station.

As mayor, several of them presided over specific decisions about the play. In 1476, Thomas Wrangwis was mayor when an important ordinance was passed specifying auditions for all actors taking part in the cycle, amateur and professional alike, and prohibiting anyone from taking a part in more than two episodes.[30] That same year, he also presided over an agreement between the Tapiters and the Weavers concerning their contributions to the Passion sequence in 1475–6.[31] In his next term, in 1484, he presided over an agreement of the Innholders to share the production of the Coronation of the Virgin.[32] Nicholas Lancaster, in his second term as mayor in 1483, settled a dispute among the sub-crafts of the Smiths concerning the play of the Temptation.[33] Richard York, also in his second term in 1482, worked with the Pinners and the Wiredrawers to settle a dispute about the performance of the Crucifixion.[34] John Tonge in his term in 1477 presided over the meeting that included the Labourers, a group of men who were not considered to constitute a craft, who were to contribute financially to the Masons for their production of the Purification of the Virgin, organizing the collecting of 'pageant money' by ward.[35]

Several of the men who attended the important meetings of the craft in the 1470s were also involved in mounting special performances for visiting royalty. In 1483, John Tonge and Thomas Wrangwis undertook to produce the Creed Play for the special visit of Richard III to York on the occasion of his son's consecration as Prince of Wales in the Minster.[36] Richard York, William Todd, John Beseley and John Shaw were all in office during the preparation of the elaborate Royal Entry for Henry VII in 1486.[37] They commissioned Henry Hudson, a poet, to devise the show that followed the pageant route to the Minster with six special tableaux for the king

4c   Leuven, Stedelyk Museum Ms Boonen, fo. 488. The mayor and companions preceded by the town waits wearing their badges.

including an appearance of the Virgin in Stonegate using the Weavers' pageant wagon of the Assumption for the set. In the following year, during Todd's mayoralty, he and York arranged for a special performance of the Corpus Christi Play in August to entertain the king who was again in the north following the Lambert Simnel uprising. At the end of that visit both men were knighted by the king.[38] Twelve years earlier, in 1475, the younger Todd is listed as the owner of two ships, the *Grace de Dieu* and the *Juliana Pilkington*, that plied the route between Hull and Zeeland.[39]

Richard York had been even more intimately connected with playmaking. As a young man, he had been one of the four pageant masters of the Mercers in 1462.[40] The detailed account for that year survives recording the building of a new costume for God and mending some of the twenty artificial angels that decorated the wagon. He ended his life as a merchant of the staple – a member of the London company as well as the one in York.[41]

Another of the company named in the document drawn up to govern the trading of the guild in the 1470s, Henry Williamson, served not as mayor but as sheriff and had also been a pageant master as a young man in

1461.[42] That year was the first occasion when the company decided to rent angel wings rather than once again repair them. It was also the year three and half yards of red buckram were used to make new banners. The buckram was bought from another member of the company who attended the meetings to draw up the ordinances, Thomas Beverlay, who the same year undertook to repair the craft's ceremonial torches.[43] Beverlay was both master of the guild and mayor in 1471.[44]

Finally, two of the Mercers named in the document rented stations on the pageant route following Thomas Scauceby's example. Wrangwis himself rented the tenth and last station at the Pavement in 1462[45] and Thomas Welles rented the fourth station in 1486.[46]

The ordinances of the company concerning trading practices were redrawn in 1495. They confirmed the fees for European trading established in the earlier ordinance and went on to make specific provision for the behaviour of their members while abroad. The master and constables were to name 'ane honest persone or ij of the company at ilk tyme when men passes over the see, that is to say, to Flaunders, Braban, and Seland, to have ful power of the maister and constables'.[47] These men were to act for the company in disciplining the members of the craft and their apprentices who were living and trading abroad.

In 1498, the company issued an ordinance requiring all ships sailing to the Low Countries or Normandy from Hull to pay the company 6s 8d.[48] Again, there was a large attendance of the members of the craft. Of the thirty-eight present, five became mayor at least once and two more sheriffs. Four had acted as pageant masters and two are recorded as renting stations for the play. More significant, however, is the presence at the meeting of six of the eight men (including the then mayor Richard Thornton, a grocer) who four years later commissioned Thomas Drawswerd, an alabaster carver of some repute, to

> . . . mak the pagiant of the dome (i.e. doom) belonging to the merchauntes newe substancialie in euery thing þervnto belonging havyng for the warkemanship and Stuff of the same vij marcs in money And his entrie free with Also the old pagiaunt . . .[49]

Drawswerd later became both master of the company and mayor. His pageant with its gabled roof and carved decorations seems to have been much more like the pageant wagons of the Low Countries than the fifteenth-century wagon with its rich cloth hangings had been.[50]

In 1536, a royal embargo was placed on the export of lead and from a document dated that year we have lists of the members of the company who intended to ship lead to the continent.[51] Of the sixteen hoping to ship to Flanders, seven had served as pageant masters as young men, one of whom, George Hall as master of the company in 1560, was in Antwerp.[52] Hall and two other men on the 1536 list became members of the London company as well. The close connections between the English traders and especially the town of Antwerp can be measured by the fact that all members of the English company were assessed to help pay for the royal entry of Philip of Spain into Antwerp in 1554.[53]

During the 1560s the play declined at home and the trade with the Low Countries became more troublesome. In 1563 we find Christopher Herbert whose house still stands near the Pavement in York and who was pageant master in 1550 and 1551, in Antwerp for an extended period trying to sort out the problems. Many of the political problems were beyond the control of traders. Their eyes turned farther east and, in 1567, a full court of the company was held in Antwerp to discuss the first serious proposals for making a major shift to Hamburg as the major port of entry to the continent.[54] English trade again returned to the Low Countries in the seventeenth century but by then the involvement of the trading crafts in their own playmaking was long past.

The merchants of York have here been used simply as an example. Throughout this period, although the London merchants dominated the trade, merchants and seamen from all the provincial ports played a vital, if subordinate role. A similar survey of the records of any of the port towns and their upland wool suppliers would demonstrate the same pattern. These men were Merchant Adventurers; they did not stay at home and the sights and customs of Antwerp, Bruges, Middelburg, Dordrecht, Leuven, Bergen op Zoom, Verre and Amsterdam were as familiar or more familiar to them as other English towns.

But what did they see in the Low Countries? Although scholarship on the drama of the Low Countries is not as advanced as the work on English drama, intriguing patterns are emerging from the ground-breaking work of the last two decades in The Netherlands.[55] The drama from the Low Countries influenced the content of English drama as well as its staging and was also important in the formation of the traditions of civic display.

The texts are still largely unedited but already the results of recent research are suggestive. Many of the plays were the result of the annual competitions among the Chambers of Rhetoric. Although there was one 'puy' or competition held in London around 1300, this feature of the culture of the Low Countries and northern France did not find fertile ground in England.[56] However, the types of plays that were written for the competitions did. The English seem to have been particularly interested in Biblical or apocryphal material that could be adapted for the many plays on such themes in English. Lynnette Muir and Peter Meredith have traced the relationship among the *Eerste Bliscap* (a play on the life of the Virgin) from Brussels (1441), a Rouen play of 1471, the *N-Town* Virgin sequence and the Valenciennes plays from the 1540s.[57] The manuscript recently identified as from Lille[58] contains many plays based on obscure Old Testament themes adapted to reflect the history of Lille and some based on parables. One such play, the Play of the Vineyard, may have York connections. A play of this name was paid for by the York city council as part of the Corpus Christi celebration in 1442.[59] Perhaps Thomas Scauceby, who was chamberlain that year, had seen the play on a recent business trip and brought a text home to be translated and performed. No other reference to a play on this theme in England survives.

Romance themes such as those in *Esmoreit*, a play becoming more familiar to English speaking scholars through performance, were a standard element in many of the plays of the rhetoricians. The romance elements in the play of *Mary Magdalene* from the Digby manuscript, one of the two East Anglian collections of saints plays and moralities, may owe a debt to the Low Countries. A possible family connection lends credence to this suggestion. The name William Blomfeld appears in association with the Fraternity of St Thomas or the merchant guild of Norwich in 1509.[60] In the next generation two Blomfelds with associations both with Norwich and with Bury St Edmunds have connections with the Digby manuscript.[61] The elder, another William, was in his early life a monk of Bury but left the monastery before dissolution and was later vicar of St Simon and St Jude in Norwich. The younger, Miles, of Bury, at some time during the sixteenth century had the Digby manuscript in his possession. His name appears on the first leaves of the plays of the *Conversion of Paul, Mary Magdalen* and *Wisdom*.[62] Miles also possessed a copy of William Blomfeld's 'Quintessens or the Regiment of Philosophy' on which he had written, among other biographical notes, that William was 'a good Latinist, partly a Gretian, an hebritian havyng also the tounges of dyvers languages as dutch and french.'[63] In their article about the early history of the Digby manuscript, Donald Baker and John Murray suggest that the plays were originally in the possession of William Blomfeld of Bury with the strong implication that he may have been, if not the author, at least the compiler of the collection that has survived. They suggest that just as Miles Blomfeld came into the possession of William's 'Regiment', so he came into the possession of the play book. William's facility with the Dutch language and the possible connection with the older merchant William adds tantalizing but inconclusive details to the possible transmission of continental influences to the plays in this collection.

The morality genre was a favourite among the Dutch and Flemish playwrights. This is in sharp contrast to the English tradition. Only four English morality texts survive before the appearance of *Everyman* in the sixteenth century, three from East Anglia. The earliest one, *The Pride of Life*, is a fragmentary play on the death of the King of the World found in a mid-fourteenth-century account roll from the Priory of Holy Trinity, Dublin.[64] The East Anglian plays are *The Castle Perseverance, Mankind* and *Wisdom*.[65] Many years ago, Professor David Bevington in an influential book called *From Mankind to Marlowe*,[66] argued that the morality genre as it changed from religious to educational and political themes during the sixteenth century was a major shaping influence on the great English drama of the end of that century. This argument has seemed less convincing, however, as the Records of Early English Drama project has progressed. Only one positive external reference has so far been uncovered to plays in this genre in the provinces, in East Redford in Nottinghamshire.[67] But Bevington's argument remains a convincing one if we recognize the morality genre from the late fifteenth century onwards as essentially an imported one. If the history of the transmission of *Everyman* from the Low Countries in a printed edition is typical of the process,[68] it is more than likely that printed texts of Dutch and Flemish plays followed the printing presses from the Low Countries to London, were translated for the English stage and became part of the metropolitan culture rather than that of the provinces.

Other major influences from the Low Countries were the great 'ommegange' – the processions of wagons, tableaux, marching giants and other mythical and traditional characters. The Renaissance paintings of such events in Antwerp are familiar to the scholarly world. More particularly, however, a lesser known civic document, the town book of Leuven (or Louvain) surviving from the end of the sixteenth century[69] has a lively series of water colour sketches that picture the entire procession in honour of the Virgin from the first marching militia, to the four orders of friars, to the cathedral clergy with the choir boys in attendance, to the pageants depicting the life of the Virgin, to St George and the dragon, to the city waits preceding the mayor and aldermen in their solemn black velvet as they march in honour of the town and the Virgin. Dogs and children dart in and out of the parade; the feet of the bearers of the giants peek out from under their skirts. In this series of pictures we have a late contemporary representation of the customs that existed in the Low Countries and much of England in the fifteenth and sixteenth centuries. It was these shows that the English merchants saw on the continent and returned home to imitate.

Although very few English towns sponsored drama performed in procession as at York, many towns had local annual processions that contained special features that were repeated year after year. The procession on Corpus Christi Day from 1498–1569 in English-occupied Dublin contained, among Biblical tableaux, a dragon, a pageant of Arthur and his knights and another of the Nine Worthies.[70] Hereford's procession included a St Katherine tableau[71] and the one at Norwich a griffin.[72]

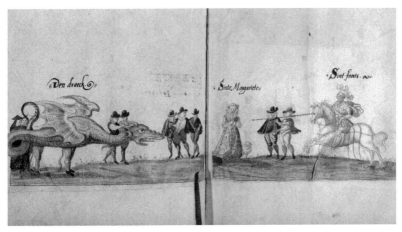

4d  Leuven, Stedelyk Museum Ms Boonen, fos. 492ᵛ–493. St George and the
dragon with St Margaret (photograph by Alexandra F. Johnston).

Other similarly exotic beasts appear in the Ipswich Corpus Christi
procession which boasted a dolphin and a bull.[73] Chester used pageant
camels, dromedaries and other beasts in their Midsummer Show as well as
giants.[74] Norwich included a giant in their greeting of Queen Elizabeth
(Woodville) in 1496.[75] Both stationary and marching giants were an
important part of London civic displays from the early fifteenth century.[76]
All of these have analogues in the 'ommegange' of the Low Countries.

The Flemish wagons undoubtedly provided a model for the northern
English pageant wagons but, as we are discovering, wagon staging of true
drama was unusual in England. The last of the Leuven drawings depicts a
play of St Katherine being performed on a booth stage made of boards and
trestles set against the wall of the church in the town square. Stages built
indoors or outdoors of boards and trestles or boards and barrels seem to
have been much more common in England than wagon plays. For
example, in the parish of St Laurence, Reading a stage was built against the
wall of the Benedictine Abbey in an open space called the Forbury to
perform Old Testament plays in the early sixteenth century.[77]

Historians of the English theatre can no longer neglect the plays and
processions of the Low Countries as a major source of analogous material
for study. The field has for too long been dominated by nineteenth-
century ideas of the importance of nations. Our scholarly parents and
grandparents lived in a world ruled by the cultures of England, France and
Germany. Belgium and Holland were the battlegrounds where the great

powers settled, or failed to settle, their quarrels. The central importance of these states for the culture of fifteenth- and sixteenth-century England went unrecognized. Only now as texts and records on both sides of the 'Middle Sea' are being discovered, edited and reinterpreted is the true picture beginning to emerge.

## Notes

1   Elza Strietman, 'The Low Countries' in *The Theatre of Medieval Europe*, Ekehard Simon (ed.), Cambridge, 1991, pp. 246–7.

2   Geoffrey Chaucer, *The Works*, F.N. Robinson (ed.) (Cambridge, Mass., 1957) I (A) 11.276–7, p. 20.

3   For detailed discussion of the English trade with the Low Countries see T.H. Lloyd, *The English Wool Trade in the Middle Ages* (Cambridge, 1977). This study ends with the decline of trade in the fifteenth century. His later book, *England and the German Hanse 1157–1611* (Cambridge, 1991), continues the story.

4   Eileen Power, *Medieval English Wool Trade*, Oxford, 1941, pp. 11–12.

5   The cultural dimensions of continental fairs is discussed by Anne F. Sutton in 'Merchants, Music and Social Harmony: the London Puy and its French and London Contexts, circa 1300,' *London Journal*, 17, 1992, pp. 1–17. For a discussion of the fifteenth- and sixteenth-century Dutch Rederijkerskamers or Chambers of Rhetoric see Strietman, 'The Low Countries'.

6   Maud Sellers, *The York Mercers and Merchant Adventurers 1356–1917*, Surtees Society 129 (1917) pp. xxxviii–ix.

7   The records of the medieval and early modern guild of Mercers and Merchants in York are still held privately by the modern descendant of the guild, the Worshipful Company of Merchant Adventurers.

8   Edward Miller, 'Medieval York' in *A History of Yorkshire: City of York, P.M. Tillott* (ed.) (The Victoria Histories of the Counties of England, University of London Institute of Historical Research, 1961), p. 71.

9   *Ibid.*, pp. 78–9.

10  *Ibid.*, p. 160.

11  The play survives in a unique manuscript that was the official civic copy. It is now in the British Library (BL Add MS 35290). The most recent edition is by Richard Beadle, *The York Plays* (London, 1982).

12  Alexandra F. Johnston and Margaret Rogerson (eds.), *Records of Early English Drama: York* (Toronto, 1979) p. 12.

13  Johnston and Rogerson, *York* pp. 17–26. For a detailed discussion of the document see Martin Stevens and Margaret Dorrell (Rogerson), 'The *Ordo Paginarum* gathering of the York *A/Y Memorandum Book*,' *Modern Philology*, 72 (1974), pp. 45–59.

14  Johnston and Rogerson, *York*, p. 54 *et passim*.

15  Johnston and Rogerson, *York* p. 25.

16  Johnston and Rogerson, *York* p. 9 *et passim*.

17  Sellers, *Mercers* p. 322. See also Francis Collins, ed. *The Register of the Freemen of the City of York*, Surtees Society, 96 (1894), p. 151. Collins is consistently one year out in his dating. Here he dates Bedale's mayoralty as 1435 when it should be 1436.

18  Collins, *Freemen* p. 117. See also Maud Sellers (ed.), *York Memorandum Book, Part II, 1388–1493*, Surtees Society, 125 (1914), p. 185.

19   Collins, *Freemen* pp. 116–7.
20   Sellers, *Mercers* pp. 40–41; *Memorandum* pp. 186–8.
21   Johnston and Rogerson, *York* pp. 55–6.
22   Johnston and Rogerson, *York* p. 61.
23   Johnston and Rogerson, *York* p. 85.
24   Johnston and Rogerson, *York* p. 93.
25   Johnston and Rogerson, *York* p. 100.
26   Johnston and Rogerson, *York* p. xxiii.
27   Sellers, *Mercers* pp. 59–63.
28   Sellers, *Mercers* p. 64.
29   Sellers, *Mercers* p. 65.
30   Johnston and Rogerson, *York* p. 109.
31   Johnston and Rogerson, *York* pp. 107–8.
32   Johnston and Rogerson, *York* pp. 133–4.
33   Johnston and Rogerson, *York* p. 105.
34   Johnston and Rogerson, *York* p. 128.
35   Johnston and Rogerson, *York* p. 115.
36   Johnston and Rogerson, *York* p. 131.
37   Johnston and Rogerson, *York* pp. 133–52.
38   Johnston and Rogerson, *York* p. 155.
39   Sellers, *Mercers* p. 72.
40   Johnston and Rogerson, *York* p. 95.
41   Francis Drake, *Eboracum* (London, 1736) p. 363.
42   Johnston and Rogerson, *York* p. 92.
43   Johnston and Rogerson, *York* p. 92.
44   Drake, *Eboracum* p. 363.
45   Johnston and Rogerson, *York* p. 93.
46   Johnston and Rogerson, *York* p. 144.
47   Sellers, *Mercers* p. 93.
48   Sellers, *Mercers* p. 104.
49   Johnston and Rogerson, *York* p. 189.
50   For a detailed discussion of the Mercer's wagons see Alexandra F. Johnston and Margaret Dorrell, 'The York Mercers and their Pageant of Doomsday,' *Leeds Studies in English*, New Series, vi (1972) pp. 11–35.
51   Sellers, *Mercers* p. 135.
52   Sellers, *Mercers* p. 164.
53   Sellers, *Mercers* pp. 151–2.
54   Sellers, *Mercers* pp. 179–80.
55   See Strietman, 'The Low Countries', for a survey of the scholarship up to 1986.
56   For a detailed account of the London puy and its analogues in the northern French provinces bordering Flanders see Anne F. Sutton 'Merchants, Music and Social Harmony.
57   Peter Meredith and Lynnette Muir, 'The Trial in Heaven in the *Eerste Bliscap* and other European Plays,' *Dutch Crossings*, 22 (1984), pp. 84–92.
58   A manuscript that seems to comprise a collection of plays written for a rhetoricians competition has been identified in a German archive and is being edited by Professor Alan Knight. This manuscript was the subject of a session at the Medieval and Renaissance Drama Society session at the Modern Language Association in New York in 1987. The papers presented there by Professors Knight, Alexandra F. Johnston and Pamela Sheingorn were published in *Research Opportunities in Renaissance Drama*, XXX (1988).
59   Johnston and Rogerson, *York* p. 60.

60    Sellers, *Mercers* p. 121.
61    D.C. Baker and J.L. Murphy (eds.), *The Late Medieval Plays of Bodleian MSS Digby 133 and E Museo 160*, EETS, ES 283, 1982.
62    D.C. Baker and J.L. Murphy, 'The Late Medieval Plays of MS. Digby 133: Scribes, Dates and Early History', *Research Opportunities in Renaissance Drama*, X (1967), p. 163.
63    Baker and Murphy, *RORD*, p. 168.
64    What survives of the text appears in Norman Davis (ed.), *Non-Cycle Plays and Fragments*, EETS SS 1, 1970.
65    They are found in the East Anglian Macro ms. The most recent edition is Mark Eccles (ed.), *The Macro Plays*, EETS OS 262, 1969. A second, fragmentary copy of *Wisdom* is also found in the Digby ms.
66    David Bevington, *From Mankind to Marlowe* (Cambridge Mass., 1962).
67    Ian Lancashire, *Dramatic Texts and Records of Britain: A Chronological Topography to 1558* (Toronto, 1984) 631, p. 128.
68    Strietman, 'The Low Countries,' pp. 246–7.
69    See Meg Twycross, 'The *Liber Boonen* of the Leuven Ommegang,' *Dutch Crossings*, 22 (1984) pp. 93–6.
70    Lancashire, *Texts and Records*, 1736 pp. 327–8.
71    Lancashire, *Texts and Records* 768 p. 152–3.
72    Lancashire, *Texts and Records* 1220 p. 235.
73    Lancashire, *Texts and Records* 790 p. 157.
74    Lawrence M. Clopper (ed.), *Records of Early English Drama: Chester*, (Toronto, 1979), p. 72.
75    Lancashire, *Texts and Records* 1225 p. 236.
76    Lancashire, *Texts and Records*, 918 p. 178; 923 p. 179; 969 p. 188.
77    See the churchwardens' accounts of the parish, Berkshire Record Office, BRO D/P 97 5/1.

# 5

# An Anglo-Burgundian Nobleman and Art Patron: Louis de Bruges, Lord of la Gruthuyse and Earl of Winchester

Malcolm Vale
*St John's College, Oxford*

Relations between England and the Low Countries in the fifteenth century have often been discussed in terms of economic activity. Anglo-Flemish commercial and mercantile connections, often mediated through Calais, were certainly highly important; but the picture is incomplete without some consideration of the political and cultural contacts between the English court and its Burgundian counterpart, located after 1450 within the Netherlandish territories of the Valois dukes, and between individuals in the service of both powers. The latter served as intermediaries between England and Burgundy: Louis de Bruges, lord of la Gruthuyse, created earl of Winchester in 1472, provides an exemplar of the interplay of politics and culture under Edward IV, Philip the Good and Charles the Bold.

There is no biography in English of this Flemish nobleman who was at the centre of much Anglo-Burgundian diplomacy and cultural activity between 1466 and his death in 1492. A study by Joseph Van Praet, entitled *Recherches sur Louis de Bruges*, appeared in Paris in 1831.[1] There has been no further general work in French or Dutch with the exception of two exhibition catalogues: *Vlaamse Kunst op Perkament* (Bruges 1981) which has a useful section by Claudine Lemaire devoted to the Gruthuyse library (pp. 207–229) and *Lodewijk van Gruuthuse. Mecenas en Europees Diplomaat, c. 1427–1492* (Bruges, 1992) with valuable contributions from a number of scholars.[2] Louis de Bruges' political and diplomatic activity as an intermediary between England and Burgundy during the period from *c.* 1466 to 1472 has been set out in some detail in a recent Oxford D.Phil. thesis by Mark Ballard on Anglo-Burgundian relations.[3] Work is also in progress in Germany and Holland under the supervision of Professors Werner Paravicini and Wim Blockmans respectively on other aspects of Louis de Bruges' role in the politics and government of the Burgundian lands.[4] But there is, to my knowledge, no synthesis in the offing which will tell us the full story of Gruthuyse's part in Burgundian and Anglo-

Burgundian history at this crucial period – which witnessed the transition from Burgundian to Habsburg rule – in the destiny of the Low Countries.

Some of the reasons for this lacuna are not hard to find: the apparent loss of the Gruthuyse household accounts, unlike those kept by the family of his wife, the Dutch noblewoman Margaret van Borsselen, means that we cannot piece together the pattern of Louis de Bruges' conspicuous consumption and expenditure.[5] The survival of the van Borsselen accounts, for instance, has enabled A. Arkenbout to reconstruct a detailed picture of daily life in the household of Louis' father-in-law, Frank van Borsselen. There is also the historiographical problem created by the concentration of Belgian historians since Pirenne on the Third Estate (burghers and peasants) at the expense of the nobility, compounded by the influence of the *Annales*. Lastly, and perhaps most seriously, the shrinking of so much historical research into nationally or regionally defined and delimited boundaries – witness the triumph of regional history in both French and Belgian universities – effectively puts the study of subjects which cross those artificial boundaries into a limbo attracting few researchers.

It has been said by Mr C.A.J. Armstrong that 'for over a decade after 1471 England saw a revival of court culture strongly influenced by Burgundy, detectable in numberless small details'.[6] Professor Gordon Kipling went further and sub-titled his book on *The Triumph of Honour* 'Burgundian Origins of the Elizabethan Renaissance'.[7] In this process of cultural change, or shift of emphasis, the role of intermediaries was crucial: Sir John Donne, Collard Mansion, William Caxton, William, Lord Hastings, Anthony Woodville, Earl Rivers and Louis de Bruges all have objects and artefacts associated with them from which the cultural and art historian can assess influence and piece together the jigsaw of 'Anglo-Burgundian' culture.[8] The court and household of Edward IV, especially after his return from his enforced exile in the Low Countries in 1470–71 became, we are told, a Burgundian institution, partly modelled upon Charles the Bold's establishment, engaged in the thoroughly Burgundian pursuits of jousting, tourneying and feasting to a degree which the court of Henry VI and Margaret of Anjou had never witnessed.[9] The Garter, in emulation of the Golden Fleece, once again became the forum for that companionship with his nobility which Edward III had successfully instituted. Edward IV became a book collector on the Burgundian pattern, although the ownership and commissioning of manuscripts had already been a feature of the English court for a long time. It was the provenance of his manuscripts which marked off Edward IV's library: twenty-five volumes of lavishly illuminated books ordered from the workshops of Bruges and Ghent, about half of them reproducing manuscripts already in the Gruthuyse library.[10] The king's taste was allegedly formed by the

5a   Windsor, St George's Chapel. Edward IV's royal pew or oratory.

volumes which he saw in Louis de Bruges' collection, whether at the
Hague, at his rural castle of Oostcamp near Bruges, or in his great
townhouse in the city itself. The role of the intermediary was here
paramount.

What is striking about this kind of so-called 'cultural' connection is that
it was to a large degree fortuitous. If Edward had not been driven by
Hanseatic ships to land on the coast of Holland at Texel, near Alkmaar, in
October 1470, where Louis de Bruges was governor, would Anglo-
Burgundian cultural and artistic relations have been of quite the same
kind?[11] If Edward had not happened to be received by Gruthuyse in his
house at Bruges, would the king's chantry chapel and oratory at St
George's, Windsor, have taken the form it did?[12] I shall revert to these
questions in a moment, but first we must briefly review what is known of
Louis de Bruges' career and his connections with England.

Born in c. 1427, son of Jean IV of La Gruthuyse, who had been a
prominent member of religious and secular fraternities at Bruges, patron of
tournaments and music, Louis de Bruges was a representative of the bi-
lingual aristocratic and patrician culture of Flanders.[13] His five manuscripts
written in the Flemish vernacular (out of 140 surviving volumes) suggest
that any tendency towards the spread of the French language as a result of
Burgundian rule did not achieve a resounding victory over Netherlandish
in the later fourteenth and fifteenth centuries.[14] Louis de Bruges first
entered the service of Philip the Good of Burgundy as an *échanson* or cup-
bearer in the ducal household in 1445. It was the conventional manner of
entry into the court circle, which was followed both by Olivier de la
Marche and Philippe de Commynes. In 1452 he became governor of
Bruges and Oudenaarde, sustaining the Burgundian interest during the
duke's bitter war with Ghent between 1451 and 1453. The patriciate of
Bruges remained loyal to Philip the Good, partly as a result of Louis de
Bruges' promotion of the Burgundian cause at that time. His services to
the dynasty led to his creation as a knight of the Golden Fleece in May
1461. By May 1463 he had been promoted to a difficult office: the
governorship of Holland, Zeeland and West Frisia. He had married into
the Dutch nobility and retained his office for fourteen years, until the
Burgundian *débâcle* of 1477. His skills of diplomacy were exercised to the
full in the rule of this area, noted for its sporadic outbursts of resistance to
Burgundian rule.[15] His first recorded connection with English affairs seems
to have been his appointment by Philip the Good as an envoy to intervene
in a proposed Anglo-Scottish marriage alliance in 1461, followed by a
further commission as envoy to Edward IV in October 1466.[16] But it was
in the course of his tenure of the Dutch governorship that he met and
harboured the near-penniless Edward and his entourage between the king's
landfall in Holland in October 1470 and his re-embarkation for England at

Flushing on 11 March 1471.[17] During that time Edward seems to have spent much more time in the company of Louis de Bruges than in that of his Burgundian relatives at court.

It was this hospitality that won Louis de Bruges his English title of earl of Winchester in October 1472. The narrative known as *The record of Bluemantle Pursuivant* tells us that Edward, arrayed in majesty before the lords spiritual and temporal in the Parliament chamber at Westminster, favourably received the recommendation of the Commons that he should reward 'the grete humanite and kyndnes of my lord Gruthuse shewed to his highnes when he was in the counties of Holand and Flaunders, the foresaid lord Gruthuse ther being present'.[18] A similar expression of gratitude had already come from Edward himself to the citizens of Bruges in a letter of 29 May 1471, when he referred to 'la bonne chiere et grandes courtoisies . . . au bien et consolation de nous et de nos gens pendant le temps que nous estions en ladicte ville'.[19] Gruthuyse's hospitality was not given without an element of risk to himself: Charles the Bold's initially lukewarm and non-committal attitude towards Edward's plight meant that Louis de Bruges' behaviour was not wholly in line with ducal policy. But his generosity was to be amply repaid by the grant of an English titular earldom in perpetuity, with a new coat of arms and an annuity of 200 pounds sterling; and by the splendid festivities that accompanied his visit, when he was in the limelight for some days at Westminster, Whitehall and Windsor.[20] It was a singular honour for one who was not a subject of the English crown and appears to have been the first grant of an earldom to a foreign nobleman since 1377, when Sir Guichard d'Angle was created earl of Huntingdon.[21]

Such are the bare facts of Louis de Bruges' English connections. A number of questions remain unanswered. First, what influence was really exerted by him over Edward IV's activities as a book collector? How was his own library formed, and how (if at all) did this affect the English royal collection? Edward clearly owed much to him, but what did he owe to England? Secondly, there is the problem of architectural influence. It has been claimed that Louis de Bruges' oratory in the collegiate church of Our Lady at Bruges had a direct influence upon the design of Edward's chantry chapel and oratory at St George's, Windsor. Finally there is the larger but related question of Burgundian influence upon English secular building in the later fifteenth and early sixteenth centuries.

Dr Scot McKendrick has recently shown that in the case of at least one of the royal manuscripts (BL, MS Royal 17F.ii) links with the Gruthuyse library were superficial 'and any claimed direct influence of Louis' collection of manuscripts on Edward IV appears unlikely in this case.'[22] Furthermore, this particular text, a version of the *Faits des Romains* known as *La Grande Histoire César*, had not entered the Gruthuyse library by the

5b  Windsor, St George's Chapel. Edward IV's royal pew: interior, west bay.

winter of 1470–71 when Edward IV might have seen it.[23] In the event, a different version came later into Louis de Bruges' possession. But MS Royal 17F.ii bears (according to Dr McKendrick) traces of the Gruthuyse arms beneath the English royal arms. The fact that these are drawn, rather than underpainted, suggests that the manuscript was originally prepared under the aegis of (but not owned by) Louis de Bruges and that he may have played some part in getting it made.[24] Whatever the case, it is clear that there was some direct connection between Louis de Bruges' activities in the commissioning and purchase of manuscripts and Edward IV's library. The famous Josephus *Antiquités judaïques* (Sir John Soane's Museum, ms 1), which bears the partially erased arms of Louis de Bruges, overpainted with those of Edward IV, is a clear example of the passage of a volume from one collection to the other by gift or purchase. Whatever else he may have been, Louis de Bruges was something of a dealer in books: his ownership of manuscripts written and illuminated before his lifetime, for example, can be accounted for partly by inheritance, but also by purchase. This seems to be the case for some of his Netherlandish books, such as his *Boek van het Kerstene Levene*, dated 1413, adorned with his arms at a much later date.[25] Even more intriguing is his manner of acquisition of ten books which were in the French royal library of Charles V and Charles VI before its dispersal in the 1420s. This, I suspect, may have owed something to his Anglo-Burgundian connections.

A key codex in this respect is a copy of Christine de Pisan's *Epitres d'Othéa*, probably produced for Isabelle of Bavaria, queen of France, between *c*. 1410 and 1420.[26] It bears the autographs of both Jacquetta of Luxemburg, second wife of John, duke of Bedford, and Louis de Bruges, as well as the mottoes of both Gruthuyse (the famous *Plus est en vous*) and Anthony, Lord Scales, later Earl Rivers: *Nulle la vault arivieres*.[27] Scales was Jacquetta's son by her second husband, Richard Woodville, Lord Rivers. As dowager duchess of Bedford, Jacquetta presumably inherited at least some of her first husband's books, probably including those volumes from the French royal library acquired by John, duke of Bedford as regent of France for Henry VI. Anthony, Lord Scales, was of course a prominent Anglo-Burgundian intermediary, and it may have been through him that Louis de Bruges acquired those volumes from the French royal library that can be identified.[28] Whether this was by gift or purchase will probably never be known, but it would not be impossible for Louis to have bought them from Scales or his mother. The Gruthuyse fortune, originally founded upon the profits of farming the tax levied at Bruges on the *gruut*, a herb used in the brewing of beer, swollen by the profits of Burgundian ducal service, may well have been deployed in this way.[29] Louis' conspicuous largesse to the heralds after his investiture as earl of Winchester in October 1472 certainly received the approbation of

Bluemantle pursuivant and his *hôtel* at Bruges still bears witness to his great wealth.[30] But the manner in which he acquired books from the former French royal library must remain a matter for speculation.

It has, finally, been suggested that the residence of Edward IV at Bruges between 13 January and 19 February 1471 may have had some influence upon English architectural history. On 7 January 1472, Louis de Bruges obtained permission from the authorities of the collegiate Church of Our Lady at Bruges to re-build in stone a wooden oratory which enabled him and his family to be present at Mass without leaving their own house.[31] There were, of course, long-standing precedents for this type of arrangement, deriving from Charlemagne's connecting gallery in the imperial palace at Aachen and finding an earlier expression at Bruges in the *transitus*, or connecting passage, linking the comital house of the counts of Flanders to the castle chapel of St Donatian.[32] This was the scene of the bloody events of March 1127, when Count Charles the Good was murdered in his oratory there. Louis de Bruges' reconstruction of his family's chapel was accompanied by pious gifts to the collegiate church, including money for repairs to the shrine of the Anglo-Saxon St Boniface and tapestries depicting the saint's life for use in the choir on feast days. The church's beadle was to be paid an annual sum from a perpetual rent for opening and shutting the oratory.[33] Louis de Bruges and Margaret van Borsselen made their will in the oratory, before notaries and witnesses, on 18 August 1474.[34] The close proximity of the church to the Hôtel Gruthuyse is noteworthy. Its great brick tower dwarfs the Gruthuyse house. A corridor or connecting gallery was constructed over an arch between the *hôtel* and the choir of Notre-Dame, terminating in the opera-box-like oratory with its glazed windows overlooking the high altar. The balcony or watching chamber, in the form of an oriel, is constructed almost entirely of wood, resting on a stone lower storey, and the interior vaulting is again wooden, decorated with paper flowers and the device *Plus est en vous*. Later medieval *de luxe* piety is well represented by the *prie-dieu* with built-in cupboards to contain service books and books of hours, with cushioned window ledges upon which to read them. In type, the Gruthuyse oratory resembles the later oratory boxes found in South German and Austrian baroque and rococo churches, reserved for nobles, patricians and wealthy burghers. The excellent musical resources of Our Lady at Bruges, patronised by the Gruthuyse family, could be appreciated from this vantage point, and it is noteworthy that Bluemantle pursuivant referred in his narrative to the fact that the mass which Edward IV and Gruthuyse heard in the king's private chapel at Windsor in September 1472 was 'melodyousely songe.'[35]

The first point to be made about the possible influence of the Gruthuyse oratory upon the royal chapel or closet in Edward IV's reconstructed St

George's, Windsor, is that Edward was unlikely to have seen the Gruthuyse oratory in its present form. He had departed from Bruges in March 1471; the oratory was not commissioned until January 1472 and not completed until 1474.[36] This does not mean that plans were not afoot for the new fixture. We know nothing about the oratory which it replaced. Whatever the case, Edward's campaign of building at Windsor, begun in March 1477 and initiated by the appointment of Richard Beauchamp, bishop of Salisbury, as master and surveyor of the king's new works in February 1473, clearly included a two-storey chapel set between two pillars of the choir arcade, as at Bruges.[37] This is entirely constructed of stone, whereas the Gruthuyse oratory (despite the terms of the foundation grant) still retains a substantial element of wood. But the principle remained the same: it would be a little too dismissive of Burgundian influence to reject all affinity out of hand.

There were, however, some English architectural precedents for two-storey chantry chapels: the best is perhaps the so-called Warwick chapel in Tewkesbury abbey (dating from 1422).[38] Watching chambers or lofts – such as the two-storeyed chapel near the shrine of St Frideswide in Christ Church cathedral, Oxford – are also found, sometimes associated with a chantry.[39] Edward IV's foundation was also to serve as a chantry, and as a place for his tomb – which was never completed. This was to have been housed beside an altar in the upper chapel in the easternmost bay of the north choir aisle at Windsor. His will of 20 June 1475 prescribed that his body be buried beneath a cadaver effigy, and over it 'a vaute of convenient height as the place will suffre it, and . . . upon the said vaute . . . a chapell or a closet with an autre convenient and a tumbe to bee made and sett there, and upon the same tumbe an image for oure figure . . .'[40] His tomb was to be of touchstone, a black marble imported from the Low Countries.[41] Moreover, we know from the building accounts for St George's for 1478–9 that Flemish sculptors were employed in the choir, carving figures of St George and the Dragon, St Edward the Confessor, and a crucifix with the Virgin and St John for the rood-loft. Dieric Vangrave and Giles Vancastell were paid for this task at the rate of 5*s* per foot-length.[42] Beside the eastern bay of the north choir aisle, a second bay was to be included in the chapel or closet. This survives more or less in the state that Edward intended, with its original stone oriel – unlike its companion, now blessed with a Renaissance-style wooden extrusion which we owe to Henry VIII.[43] From the oriel of the western bay, it is quite possible to see the high altar, and it was perhaps here that the 'places for 13 personnes to sit and knele in' near to his tomb, which Edward prescribed in his will, were to be found.[44] In their will, observing an agreement with the Tailors' guild, Louis de Bruges and his wife had endowed thirteen aged and indigent tailors, who were also to attend masses

5c   Bruges, Hotel Gruthuyse (Gruuthuse-palais). Passage from Gruthuyse's *hôtel* to the choir of Notre-Dame (Onze-Lieve-Vrouw), showing archway.

5d   Bruges, Hotel Gruthuyse
(Gruuthuse-palais). Passage from
Gruthuyse's *hôtel* to the choir of Notre-
Dame (Onze-Lieve-Vrouw)(exterior
detail).

which were to be said near his tomb in the choir of Our Lady at Bruges.[45]
But such provisions were not uncommon in wills of the time. At Windsor,
both oriels were to become parts of the royal pew under Henry VIII, and
were to be subject to the attentions of George III. But sufficient evidence
survives to form an impression of Edward IV's scheme.

The Windsor accounts suggest that work on the royal chapel was
nearing completion by January 1484, because ironwork fittings for the
'king's closet' including 'cymenting barris, swevilles, and steybarris' were
then provided.[46] These items in turn suggest that the oriels were glazed,
with some hinged panes, so that divine office and mass could be heard
from them, as at Bruges. Access to Edward's chapel was by a spiral staircase
within an external stair-turret whose door was reached from the north
choir aisle via the vestry, and thence out through the cloisters to the royal
lodgings.[47] There was apparently no purpose-built *transitus* or connecting
passage for the royal household until a much later date. But the chapel was
intended to be a self-contained entity, as was Louis de Bruges's oratory,
sealed off from the choir aisle by John Tresilian's magnificent iron gates on
the west side and by a screen on the east.

To argue that Edward IV's chantry chapel, tomb and closet at Windsor
was a direct product of his visit to Bruges in 1470–71 would be a

5e   Bruges, Notre-Dame (Onze-
Lieve-Vrouw). Gruthuyse oratory.

distortion of the evidence. Architectural enterprises of this sort were in any case derived from a multiplicity of influences, and the role of the master mason – the very accomplished Henry Janyns of Burford – must not be underestimated.[48] But England shared many things with its European neighbours and later medieval culture cannot be said to have been dominated by the national characteristics discerned (or were they invented?) by the great scholars of the last century. We should not ignore the evidence of Flemish and Dutch influences, for example, on English domestic architecture at this time. The brick-built castle, palace or country house – Tattershall, Caister, Hurstmonceux, Sheen, Richmond, Otford, Ockwells Manor – owed much to Burgundian connections and it was no coincidence that the master of the brickwork at Tattershall was one Baldwin, probably a Dutchman.[49] The Hotel Gruthuyse is of course a brick construction – with elaborate patterning and tracery made wholly of bricks – dressed with stone, and the pinnacled gables of the Low Countries were to find an echo in much English vernacular building of the period.[50]

But further work is required on this subject, as it is on the role of Louis de Bruges and his contemporaries as intermediaries between England and the Burgundian lands. Yorkist England was in no sense a mere cultural annexe of the Burgundian dominions – its ecclesiastical architecture,

5f   Bruges, Notre-Dame (Onze-Lieve-Vrouw). Gruthuyse oratory. Engraving of front and sides of pew (The Conway Library, Courtauld Institute of Art).

literary and musical activity all refute this notion – but due weight has to be given to the affinities and alliances between the two north-west European powers as French influences progressively declined. Could it be that the vigorous vernacular culture of the Netherlandish-speaking Low Countries also had some impact upon the burgeoning of English vernacular art and literature? At the level of the court and noble household, there seems no doubt that Burgundian precedents and models were much prized. These demanded wealth: as Sir John Fortescue told Edward IV, a successful ruler was obliged to spend prodigiously on 'rich cloths, rich furs . . . rich stones . . . and other jewels and ornaments . . . rich hangings and other apparell for his houses; vessels, vestments, and other ornaments for his chapel . . .'[51]

The example of the Burgundian nobility – the Croy, Lalaing, Lannoy, Nassau, Brimeu, Renty, and Gruthuyse, to name only a few – demonstrated the manner in which a ruler might both impress and control his nobles.[52] There was no noble-led civil war of lasting significance within the Burgundian lands before the advent of the Habsburgs: Louis de Bruges' tenure of office in Holland seems to have witnessed some abatement of the vicious factional strife seen there in 1456; nor was there a War of the Public Weal, or similar magnate revolt, in the Burgundian Netherlands before 1484.[53] Louis de Bruges may have provided Edward IV with a model for the kind of service nobility, bound to the ruler by office-holding and membership of his household, that might have been created in England. That, apart from mere friendship, was perhaps one reason for the favour which Edward showed him. Lastly, to have a second permanent representative – as well as his sister – at the court of Burgundy, prepared to act on his behalf and support English interests (as Louis de Bruges did after 1472) was much to Edward's advantage.

## Notes

1   J.B.B. Van Praet, *Recherches sur Louis de Bruges, seigneur de la Gruthuyse, suivies de la notice des manuscrits qui lui ont appartenu, et dont la plus grande partie se conserve à la Bibliothèque du Roi* (Paris, 1831).

2   C. Lemaire and A de Schryver (eds.), *Vlaamse Kunst op Perkament* (Bruges, 1981); M.P.J., Martens (ed.), *Lodewijk van Gruuthuse. Mecenas en Europees Diplomaat ca. 1427–1492* (Bruges, 1992). French summaries of the Dutch text are included in the latter volume. The exhibition for which it serves as a catalogue was held in the Hôtel Gruthuyse (Gruuthusemuseum) and the Church of Our Lady (Onze-Lieve-Vrouwekerk) at Bruges (19 Sept.–11 Nov. 1992). In this article I have normally adopted the French forms of Flemish proper- and place-names because of their more general currency in contemporary English usage.

3   M.H.A. Ballard, *Anglo-Burgundian relations, 1464–1472* (Oxford D. Phil. thesis, 1993), especially chapters 1–3.

4   The work of H. Kruse (Kiel), J.W. Marsilje and M.J. van Gent (Leiden) is relevant in this respect. For the situation in Holland and Zeeland during Gruthuyse's stadholdership see H.P.H. Jansen, *Hoekse en Kabeljauwse twisten* (Bussum, 1966) and J.W. Marsilje (ed.), *Bloedwraak, partijstrijd en pacificatie in laat-middeleeuws Holland* (Hilversum, 1990).

5   See A.A. Arkenbout, 'Das tägliche Leben des Frank van Borsselen (†1470)' in H. Appelt (ed.), *Adelige sachkultur des Spätmittelalters* (Osterreichischen Akademie der Wissenschaften, Vienna, 1982), pp. 311–26; S.W.A. Drossaers, *Het Archief van de Nassause Domeinraad*, II (The Hague, 1955), pp. 79–82, 207–8.

6   C.A.J. Armstrong, 'The Golden Age of Burgundy. Dukes that outdid kings' in A.G. Dickens (ed.), *The Courts of Europe. Politics, patronage and royalty, 1400–1800* (London, 1977), p. 56. The most recent study of the English court at this period is R.A. Griffiths, 'The king's court during the Wars of the Roses' in R.G. Asch and A.M. Birke (eds.), *Princes, patronage and the nobility. The court at the beginning of the modern age, c. 1450–1650* (Oxford, 1991) pp. 41–67 which attributes less influence to Burgundian example and practice.

7   G. Kipling, *The Triumph of Honour. Burgundian origins of the Elizabethan Renaissance* (Leiden, 1977). Kipling argues (p. 3) that 'much of what we have been content to label "Italian" in Tudor art, literature and society may more accurately be traced to Lowlands Burgundy'.

8   For a general view see C.A.J. Armstrong, 'L'échange culturel entre les cours d'Angleterre et de Bourgogne à l'époque de Charles le Téméraire' in his *England, France and Burgundy in the fifteenth century* (London, 1983), pp. 403–17. Also K.B. McFarlane, *Hans Memling* (Oxford, 1971).

9    For a good example, see N. Williams, 'The Tudors. Three contrasts in personality' in *Courts of Europe*, pp. 147–67.

10   J.M. Backhouse, 'Founders of the Royal Library: Edward IV and Henry VII as collectors of illuminated manuscripts' in W.M. Ormrod (ed.), *England in the fifteenth century. Proceedings of the 1986 Harlaxton Symposium* (Woodbridge, 1987), pp. 23–41; M. Kekewich, 'Edward IV, William Caxton and literary patronage in Yorkist England', *Modern Language Review*, LVI (1971), pp. 481–7.

11   For the chronology of Edward's journey see J. Huizinga, 'Koning Edward IV van Engeland in Ballingschap', in his *Verzamelde Werken* (Haarlem, 1948–53), iv, pp. 183–95.

12   See Armstrong, 'The Golden Age of Burgundy' in *Courts of Europe*, p. 56: 'the Gruuthuse oratory at Bruges provided Edward . . . with the model for his royal pew at Windsor, . . . evidence of the impression which Burgundy had made on him during his short exile (1470–71)' and accompanying plate.

13   The most recent attempt at a biography of Louis de Bruges is to be found in Martens, *Lodewijk van Gruuthuse*, pp. 13–43. For the role of the Gruthuyse family as patrons of music and their membership of confraternities see R. Strohm, *Music in late medieval Bruges* (Oxford, 1985), pp. 42–8, 67–72, 83–4; for Louis de Bruges and the tournament see M. Vale, *War and Chivalry* (London, 1981), pp. 66–7, 84 and plate 7, and 'Le tournoi dans la France du Nord, l'Angleterre et les Pays-Bas' in *Théâtre et Spectacles hier et aujourd'hui. Moyen Age et Renaissance* (Actes du 115e Congrès National des Sociétés Savantes, Paris, 1991) pp. 69–70; also P. De Gryse in *Lodewijk van Gruuthuse*, pp. 87–92.

14   C. Lemaire in *Vlaamse Kunst op Pergament*, pp. 211, 224–6. See also C.A.J. Armstrong, 'The language question in the Low Countries' in *Europe in the late Middle Ages*, J.R. Hale, J.R.L. Highfield, B. Smalley (eds.) (London, 1965), pp. 392–3, 402–6. For what follows see Martens, 'De Biografie van Lodewijk van Gruuthuse' in *Lodewijk van Gruuthuse*, pp. 13–26.

15   See Van Praet, *Recherches*, pp. 1–24; Martens in *Lodewijk van Gruuthuse*, pp. 13–32; *Inventaire des Archives de la ville de Bruges. Chartes*, ed. L. Gilliodts-van Severen, VI (Bruges, 1876) pp. 34, 62, 156, 204–5; H. van Papendrecht, *Analecta Belgica*, II, i (The Hague, 1743), pp. 30, 35. The Burgundian government of Holland in the fifteenth century is also discussed in J.D. Tracey, *Holland under Habsburg Rule, 1506–1566. The Formation of a Body Politic* (Berkeley – Los Angeles – Oxford, 1990), pp. 9–32.

16   See Martens in *Lodewijk van Gruuthuse*, p. 21; F. Madden, 'Narratives of the Arrival of Louis of Bruges, Seigneur de la Gruthuyse, in England, and of his Creation as Earl of Winchester, in 1472', *Archaeologia*, XXVI (1836), p. 268.

17   Huizinga, 'Koning Edward IV van Engeland in Ballingschap', pp. 184–5; Martens in *Lodewijk van Gruuthuse*, p. 25.

18   'The Record of Bluemantle Pursuivant' in C.L. Kingsford, *English Historical Literature in the fifteenth century* (Oxford, 1913), p. 382.

19   *Inventaire des Archives de . . . Bruges*, VI, p. 62.

20   W. St John Hope, 'On a grant of arms under the Great Seal of Edward IV to Louis de Bruges, seigneur de la Gruthuyse and earl of Winchester, 1472, with some remarks on arms of English earldoms', *Archaeologia*, LVI (1898), pp. 27–38; 'Record of Bluemantle Pursuivant', pp. 383–8. The original grant of arms is now London, British Library, MS Egerton 2830.

21   M. McKisack, *The Fourteenth Century, 1307–1399* (Oxford, 1959), pp. 399, 424. He died in 1380. My thanks are due to Dr Chris Given-Wilson for reminding me of this creation.

22   S. McKendrick, '*La Grande Histoire César* and the manuscripts of Edward IV' in P. Beal and J. Griffiths (eds.) *English Manuscript Studies, 1100–1700* (Oxford, 1990), p. 120.

23   McKendrick, 'La Grande Histoire César . . .', pp. 20, 22.
24   For this, and for what follows, see McKendrick, 'La Grande Histoire César . . .', pp. 124, 127.
25   Brussels, BR, MS II.280. It is dated by its explicit (in Latin and Flemish) on fo.102r and is in an original fifteenth-century binding with clasps adorned with the Gruthuyse arms. The representation of the Gruthuyse arms on fo.3r is identical to that found in another Gruthuyse MS of c. 1470 (Brussels, BR, MS 15.657). This is a Flemish treatise in verse on the childhood of Christ, ascribed to the year 1358.
26   London, British Library, Harleian MS 4431.
27   See Madden, 'Narratives of the arrival . . .', pp. 271–4.
28   For the milieu in which this literary activity took place see, most recently, J. Hughes, 'Stephen Scrope and the circle of Sir John Fastolf: moral and intellectual outlooks' in C. Harper-Bill (ed.), The Ideals and Practice of medieval knighthood. IV (Woodbridge, 1992), pp. 133–5. Also C.C. Willard, Christine de Pizan. Her Life and Works (New York, 1984), pp. 214–15.
29   See Lodewijk van Gruuthuse, pp. 49–51 and J. De Smet, 'Het gruitrecht te Brugge', West-Vlaanderen, VI (1957), pp. 2–3.
30   'Record of Bluemantle Pursuivant', pp. 383–4; for the Gruthuyse palace see V. Vermeersch, Guide musée Gruuthuse (Bruges, 1970) and K. Verschelde, 'Het Hof van Gruuthuse en zijn aanhorigheden', Ron den Heerd, XV (1880), pp. 177–9, 186–8, 195–7, 204–6, 282–5, 313–15, 321–3, 355–7; L. Devliegher, Les maisons à Bruges (Liège, 1975), pp. 59–67.
31   For the oratory and its history see Van Praet, Recherches . . ., pp. 12–13 (7 Jan. 1472); P. Beaucourt de Noortvelde, Description historique de l'église collegiale et paroissiale de Notre-Dame à Bruges (Bruges, 1773) pp. 40, 67, 108; L. Devliegher, 'De bidkapel van Gruuthuse te Brugge', Gentse Bijdragen tot de Kunstgeschiedenis, XVII (1957–8), pp. 69–74; and, most recently, Martens in Lodewijk van Gruuthuse, pp. 39–42.
32   See Galbert of Bruges, The Murder of Charles the Good, tr. and ed. J.B. Ross (Toronto, 1982), pp. 58–9, 175–6, 318–20.
33   Van Praet, Recherches . . ., p. 13; Martens in Lodewijk van Gruuthuse, pp. 39–42, 47–8.
34   Van Praet, Recherches . . ., pp. 332–6; Lodewijk van Gruuthuse, p. 47.
35   See R. Strohm, Music in late medieval Bruges, pp. 42–50; 'Record of Bluemantle Pursuivant', p. 386. For the Gruthuyse patronage of music at an earlier date, see K. Heeroma and C.W.H. Lindenberg (eds.), Liederen en Gedichten uit het Gruuthuse Handschrift (Leiden, 1966) and the account of the Gruthuyse song-book (c. 1395), which Louis de Bruges inherited from his father, in Lodewijk van Gruuthuse, pp. 161–3. Some of the songs (with Netherlandish lyrics) from this manuscript have been recorded by the Paul Rans Ensemble (CD/1170 EUFODA).
36   See Lodewijk van Gruuthuse, pp. 39–40; Bruges, Rijksarchief, Fonds Onze-Lieve-Vrouw, Oud Archief, Charter prov.nr.1385 and 721, fos. 9–14. For illustrations of the oratory and tomb (now destroyed) of Louis de Bruges and Margaret van Borsselen, see J. Gailliard, Inscriptions funéraires et monumentales de la Flandre Occidentale. I. Arrondissement de Bruges, 2. Bruges, Eglise de Notre Dame (Bruges, 1866) pp. 70–71; BR, MS II.3623F, fos. 17–20 (Van Tieghem and Gailliard's collection of tinted drawings); and V. Vermeersch, Grafmonumenten te Brugge voor 1578, II (Bruges, 1976), pp. 265–73.
37   See W. St J. Hope, Windsor Castle. An Architectural History, II (London, 1913), pp. 377–8. I am indebted to Mr H.M. Colvin for his comments, to the Dean of Windsor for permission to inspect the royal pew and chantry chapel and to Dr Eileen Scarff (Archivist to the Dean and Chapter) and Mrs Enid Davis (Assistant Archivist) for their help.
38   See F.H. Crossley, English Church Monuments, 1150–1550 (London, 1921), p. 76 and plates on pp. 80 and 114.

39 Crossley, *English Church Monuments*, p. 76; *An Inventory of the Historic Monuments in the City of Oxford* (Royal Commission on Historic Monuments, London, 1939), p. 43 and plate 90.

40 See H.M. Colvin *et al.*, *The King's Works. The Middle Ages*, II (London, 1963), p. 887 and St John Hope, *Windsor Castle*, II, pp. 376–7 where the will is printed.

41 *King's Works*, II, p. 887. Although it was never used for the king's tomb, the stone had been unloaded at London, because the Issue Roll for 22 Edward IV contains a payment for the repair of a crane there which had been damaged by its weight (St John Hope, *Windsor Castle*, II, p. 381, n. 42).

42 London, PRO, E.101/496/17, printed in St John Hope, *Windsor Castle*, II, p. 399 and discussed on p. 429.

43 St John Hope, *Windsor Castle*, II, pp. 427–8.

44 St John Hope, *Windsor Castle*, II, pp. 377, 419, 421–2.

45 Van Praet, *Recherches. . .*, p. 333; Martens in *Lodewijk van Gruuthuse*, p. 42 and pp. 47–9.

46 St John Hope, *Windsor Castle*, II, pp. 382, 405.

47 *King's Works*, II, p. 312; St John Hope, *Windsor Castle*, II, pp. 419, 422.

48 St John Hope, *Windsor Castle*, II, p. 378.

49 See J. Evans, *English Art, 1307–1461* (Oxford, 1949), pp. 128–30, where other examples are also cited.

50 For instances, see Kipling, *Triumph of Honour*, pp. 3–10.

51 J. Fortescue, *The Governance of England*, ed. C. Plummer (Oxford, 1885), pp. 125–6.

52 C.A.J. Armstrong, 'Had the Burgundian government a policy for the nobility?' in *England, France and Burgundy in the fifteenth century*, pp. 224–7.

53 See, for example, W. Blockmans, 'Autocratie ou polyarchie? La lutte pour le pouvoir politique en Flandre de 1482 à 1492, d'après des documents inédits', *Bulletin de la Commission royale d'Histoire*, CXL (1974), pp. 257–368.

6

# The Wall-paintings in the Chapel of Eton College[1]

Andrew Martindale
*University of East Anglia*

*This paper was delivered in the chapel of Eton College by kind permission of the Provost and Fellows. It was not possible, in that context, to introduce comparative visual material into the discussion; hence it was also impossible to pursue very deliberately the main theme of the symposium – England and Europe. In what follows, not very much is said about style; neither was it possible to make much of the late-medieval world of shared expectations, shared impressions and shared images to which some of the other speakers referred during the symposium. There were, however, compensations. There is never any adequate substitute in the history of art for being directly in the presence of what is being studied; and it was possible to lay unusual emphasis on the architectural context and function of the paintings. It was also possible to comment directly on the method of storytelling, to say something about the choice of stories – and to speculate about the significance of the paintings in relation to the likely audience.*

In any study of the Eton wall-paintings, it is necessary to come to terms with an initial paradox. Standing or sitting near the present organ screen (Fig. 6a), one is simultaneously in the choir of a collegiate church and in the nave of a parish church.[2] That needs to be explained; and this can only be done with some reference to the early history of the institution. Henry VI founded Eton in 1440. After some initial revision in the size of the establishment, the numbers of the foundation members eventually stabilised in 1443 at 10 chaplains, 10 clerks, 16 choristers, 70 scholars, a schoolmaster, an usher and 13 poor men. In 1448 and 1449, the first plans for the buildings were substantially revised and enlarged. Whatever had already been built was demolished; and one reaches the start of the existing building.[3]

There can be little doubt that, could Henry VI revisit Eton and be transported directly into the chapel choir, he would now find in general terms what he expected. He might be mildly surprised by the vault (put up in 1957), by the stained glass of Evie Hone and John Piper and by the organ which would certainly be bigger than any organ he had ever imagined. But the general layout and disposition of high altar, stalls, screen and organ loft in broad outline follow his plans.

6a   Eton College Chapel. General view of the interior looking west.

When, however, the resuscitated monarch went through the arch beneath the organ, he would be dismayed by what he found. Here it should be explained that Eton was a collegiate foundation with parochial responsibilities. Henry had accepted those responsibilities and had projected for parish use a nave with flanking aisles which, had it been built, would have been one of the largest naves in England.[4] Henry's intentions, in fact, had a massive scale. In terms of size, the college was in the same league as the Charterhouse at Pavia and well beyond the scale of a church such as that at Brou.[5]

Moreover, in 1448 Henry made substantial provision for the future of the construction.[6] This, of course, did not go according to plan. The building proceeded spasmodically, affected by the political fortunes of the king; and in 1461, when Henry was deposed, the whole enterprise nearly came to an untimely end. In 1463, a bull of Pius II dissolved the new college as, in old UGC parlance, a 'pallid growth', the resources being annexed to Edward IV's foundation of St George's Chapel in Windsor Castle.

Clearly that was not the end of the story. Eton luckily had an extremely able Provost, Westbury; and a capable and powerful protector, William Wayneflete, Bishop of Winchester. By means which remain in detail unclear, the apparently irreversible was reversed; the papal bull of 1463 was rescinded by another bull of Paul II (1470), and gradually the college was brought back into royal favour. Building was resumed in 1469, the bills being sent to Wayneflete; and the fabric of the chapel, as it now is, was probably finished by 1482.[7]

It was however a very different building from that originally planned. In substance the former collegiate choir was completed; but, for the rest, Wayneflete did two conflicting things. The huge nave was abandoned and in its place Wayneflete set a transverse antechapel of the sort pioneered at New College, Oxford. (His own foundation of Magdalen College received a very similar chapel and antechapel during precisely the same years.) Both the New College and the Eton antechapels originally had altars in them;[8] and it may have originally been thought that this arrangement would suffice for the Eton parishioners. In the event, however, the final arrangements were rather different; and when Wayneflete contracted for a *pulpitum* in 1475, that screen and gallery were set not where the present organ is but halfway down the former choir.[9] The marks left by the coving of the loft are still visible in the painted decoration. For over two centuries,[10] the collegiate body had the space to the east of that division; and the part of the church to the west would have been technically the parish church – although in practice it must have been increasingly invaded by those schoolboys, the commensals, who were not scholars and therefore had no right to a seat in the choir. The paintings were therefore for the immediate consumption of a group of persons other than those sitting in the choir.

The scenes were painted at some point between 1477 and 1487.[11] Originally there were two tiers of paintings,[12] which extended up to the stone moulding running beneath the windows (Figs. 6b & 6c). Most unfortunately, a sequence of disasters since their rediscovery in 1844 has

6b   Eton College Chapel. South wall, general view.

6c   Eton College Chapel. North wall, general view.

reduced the two tiers to one on each side (with the exception of a small section in the south-west corner – S.A.VIII). Partial records were, however, made in the 1840s and more or less the complete programme is known. There are indeed drawings of the lower halves of the now-lost upper scenes.[13] The whole composition is finished at the eastern end by a strip of fictive damask. This continues along the bottom behind the nineteenth-century choir stalls as a band about 24–30 inches broad.[14] Beneath that it seems likely that the wall was faced with panelling. Perhaps it should be added that, according to the conservator's report, the medium of the paintings is linseed oil. The colour is, somewhat unexpectedly, applied directly to the primed stone wall-surface.[15]

In any comment on the style of the paintings, it has to be emphasised how difficult it is to find suitable comparative material of any sort, anywhere. Eton chapel really is distinguished in its possession of perhaps the finest quality fifteenth-century mural paintings anywhere in Europe outside Italy. It must be admitted that this is almost entirely the result of the political misfortunes already outlined. The enormous flat area beneath the windows was not originally intended for painting – according to Henry's original plans, it would have been masked by the stall canopies. The revised circumstances of *c.* 1480 presented those involved with an unpremeditated and, for the fifteenth century, perhaps unprecedented challenge – a very large blank masonry surface totally devoid of the usual perpendicular decorative adjuncts of blind panelling and tracery.[16] The conventional answer to this challenge would have been some sort of covering of textile hangings. The choice of wall-paintings is unexpected and is likely to have been prompted by two considerations. Paintings were almost certainly cheaper than textiles; they were also more durable. At the same time, the choice must have been facilitated by the availability of men who could execute the job – men who were not only able to paint extremely competently but were also able to 'think big'. It is the antecedents of these men that are hard to isolate. For, whereas it is clear that their style is in some sense 'Flemish', the surviving comparative material in the Netherlands is almost all on a much smaller scale – paintings either on panel or in manuscripts. The 'placing' of the paintings is also hampered by the comparative rarity of the subject-matter; there is no very clear illustrative tradition for the 'miracles of the Virgin'.[17]

The scheme as a whole looks superficially like sculpture. Indeed, the alternation of narrative scenes with large figures standing in niches has a few sculptural parallels – as in the early sixteenth-century choir screen of Chartres Cathedral.[18] The standing figures are certainly meant to look sculptural; and the skill with which they and their plinths are foreshortened so that they appear to be above the eye-level of the viewer is extremely sophisticated. The management of the lighting should also be noticed – giving the impression of a smooth flow of light coming from the west.[19] Control of structure through light and perspective was, of course, a commonplace of Italian wall-painting by *c.* 1480 (this is the age of Mantegna and Ghirlandaio). The Eton paintings act as a reminder that non-Italians were equally concerned about these effects.

Grisaille painting in itself is, nevertheless, far commoner north of the Alps than south. It is not unknown in Italy – there are, indeed, some teasingly and suggestively similar secular wall-paintings of *c.* 1460 from the castle of Roccabianca painted in grisaille.[20] But the taste for these black-and-white effects has a long and continuous history in the north from *c.* 1300. During the fourteenth century, it appears to be principally a Parisian fashion and is found in both sculpture and manuscript painting. Its scope expanded vastly in the Netherlands during the first half of the fifteenth century, the impetus coming from Robert Campin, Jan van Eyck and Roger van der Weyden. At the same time, its ambiguity increased, so that here at Eton, for instance, it is often hard to tell whether one is meant to be looking at 'grey' human beings or 'lively' stone sculpture. The general impression may, indeed, be lapidary; but there are frequent flashes of colour (both in the faces and in the architecture) which tend to undermine this effect in the detail. It may with some confidence be suggested that part of the perceived skill of this sort of painting lay in the artist's ability to maintain this ambiguity.

Ever since these paintings were first seriously discussed (by M.R. James and Professor Tristram), it has been agreed that the two walls cannot have been designed by the same artist. For those scenes which have survived are constructed in different ways and demonstrate different sets of interests. (It is unfortunately much harder to form a view on the two upper rows of scenes, where only the lower part of each scene was recorded.)

The artist who painted the north wall liked space; and he liked

interesting settings. If a distant landscape was possible, he put one in. If the
action took place indoors, he showed an enclosed chamber. His figures
tend to be set out in a rational way behind a proscenium arch so that in
most cases it would be possible to attempt a ground-plan of the action (Fig.
6d). In relation to their settings they are modest in size, being somewhat
elongated (Fig. 6e). The faces are rarely strongly characterised or
differentiated, the heads being, on the whole, proportionately rather small.

6d  Eton College Chapel. North wall, third scene from the west, NB VI: the
miracle of the candle.

6e   Eton College Chapel. North wall, sixth scene from the west, NB III: the knight who sold his wife to the devil (part i).

The figures are, too, arranged rather flatly within the picture-space; and, perhaps surprisingly for someone apparently interested in spacial clarity and definition, there is no strong foreshortening. In general terms, this would seem to be the art of the late studio of Roger van der Weyden (who died in 1464). It is reasonably close to Dirk Bouts (who died in 1475); and although it is hard to find any *very* close parallels, that seems to be the general milieu from which this artist emerges.

In many ways, the artist of the south wall seems to have had opposite interests. Space and setting play very little part in the scenes. By contrast, the figures themselves have a very marked importance. In fact, the action is dominated by very large figures, crammed together and brought forward towards the front of the stage. Indeed, in the opening scene, the Empress's horse overlaps the front of the stage and appears to be walking out into the church (Fig. 6i) – a conceit one might expect to find in sixteenth-century Italy but hardly in fifteenth-century England. Again, in the fifth scene, the Empress's boat is being punted and propelled in strong foreshortening towards the spectator. By contrast with the north side, the figures on the south often

6f   Eton College Chapel. South wall, sixth scene from east, SB VI: the knight's brother is healed of leprosy.

have very strongly characterised faces, whether as bad, good or merely sick (Figs. 6f and 6g). This style is rather harder to pin down – and the issue leads to the problem of their date relative to the scenes on the opposite side.

It has been argued – not very specifically – that the absence of 'space' in the scenes on the south means that they are rather more 'old-fashioned' than those on the north. It has also been argued (again not very

6g Eton College Chapel. South wall, third scene from east, SB III: the empress is rescued by a knight.

specifically) that the southern compositions are reminiscent of tapestries. These arguments tend towards the conclusion that they are earlier than the scenes on the north. The 'tapestry' observation is indeed of some interest, especially since the paintings appear in some sense to be doing the job of wall-hangings (see above). No fifteenth-century tapestry survives which looks like the Eton paintings; but the structure of the much earlier Angers Apocalypse tapestries (1370s) is not dissimilar. Both schemes unfold the narrative in two tiers of scenes set within an architectural framework; and in both, the narrative is interspersed with large figures set vertically in illusionistic niches. It is not, in fact, possible to be certain that there were *never* any tapestries which looked like the Eton paintings; and, as a result of subsequent losses and destruction, there is indeed a whole area of Flemish art relating to large-scale composition – wall-painting, tapestry, stained glass – about which information is scanty. Speculation along these lines does not, however, help with the relative dates of the Eton paintings.

For it is also possible to argue that the artist who painted the south wall was thoroughly up to date in his style. There are similarities to the work of another Burgundian court painter, Hugo van der Goes, who died in 1482 and who during the 1470s was at the peak of his career. Hugo certainly tended to distort the spatial conventions established, for instance, within the painting of Dirk Bouts; and he produced some grotesquely characterised faces. Thus, the differences between the paintings – north and south – suggest merely the presence of two designers working in contrasted but near-contemporary styles – and within an agreed and unified architectural framework.

Something must now be said about the choice and arrangement of the stories – and of how they were meant to be read. In the first place there is a crude distinction relating to the sexes. The upper rows featured virtually entirely male saints and prophets, and miracles affecting male subjects (the exceptions relate to the Virgin herself). The lower rows are correspondingly female-oriented. Beyond that general distinction, it is difficult to discover any further general principles. The stories, with the exception of the scene of the Assumption and probably a representation of the Annunciation, all relate to miracles and wonders wrought after the death of the Virgin and through her intercession.

There were various texts for the *Miracles of the Virgin* to which those planning the decoration might have turned.[21] Fortunately, one is saved a lot of needless speculation by the fact that underneath each picture there is or was an inscription. That inscription gives a brief résumé of the story and also quotes – almost literally – chapter and verse for its source. As M.R. James pointed out, there are two works to which one is referred.[22] Of the twenty-four miracles, sixteen come from the *Speculum Historiale* of Vincent of Beauvais and five from the *Legenda Aurea* of Jacopo da Voragine. Two stories are uncertainly identified and probably come from Vincent

(N.A.IV and V). It may be assumed that the choice of these two great thirteenth-century compilations was governed particularly by accessibility – that is, most good libraries would have had them in the late-fifteenth century.

Jacopo and Vincent between them offer a wide range of miracles.[23] Jacopo has twenty, Vincent fifty-eight. Thus, allowing for some overlaps, there would have been some sixty to seventy stories from which to fill the thirty-two spaces at Eton. In fact, the choice was far more restricted than that because at some stage it was decided to devote one entire line (S.B. I–VIII) to one of Vincent's longer so-to-say three-chapter stories;[24] and another story (N.B.III–IV) was set out in two separate scenes.[25] So in the end a mere twenty-three stories are told. The principles by which twenty-three stories were selected out of a possible sixty-five (or thereabouts) remain mysterious; and sensible comment is inhibited by a number of factors. There is in any case the historical problem of catching in the twentieth century the resonances of a fifteenth-century patron choosing from a thirteenth-century text. There is also the problem of the presumed audience – was it the parishioners of Eton or Waynflete's schoolboys? Surveying the range of miracles which were 'available' it is perhaps possible to say that the more socially and morally problematic were apparently excluded. Thus we do not find on the walls of Eton the story of the mother who had a child by her own son;[26] nor the story of the abbess who had a child by her steward;[27] nor the story of the knight who, on the way to a tournament, persuaded the parents of a very beautiful girl to sell her to him for one night.[28] (There is however a convicted thief and robber who gets saved on the gibbet).[29]

Perhaps the main feature of the Eton stories is the simplicity of their story-line. The good and the bad are easily distinguishable. Thus there are two 'bad' Jews (S.A.II and VIII) and one 'good' (repentant) Jew (N.B.IV). There is a 'bad' gambler who swore (N.B.II); and a 'good' painter who insisted on making his devils as ugly as possible (N.B.III). There is, indeed, a reprehensible knight who, in order to support his life-style, sells his wife to the devil (N.B.III and IV (Fig. 6e)); but she is retrieved before anything terrible happens – and the cause of his original financial difficulties was apparently in part his generosity.

Like all good narrative paintings, the scenes encourage question and answer – what is happening there? why is that like that? In this case, the process presupposes either literacy or access to literacy. For very often the scenes are not in themselves fully explanatory; and it is necessary to read the words beneath and to refer to the texts quoted in order to understand what one sees. The precision with which the reader is referred to texts is indeed one of the unusual features of the Eton paintings, though it was in fact sensible to provide access to glosses for scenes which would to most people have been unfamiliar; and since this process of cross-reference was apparently intended by the planners, it is of some interest to see how it works in practice.

The seventh scene on the north side (lower row) shows a woman kneeling before an image of the Virgin and the Christchild (Fig. 6h). Her left hand reaches up to the child. On the extreme left stands a boy; and in the centre a woman, presumably the same one, kneels before a half-opened box, inside which is apparently either a baby or a doll. The inscription says 'How a certain woman through the son of the blessed Virgin merited that her own son be freed from prison and restored to her – see the Legends of Saints.'[30] Now neither the picture nor the inscription tell one what is happening; and it is essential to follow up the reference and find out what the Golden Legend has to say. Here it is:[31]

6h  Eton College Chapel. North wall, second scene from the west, NB VII: the woman who took the image of the Christchild as hostage.

There was a certain woman who, deprived of the solace of a man, had an only son whom she worshipped tenderly. By chance, that son was captured by enemies and imprisoned and chained in captivity. When she heard this, the woman wept unconsolably and besought the Virgin, to whom she was greatly devoted, with importunate prayers that she would liberate her son. Nevertheless, seeing that this produced no results, she went alone to a church in which there was an image of the Virgin and, standing before the image, addressed it with these words 'Blessed Virgin, I have often asked you to liberate my son and up till now you have brought no help at all to a miserable mother. I have implored your protection for my son and I perceive up till now no results. Therefore, just as my son has been taken from me, I also shall take your son from you and keep him in my custody as a hostage for my son.' Saying this, she went closer and, removing the image of the boy which the Virgin had in her bosom, went home; and taking that same image of the boy, wrapped it in very clean cloth and hiding it in a chest shut it carefully with a key. For she rejoiced to have a good hostage for her son and she kept that hostage carefully. And – behold – the following night the blessed Virgin appeared to the youth and, opening the door of the prison, ordered him to leave, saying to him 'Tell your mother, son, that she should return my son just as I have returned hers.' The youth departed and came to his mother and told her how the blessed Virgin had freed him. She, greatly rejoicing, took the image of the boy and, going to the church, returned the Christchild to the Blessed Mary saying 'I give you thanks, my lady, because you have returned to me my only son; and now I return your son to you, acknowledging that I have received back mine.'

The painting to which this refers remains mildly ambiguous – is the woman shown removing or returning the image? Nevertheless the process which has just been rehearsed holds good for all the paintings. One looks at the scene; one wonders what it is all about; one reads the inscription and then goes to a library to look up the text. If one cannot read, one asks someone who can. Since one is in the nave of a parish church, one may, I think, assume that many of the scenes formed the focus of simple sermons. It is also quite likely that texts and pictures formed the basis for instruction in Latin for the Eton scholars; though unfortunately nothing is known about the fifteenth-century curriculum at Eton, nor of the standards of Latinity which were coaxed into the scholars.

One of the illustrative problems which emerges from this is that of indicating a whole narrative in a single scene. The device is often used of making the same person appear more than once so that, in effect, one gets

two episodes within the same picture. This happens several times at Eton –
for instance in the adjacent scene in which a dead woman is resurrected to
confess an undisclosed sin (N.B.VIII). In one instance, this process of
compression is reversed – where the knight sold his wife to the devil to
raise cash (N.B.III–IV (Fig. 6e)). It is not at all clear why this story was
selected for expanded treatment; but it is extended to cover two spaces.
Even less clear is the rationale underlying the choice of subject on the
surviving south wall which is entirely devoted to a single story – that of the
betrayed Empress. Since most of the rest of this paper is devoted to a
consideration of these scenes and since the story is likely to be unfamiliar,
some explanation is necessary.

  The heroine is a beautiful and pure Empress who had a particular
devotion to the Virgin.[32] According to the inscription beneath the first
scene, she is here saying goodbye to her devoted husband who is about to set
off on a pilgrimage (Fig. 6i). One has, however, to go to Vincent of Beauvais
to understand what is happening on the right. In the Emperor's absence, his
brother made unwelcome advances to the Empress; and she, to escape him,
kept him in honourable confinement in a tower. The inscription under
scene two (Fig. 6i) says 'Here the returning emperor orders his falsely-

6i  Eton College Chapel. South wall, first two scenes from east, SB I and II: the
emperor goes on pilgrimage, leaving his wife who shuts up his brother in a tower;
the brother falsely accuses the empress, who is led off to execution.

accused wife to be led off to a wood and there beheaded.'[33] It has already been discovered that the captions by themselves do not always fully explain what is happening; and it is necessary to follow up the reference to Vincent to find out that the brother had been released from his tower prematurely, that he had ridden out to greet the returning Emperor and that he had poisoned his mind against the Empress. Thus when husband and wife met and she greeted him, the Emperor, instead of returning her kiss, struck her (see the picture). The third inscription is fragmentary but in any case one can move more quickly through the rest of the story. In the third scene (Fig. 6g), the execution party having taken the Empress into the middle of the forest, were preparing to rape her before cutting off her head. At that point, an unknown knight with a great company of followers hears her cries for help and rescues her – but fails to recognise her as the Empress. For the fourth scene, it is necessary to know in advance (see Vincent) that she had been employed by the knight to nurse his infant son and that the knight had a brother who had fallen in love with her. When repulsed, this brother also turned nasty and – here one reaches the picture – murdered the infant son, putting the corpse plus bloody knife in the Empress's bed. For this the Empress is exiled to a remote island (scene five); and here at last the Virgin appears to her in a dream and tells her that her sufferings are over and that she must gather large quantities of the herb on which her head is resting. She returns (scene six) to the land of the knight where it is found that the herb cures leprosy (Fig. 6f). By an amazing coincidence, the wicked brother has contracted the disease. In return for a complete confession of the crime, he is cured. Eventually the Empress returns to Rome (scene seven) still armed with supplies of the herb. There she finds that the Emperor's brother has also contracted leprosy (Fig. 6j). He too is promised a cure if he will confess all before the Pope and Cardinals (the Pope and one cardinal are visible in the background.) This duly happens and she is reconciled to the Emperor. However (scene eight) she finally decides to renounce the world and her husband and to become a nun.

This is one of the longest stories associated with the Virgin. It apparently belongs to an extended family of Empress stories[34] and its appeal is not difficult to appreciate. Readers (and viewers) are transported into a world of aristocratic highlife complete with dramatic reversals of fortune and an imperial dimension. It is literally great stuff. It must have delighted the eyes of generations of schoolboys up to the moment in 1560 when it was whitewashed; and it has continued to perform the same service since its re-exposure in 1923. It has always occupied a very substantial proportion of the available space in the chapel but perhaps the story itself offers the best explanation of and justification for this position of honour.

Nevertheless in the context of the 1480s, it cannot escape notice that the Empress story has an uncomfortable emphasis on gullible rulers,

6j   Eton College Chapel. South wall, seventh scene from the east, SB VII: the emperor's brother confesses his sins and is healed of leprosy.

corrupt brothers, wronged queens and murdered nephews. Moreover it has been pointed out that, in scene seven, the wicked brother who is having the truth squeezed out of him in return for his leprosy-cure has around his neck a chain with a prominent pendant (Fig. 6j). This takes the form of a sunburst with, beneath it, a crescent; and although the meaning of the crescent has not been explained, the sunburst has been interpreted as a Yorkist emblem.[35] It seems necessary to ask, therefore, whether the spectator is not being presented with a small anti-Yorkist joke? If this were the case, it would severely limit the dates at which it could have been painted. Within sight of the walls of Windsor Castle, it would arguably have been unwise to do this under Edward IV and suicidal under Richard III. There remains the period between 1485 and 1487 when, with the change of régime, the college – or someone in the college – might have felt prompted to reveal somewhat indirectly their feelings about the family which had deposed and murdered its founder.

This line of argument would have some consequential effects on the dating of the paintings. Painted work of some sort already existed in the 'nave' of the church by 1482;[36] and it is known that painters were working in the church in 1486–7.[37] Although James thought that work on the wall-paintings went on throughout the whole of this period, it is possible that the north wall was painted *c.* 1480; and that the south wall (or at least the Empress story) was painted in 1486. Such a pause in the work would have to be explained in relation to Wayneflete but for possible explanations (e.g. shortage of funds) there is no direct evidence. Such a pause would, however, explain the break in the style.

There are manifestly many uncertainties about all this and I shall conclude with a further uncertainty by saying something about William Baker. He is a painter who has intermittently considerably exercised historians. He makes his only appearance in the account role for 1486–7 – which contains in effect the only substantial notice of painting activity in the chapel during the whole medieval period. It seems to be a tidying-up account; and since Wayneflete himself died in 1486, James reasonably proposed that bills which ought to have been paid by the bishop were suddenly presented for payment to the college bursar.[38] The account, annotated in the margin *pictura ecclesiae*, is for a list of pigments (total 31*s* 6*d*), some gold for goldleaf (4*s* 6*d*), administrative expenses connected with their purchase (3*s* 8*d*), wages for an unspecified number of painters over an unquantified period of time (8*l* 7*s* 4*d*); and finally a small account for the additional purchase of pigments (3*s*) from a man called William Baker noted as *ipse pictor*. Earlier in this century William Baker attracted considerable attention partly because names attached to surviving work tend to be in short supply in English medieval art. It was also because significant painting in England tends to be by men with names like Hermann Scheere, Holbein and Van Dyck; and William Baker sounded as if he might have been English. These concerns are nowadays perhaps less pressing. Whether one is dealing with William Baker of London or Villem Becker of Bruges it seems reasonably certain that neither wall has its stylistic antecedents in England. There remains however some uncertainty over the significance of the colours which were bought for 31*s* 6*d* and 3*s* respectively. It has reasonably been inferred that Baker (*ipse pictor*) had been working with them; and it is therefore necessary to ask whether they (and he) could have been employed in the painting of the walls.

The relationship between the list of pigments and the wall-paintings is ambiguous.[39] It needs, in fact, a detailed study in order to determine the extent to which there is any relationship at all.[40] The colours listed are not incompatible with the paintings; but the quantities are strange. Thus the purchase of ¾ lb of gold might have been expected to cover at least 20 sq.m. of surface; ¾ lb of vermilion might cover *c.* 12.5 sq. m., 5 lb of ochre 85 sq. m.; 10 lb of white and red lead (undifferentiated in the bill as to quantity) might cover *c.* 150 sq. m. This last entry might well be linked to the paintings, though the absence of a definitively black pigment remains to be explained or glossed; and the largest single item of expenditure (xs.xd) was on copper green (viridian/verdigris). In the end, one is left with the impression that the colours for which the college footed the bill were used for a great many jobs in addition to the 'paintings' here being considered; and that the description of the task – *diversi pictores* working on the *pictura ecclesiae* – should probably conjure up the image of a lot of painters working all over the building at a variety of tasks generally designed to embellish the basic structure. Some of this embellishment is likely to have included the wall-paintings.

Nor does this clarify the status of William Baker. James saw him as *the* painter in 1486–7 (*ipse pictor*). If, however, he was being singled out for special and meritorious mention from the group *diversorum pictorum* of the previous sentence, *ipse* is an odd word to use.[41] *Magister* or *principalis* would have done better; and it seems more likely that, as used here, *ipse* glosses the adjective *proprius*. That is to say, the colours in question (3*s* worth) were the personal property (*proprii colores*) of that particular painter (*ipse pictor*) called William Baker (*scilicet Willelmus Baker*). Whether he was a 'great artist' or a fifteenth-century 'colour-man' – or something in between – remains in doubt; and this situation is likely to continue until, either in paintings or archives, he turns up in some other context.

*The illustrations for this paper are reproduced by kind permission of the Royal Commission on Historial Monuments for England. The copyright is vested in the Crown.*

## Notes

1 My interest in these paintings dates from about thirty years ago, when I was requested to lecture on them at the Courtauld Institute. At that date, little had been written on them beyond what had been said by M.R. James and Maxwell Lyte. This was sound as far as it went but also unsatisfactory. It was elementary by modern standards in its discussion of 'style' and incomplete in its views on the liturgical arrangements in the chapel and on the function of the paintings. I did some research on these last aspects of their history (see note 2) hoping to return in due course to the paintings themselves. Other interests overtook these studies; but in 1992, they still do not appear to have become the focus of anyone else's interest. The paintings have indeed been noticed in various contexts; but a general study is still lacking. Time has not however stood still. During the intervening period, a magnificent programme of conservation

has been brought to conclusion (1961–75) by Miss Pauline Plummer.

2   For the architectural and liturgical history of the chapel and its choir, see A.H.R. Martindale, 'The early history of the choir of Eton College Chapel', *Archaeologia*, CIII (1971), pp. 179–98.

3   The building history of the college is to be found in R. Willis and J.W. Clarke, *The architectural history of the University of Cambridge* (Cambridge 1886, reprint 1988), 1 *passim*. For the history of the college, see H.C. Maxwell Lyte, *A history of Eton College (1440–1898)* (London, 1899). The statutes of the college were printed by J. Heywood and T. Wright, *The ancient laws of the fifteenth century for King's College, Cambridge and for the public school of Eton* (London, 1850).

4   Willis and Clarke *Architectural history*, p. 365. In the third and largest design the nave was to be 168 × 40 ft. The total length of the church was to be 318 ft.

5   The Certosa was founded in 1396; the monastery at Brou was founded in 1508.

6   Henry's intentions were expressed in the document known as the 'Will', see Willis and Clarke, *Architectural history*, p. 353.

7   *Ibid.*, pp. 410–11.

8   The Eton evidence is contained in various wills, for which see Maxwell Lyte, *A history*, pp. 95–6.

9   Martindale, 'The early history of the choir', pp. 189–93.

10  Until the refashioning of the choir in 1699.

11  Much of the documentary evidence for painting was printed in M.R. James and E.W. Tristram, 'The wall-paintings in Eton College Chapel and in the Lady Chapel of Winchester Cathedral', *Walpole Society* XVII (1928–9) pp. 1–43. James showed that the college employed painters intermittently from 1479 to 1487 – though the first mention of wall-paintings comes only in 1482. Since then, the discovery of a fragment of the account roll for 1477 shows that five painters were working in the college in that year, though the nature of their job is not given (I am indebted to Mr Patrick Strong and Mrs Penny Hatfield for this information. The fragmentary roll is now numbered BR/K16).

12  James instituted a simple numbering system to which I have adhered. The paintings are referred to as N(orth), S(outh), A(upper), B(lower), (number) I–VIII (for the scenes) and (number) 1–9 for the figures, both counting from the east. Thus N.B.VII will be found to be the *Miracle of the Christchild held as hostage.*

13  Drawings of the walls were made, probably in 1847, by R.H. Essex and are preserved in the College Library. They show the two upper rows still half-intact. They are illustrated in James and Tristram, 'The Wall Paintings in Eton College Chapel', plates I–III.

14  Information kindly supplied by Pauline Plummer and acquired while she was working on the conservation.

15  This detail comes from the conservation report of Pauline Plummer who kindly gave me a copy. She noted the presence of masons marks still visible in the stone surface, a reminder that this stretch of wall was, in the original intention, to be left bare but concealed behind stall canopies (see below). Failure to plaster this surface before painting remains mildly surprising, perhaps reflecting some otherwise unrecorded need for urgency.

16  This observation was emphasised during the session at the conference by Dr Christopher Wilson who pointed out that it was to a considerable extent responsible for the difficulty of finding parallels for the Eton paintings elsewhere in contemporary Northern Europe.

17  But see G.F. Warner, *Miracles of Notre Dame collected by Jean Miélot* (Westminster 1885) and A. de Laborde, *Les Miracles de Notre Dame compilés par Jehan Miélot* (Paris 1929). The three manuscripts published in these works – Paris B.Nat. MSS Fr. 9198 and 9199 and Oxford Bod. Lib.MS. Douce 374 – contain copious illustrations produced probably during the third quarter of the fifteenth century. In choice of miracle stories, there is considerable overlap with the Eton series. Iconographically, however, they seem almost

entirely independent. By contrast, they are stylistically related. In particular, the grisaille technique of Fr. 9199 may be compared to the paintings on the north wall for the heightening of the faces with colour and the touches of colour in the architecture.

18    The screen which encloses the choir at Chartres was designed *c.* 1520 by Jean Texier. The carvings were completed over a long period which ended in the early eighteenth century. See E. Houvet *An illustrated monograph of Chartres Cathedral* (Chartres, 1947) pp. 65–9.

19    It was indeed this peculiarity of the notional flow of light which originally prompted me to question the position of the late fifteenth-century *pulpitum.*

20    They are now in the Castello Sforzesco, Milan; and they tell the story of Griselda. They have nothing stylistically in common with Eton.

21    For instance, the thirteenth-century compilation of Gautier de Coinci. See V.F. Koenig (ed.), *Les miracles de Nostre Dame par Gautier de Coinci* (Geneva-Lille, 1955–70). About 80 manuscripts survive of this work, testifying to its popularity.

22    James and Tristram, 'The Wall Paintings in Eton College, Chapel', p. 16.

23    Neither text is widely available. The *Speculum* of Vincent was printed in Douai in 1624 and this information is taken from the photostatic reprint (Graz, 1964–5). The edition of the *Legenda Aurea* which is used here is that of T. Grässe (Dresden and Leipzig) 1846.

24    Vincent *Spec.Hist.* Bk.VII, chaps 90–92.

25    *Leg.Aurea* chap.119, para. 3.

26    Vincent *Spec.Hist.* Bk.VII, chaps 93–5.

27    *Ibid.,* Bk.VII, chap. 86.

28    *Ibid.,* Bk.VII, chaps 102–3.

29    *Ibid.,* Bk.VII, chap. 116.

30    *Qualiter mulier quedam per filium beate Virginis suum filium de carceribus liberatum sibi restitui meruit legenda sanctorum.* James has *sibi restitutum invenit,* but this appears to have been a misreading.

31    See *Leg.Aurea* chap. 131, para. 4.

32    For the full text, see Vincent *Spec.Hist* Bk.VII, chaps. 90–92.

33    James, 'The Wall Paintings in Eton College Chapel', p. 24, expanded what is now a very badly damaged and incomplete inscription. Missing letters are here put in square brackets. *Hic redie[ns imperator] accusat[am] falso sibi u[xorem jubet in silvam] deduci et decapitari [Vincentius li.8 cap . . .]*

34    James, 'The Wall Paintings in Eton College Chapel', p. 23, drew attention to the similar though not identical plot of the story told by Chaucer's Man of Law.

35    This was pointed out by Pamela Tudor-Craig in her exhibition catalogue *Richard III* (London, 1973), p. 21.

36    James and Tristram, 'The Wall Paintings in Eton College Chapel', p. 2. As noted already, it is now known from a fragmentary account roll that five painters were active in the college in 1477.

37    *Ibid.,* p. 3.

38    *Ibid.*

39    The list will be found printed in full in James and Tristram, 'The Wall Paintings in Eton College Chapel', pp. 3–4.

40    Professor Stephen Reece-Jones, formerly Director of the conservation laboratory at the Courtauld Institute of Art, has kindly given some preliminary advice on this problem. The figures offered here represent a tentative essay in elucidation. They are based on the known chemical and physical values of some of the identifiable pigments combined with data relating to paint thicknesses observed in fifteenth-century Flemish painting. I hope that a more complete study will follow.

41    James and Tristram, 'The Wall Paintings in Eton College Chapel', p. 4. The final entries run *Et pro laboribus diversorum pictorum in opere predicto viii li.vii s. iiij d. Et pro diversis aliis coloribus ocupatis de coloribus propriis ipsius pictoris scilicet willelmi baker iij s.*

# 7

# Cross-channel Trade and Cultural Contacts: London and the Low Countries in the Later Fourteenth Century[1]

Vanessa Harding
*Birkbeck College, University of London*

The English customs accounts of the fourteenth and fifteenth centuries offer a number of insights into the cultural contacts between England and the countries with which it traded. Besides the broad economic issues, of direction, value, and volume of trade, and the identification of the merchants and mercantile associations, we can see what goods and commodities for daily use, elements in a shared material culture, were exchanged; and we can also begin to identify, in the operators of ships and their patterns of behaviour, an important community whose whole existence was dependent on the high level of interchange. It is well known that by the end of the fifteenth century much of England's overseas trade was channelled through London to Antwerp;[2] the strength of London–Low Countries trade a century earlier is perhaps less widely recognized. Hanseatic cogs, Venetian galleys, and the Gascon wine fleet may have constituted the largest ships with the bulkiest and most valuable individual cargoes, but most ships putting into London in the late fourteenth century had not come so far. A high proportion of London's overseas trade was with the shores immediately opposite, the Low Countries and northern France. The main customers for English wool, still London's most important single export despite the damage caused by wars, embargoes, and heavy export duties, were the clothmaking towns of Flanders. The shops and warehouses of the same towns, and especially Bruges, and the fairs of Brabant, furnished many of the goods desired by English consumers (textiles, metalwares, small manufactures, spices and luxury foods), some produced locally but others brought thither for exchange. Some of London's basic food needs (fish, beer, fruit and vegetables) were met from the produce of Holland and Zeeland.[3] A large number of relatively small ships and shippers took part in this cross-channel trade and it is their activity, and the importance of this trade for London, that this paper seeks to illuminate.

The study is based on a number of itemized or 'particular' customs accounts for the import and export of wool, cloth, wine and other commodities. The customs accounts are well known and need little introduction, except perhaps to reiterate that, because of the volume of trade passing through London, each duty had its own group of collectors and administrators, who rendered separate accounts to the Exchequer. Thus there were separate accounts for the custom on the export of wool, woolfells, and hides; for the custom on imported wine; for the New or Petty Custom, paid by alien merchants on their imports and exports other than wine or wool, from 1303, and by alien and denizen (native English) merchants on exports of cloth, from *c.* 1357; and for subsidies on all goods imported or exported by aliens and denizens, which only became a permanent feature in the late fourteenth century. Only a handful of particular accounts survives for fourteenth-century London, and there is no single year for which accounts from all branches of the Customs can be found, so conclusions about patterns of voyages and the actual business of handling goods can be only partial. Nevertheless the coverage of surviving accounts is wide enough to permit some general observations.[4]

The second half of the fourteenth century was a period of restructuring and redirection for English overseas trade, following the difficulties of the mid-century, when plague and war interrupted established patterns.[5] The wool export trade reached its last peak, in the 1360s, and entered a long decline; exports of English cloth took off from a low start and between 1370 and 1400 increased from fewer than twenty thousand cloths a year to more than forty thousand.[6] The Anglo-Gascon wine trade made a modest recovery from its mid-century low, but never again reached the heights of the early fourteenth century. In the long run, the growth of the cloth export trade at the expense of wool was a major factor in London's increasing dominance of English overseas trade, but even at this date the city had a commanding position. In the 1370s some 40 per cent of English wool exports, 15 to 20 per cent of cloth exports, and 40 per cent of wine imports paid custom in London.[7] It is difficult to assess the value of trade in other commodities, but in 1370/1 London's imports and exports excluding wool and wine but including cloth were valued at £130,639, or 60 per cent of the total for England as a whole (£217,463).[8]

The 1380s and 1390s saw English wool exports decline absolutely, and cloth exports rise; London's share of wool exports may have declined also, but its share of cloth exports increased and its total cloth export grew from two and a half to three thousand cloths per annum in the last years of Edward III to ten to fifteen thousand in the early years of Henry IV. The trend in other imports and exports is obscured by exemptions and uncertainties, but the value of alien trade in London appears to have remained at around £40,000 per annum until the turn of the century. Figures for the early years of Henry IV suggest a marked decline thereafter, both in the value of alien trade and the overall value of trade revealed in the subsidy valuations.[9]

The volume of shipping required to carry these goods was considerable. In 1380/1 the wool export alone (9,132 sacks) was carried in 186 ships; in 1397/8, when it had fallen to 4,985 sacks, it still required 91 voyages.[10] Tentative estimates of the total number of ships visiting London can be made from overlapping Subsidy and Petty Custom accounts for 1390/1. In the period 6 March to 21 November 1390, 459 ships arrived in London with cargoes liable for the subsidy of 6*d* in the £. In the same period a further 35 to 45 ships arrived without dutiable goods but paid custom on an export cargo. The account covers part of two normal Exchequer years, but over a period of twelve months a total of around 650 ship-visits is plausible.[11] In the Exchequer year Michaelmas 1390 to Michaelmas 1391, 443 ships brought goods liable to the Petty Custom (alien imports, excluding wine). Allowing for wine ships, for ships carrying denizen-owned foreign imports, and for ships carrying English goods to or from other English ports, the total number of ships visiting London in that year could have been between 730 and 750.[12] The year 1384, the only other year for which a calculation is possible, may have been quieter: in the period 1 July to 29 September only 98 ships arrived, and the year's total is unlikely to have been much more than 450.[13]

How many of these voyages were made to or from ports directly across the Channel? London's fourteenth-century particular customs accounts do not name the latest port of call of ships arriving in London, nor their destination on leaving, but trade in some commodities is recorded in such a way that we can at least identify a number of contacts with particular places. The wool trade is the most obvious case: the operation of a foreign Staple system from 1363 onwards meant that in most years almost all the wool exported from London went to Calais or, from 1384 to 1388, to Middelburg. In the first five years of the restored Calais Staple (1371–6) the percentage of London's total wool export going there rose from 26 per cent to 74 per cent, and from then until 1400, apart from periods when the Staple was being relocated or the system temporarily suspended, less than 10 per cent of London's wool exports was directly shipped anywhere else. In several years the customs accounts record no exceptions from the Staple. All of the 186 ships recorded as exporting cargoes of wool in 1380/1 were destined for Calais, as were 89 of the 91 recorded in 1397/8 (the other two being Venetian galleys headed for the Mediterranean).[14] Some of the wool not sent to the Staple was nevertheless being shipped to the Low Countries: in 1371/2, 5,781 sacks of wool were exported from London by aliens, under licence, to Zeeland and Holland.[15] It seems probable that in the 1350s and 1360s, before the establishment of the overseas Staple, wool exporters were using a number of Low Countries ports, and did not immediately change their habits, but that as time went on the costs of not trading directly with the staple port grew. Only a relatively small quantity of wool was shipped directly from London to the Mediterranean in the 1390s (between 1 per cent and 7 per cent of a decreasing total); the rest of the wool ultimately destined for Italy must have gone either from Southampton, or to the Staple and then been re-exported by land or sea. The numbers of ships needing to visit Calais decreased, however, as the wool export itself declined, from around 200 ships in 1370 to fewer than 100 by 1400.[16]

Another branch of the customs system which records direct trade between London and the Low Countries is the New Custom on imports of alien wine. As well as the large annual import of Gascon wine, a trade dominated by English and Gascon vintners, small quantities of 'Rhenish' wine (numbered in hundreds rather than thousands of tuns) were imported into London.[17] Its place of origin and the constraints of transport meant that Rhenish wine could only pass to England through the markets or ports of the Low Countries. Almost all the surviving customs records deal solely with wine imported by aliens, but when comparisons are possible they suggest that alien merchants dominated the trade: in 1371/2 aliens imported 201 tuns of Rhenish wine (80 per cent of the total) and denizen merchants only 52.5 tuns (20 per cent).[18] The number of ships involved in this trade in any one year was not great, but was larger than might be expected from the small import total: individual shipments were often quite small and sometimes made up part of a mixed cargo. The total Rhenish wine import of 253.5 tuns in 1371/2 was carried in 30 ships; in other years, alien imports alone, which varied considerably in quantity, came in between 10 and 40 ships. The records of this trade in part answer the question of the return cargoes of ships carrying wool exports, since where there is enough data for comparison the same names of ship-masters occur in wool and wine customs accounts, suggesting that the two were complementary; of 101 ship-masters carrying wool from London in 1365/6, at least 16 brought wine cargoes into London in 1366/7.[19]

Trade in other commodities also indicates a high level of interchange between London and Low Countries ports. Analysis of the 459 dutiable cargoes discharged in London in the period 6 March to 21 November 1390[20] suggests that half to three-quarters of all the ships arriving in London had taken on all or part of their cargo in Low Countries ports and markets. Twenty-four cargoes included goods of named Netherlandish origin (Dutch, Flemish, or Brabantine linen, for example); 141 cargoes comprised characteristic products of the Low Countries and South Germany (beer, tiles and earthenware, vegetables, Rhenish wine, Cologne thread, metal wares, small manufactures). Fifty-six ships brought fish only, probably from

North Sea fisheries. Ten ships brought nothing but woad, grown in Flanders and Picardy but also in southern France. One hundred and thirteen ships had cargoes of mixed origin, including some Baltic, Mediterranean, Spanish and south French goods together with products of other parts of Europe including possibly the Low Countries. Only a quarter of the ships (112) were loaded only with goods originating outside the Low Countries, unmixed with products of other areas, and even some of these cargoes might have been made up of goods purchased in Bruges or the Antwerp fairs. Men with English, Dutch or Flemish names imported Mediterranean goods into London, and we know that English merchants had not, at this date, penetrated the Mediterranean to buy them there. English merchants also bought Baltic goods in the Low Countries for re-export to England. As illustrations of this kind of activity, in 1385 three London merchants lost a cargo of *baterie* (beaten metal wares), rock alum and Cyprus cotton to privateers while it was being shipped from Zeeland to London;[21] also in 1385, an English skinner bought beaver, otter and other furs from Rupert of Cologne, presumably a Hanse merchant, in Middelburg, then the wool Staple, for export back to London.[22] For the majority of ships trading into London, therefore, a call at one or more Low Countries ports was obviously either a necessity or a profitable opportunity.

There are few indications from the English end which ports were most used in this cross-channel trade, apart from the obvious ones of Calais, Middelburg, and Sluis. Ships may have visited more than one port: it is unlikely that Calais was able to supply adequate return cargoes for the wool export, and probably many ships went on from there to ports in Flanders, Brabant and Zeeland to collect goods for England. Some woolships headed for Calais may also have carried English cloth for which they sought a market. Though exported to many areas, including Spain, south-western France, and the Baltic, English cloth was not welcome in cloth-producing Flanders; Hanse merchants were permitted, after much wrangling, to ship packed English cloth through Flanders and on to their own home towns, from 1359, and Genoese merchants apparently obtained the same privilege in 1395, but otherwise English cloth imports to Flanders were banned. Even accidental landings, as a result of storm or distress, were liable to confiscation.[23] About two-thirds of all ships leaving London in the 1380s and 1390s carried some English-made cloth, and though undoubtedly some of this cloth belonged to Hanse merchants, and so could go to Sluis, and some went directly to areas outside the Low Countries, much of the rest must have been sent to Brabant and Zeeland, which offered the possibility of sale.[24] As cloth exports grew and wool declined, a higher proportion of ships probably avoided Calais altogether and sailed direct to Middelburg or Antwerp.

Goods for and from Bruges and Ghent were trans-shipped at Sluis, and other ships may have made rendezvous there. In 1339/40 the king's butler trans-shipped some 250 tuns of wine from four ships into shouts or riverboats at Sluis, in order to send it on by boat to Damme and Ghent and by cart to Tournai for the king's use.[25] In 1380 a *hakebot*, freighted by an English merchant with goods from Flanders for London, was boarded by men of Sluis as it lay in the road outside the port; another English-owned cargo was seized in the same year as it was being shipped from the fair of Antwerp to Sluis.[26] Relations with different ports were complicated by the political situation, as England picked allies against the French from among the towns and counties of the Netherlands, and officials found it hard to distinguish which Netherlanders were friends and which enemies. The establishment of the Staple at Middelburg and hostility between England and Flanders in the early 1380s may have drawn more trade towards Holland and Zeeland; a case in 1387 alleged that there were many ships then sailing from *Caunfer* (Veere, in Zeeland) to London, and also, less encouragingly, that many English merchants had been drowned and lost their lives in the past two years on the journey between England and Zeeland and in the straits of Holland.[27]

The accounts suggest that the ships trading into London represented several different kinds of enterprise. Some were very small ships, with cargoes of low value and limited variety, part or all of which was owned by the ship's master; several of these could have been Dutch, such as the ship of Peter Masse, carrying 10,000 bakestones[28] (18 July 1384), or that of Clays Johanson (19 July 1384), with earthenware dishes, bakestones, Holland linen cloth, and beer. Johanson's export cargo was one and a half cloths, which he owned; Masse's exit is not recorded, but in both cases they could have been exporting wool or woolfells as well, not noted in the subsidy account. The masters of ships bringing fish (not stockfish) also often owned part or all of the cargo: John Harry owned 1,000 of the 21,000 mackerel and conger imported in his ship on 4 July, while Peter Baroldeson owned the 6,000 eels which comprised his whole cargo on 29 September.[29] In 1390, when a longer period (March to November) is covered by a subsidy account, it is clear that several masters concentrated on importing fish alone, though it did not all belong to them; their recorded export cargoes consisted principally of cloth, though they may also have carried wool.[30]

These small entrepreneurs, trader-masters, contrast with the majority of ship-masters, who carried larger and more mixed cargoes, but few or no trade goods of their own. Their role was principally that of carrier or provider of transport, to a range of merchants, and some of them recur several times in a single customs account or in several different accounts.

The wool custom accounts show a few masters making repeated journeys: in 1380–1, though 71 ships carried only one wool cargo out of London, 20 carried 2, 5 carried 3 cargoes, 3 carried 5, 3 carried 6, one 8, and one ship carried 9 separate cargoes of wool.[31] The subsidy accounts confirm this pattern: in 1390, 296 ships made at least 459 visits, most therefore coming only once but nearly a quarter coming two or more times, and some up to five times.[32]

The Petty Custom and Subsidy accounts also show what goods were being imported in the ships that carried the wool exports away. Robert Staverle, who carried six wool cargoes in 1380/1, visited London at least three times in the summer of 1384, bringing linen cloth, metalwares, flax, and canvas on two occasions and garlic and tallow on a third; his only recorded export cargo was one of cheese and butter, so he may also have carried wool this year. Staverle occurs again in 1391, with an export cargo of broadcloth and serge.[33] William Skantyloun's ship carried five wool export cargoes in 1380/1; in 1384 he imported one large cargo (18 July) made up principally of linen and wax and another (13 September) with some linen and wax, and also silk and silk cloths, metalwares, and some Baltic skins. His export cargo on 26 July included some 90 broadcloths, 97 dozen caps, and 900 lb tin.[34]

Though some merchants shipped goods with the same master on more than one occasion, most used several ships, and do not appear to have formed exclusive relationships with masters. The goods carried by Staverle on 18 July 1384 belonged to four different merchants; three of these also owned goods in his ship arriving on 16 August, but another four merchants also shipped goods. The three who owned goods on both ships also imported goods on other ships arriving on 18 and 28 July, and 16, 18, and 24 August, suggesting that they simply bought space on the most convenient ship, and for reasons of security distributed their goods among several sailing at about the same time.[35]

The customs account entries list imports under headings such as '*de navi Johannis Brounswyn*' and the date, and exports under '*in navi* (etc.)'. It has been assumed here that the person so named was the master of the ship, responsible for the merchandise and custom, but not necessarily full owner of the vessel itself. Certainly some masters were owners, and some merchants owned ships which other men commanded for them, but information is scanty, and such as it is relates mostly to men and ships engaged in Spanish or longer-distance trade, partly because the complexity of arrangements for long voyages was more likely to result in litigation and hence record.[36] It seems probable that many of the small Dutch master-traders, and some at least of the masters of larger ships engaged in cross-channel trade, were owners or part-owners of their ships, but certainty is not possible.

The customs accounts give few clues to the types of ships engaged in trade with the Low Countries. The largest ships to be found in London in the late fourteenth century were Hanseatic cogs, Venetian galleys, and the English, Gascon, and Spanish ships, some of which carried over a hundred tuns, which brought Gascon wine to London.[37] Some of these large ships may also have called at Low Countries ports before or after visiting London. One of the largest ships carrying Netherlandish goods to arrive in 1384 was that of Laurence Chesse: it contained 66 barrels of pitch, woad, iron, and other goods, 20 thousandweight of woad, madder, flax, and copper, nearly 2,000 lb of *baterie*, several thousand Baltic furs, several thousand ells of linen cloth from Westphalia, Flanders, Hainault, and Zeeland, and a small quantity of Italian silk textiles. Chesse's recorded export cargo was less than 50 quarters of grain, 25 cloths, and 900 boards of wainscot, but perhaps he carried wool as well.[38] He had exported a cargo of 115 sacks of wool (weighing about 19 tons) in 1381, one of the largest loads that year, and reappeared in 1390, with a cargo of (Gascon) wine, suggesting that he engaged in more than cross-channel carrying.[39]

Chesse was clearly one of the larger carriers, and the majority of ships were smaller. Cargoes of Rhenish wine were rarely over 40 pipes (equivalent to 20 tuns capacity), and often much less; only a small number of ships carried over a hundred sacks of wool, though in both cases other goods may have been carried as well.[40] Most ships were probably not more than 40 tuns (capacity), and a few brought cargoes of less than half this. Twelve other ships paid custom on the same day in 1384 as Laurence Chesse's ship; although it is hard to equate weights and capacities, the next largest cargo after Chesse's was under 40 tuns (30 tuns of wine, 6 barrels of tar and 3,500 lb madder); the smallest, apart from one ship that apparently arrived empty, carried about 8,000 ells of linen and canvas, 400 lb flax, and 750 lb *baterie*. The other cargoes ranged in size between these, mostly towards the upper end.[41]

A list of ships released from arrest in London in 1346 may indicate a typical range of sizes and types. It comprised the ship of Peter Mesedagh called *hegebot* of 10 tuns burden (*et est ponder' x dol'*), and the ship of Lambert Flake also called *hegebot* and of the same tunnage; three ships called *craer* belonging to Laurence Outresson, Nicholas Souk, and Peter Lambyn, of 20, 25, and 30 tuns respectively; and two ships called *holkschyp*, of Peter Semel and John Peresson, of 20 tuns each.[42] The *hegebot* or *hakebot* may be a Flemish kind, as there are many references in the wine custom accounts to *hakebots* of Sluis and Bruges carrying Rhenish wine, and the *hakebot* of Walter Reyns of Flanders and the *navicula vocata hakebot* of John Joye of Flanders were arrested by the Searcher in 1356/7.[43] A *hakebot* was also being used to ship goods from Sluis to England in 1380.[44] The name may originally have denoted a fishing vessel using hook tackle, but it was obviously more widely used than that.[45]

The crayer is likely to have been a similar kind of ship, perhaps slightly larger, and also perhaps associated with fishery. William son of Roger de Bernes, fishmonger, had a share in a *craer* called *Andreu* of London in 1348–9; John Longeneye, fishmonger, had a share in a *creyer* in 1383. A crayer was used to carry 41 tuns and 1.5 pipes of wine from Sandwich to London in 1374.[46] The *holkschyps* mentioned in 1346 are too small, at 20 tuns, to be the great trading ships known as hulks; possibly they were identical with the *hocscip* (hook-ship) of Flanders, a Flemish fishing vessel, mentioned in the account of customs on fish in *Liber Albus*.[47] Another small ship engaged in river-carrying and in coastal and cross-channel trade was the *farecost*.[48] The shout or *schuyt* was a river-boat, much used on the Thames as well as in the Low Countries (from whence the name derives), especially for transferring goods from seagoing ships to quayside. Its capacity appears to have been about 20 tuns of wine.[49]

The fifteenth-century ship excavated at Blackfriars, with a waterline beam of some 5 m and a draught of 1 m, may be typical of river-boats and smaller seagoing ships of the later medieval period. It had a single mast, stayed in several places, and probably carried a single square sail on a yard at the masthead.[50] A boat arrested in London in 1356 illustrates the simple equipment of such craft: it had one mast, a sail-yard with sail, two anchors, a cable, a hawser, two oars and a gaff or sprit (*spret*). It was arrested because the master, Thomas Stacy of Faversham, was thought to be exporting 20 oxhides without paying custom, so it was presumably capable of going to sea.[51]

The contents of ships give some clue to late-fourteenth-century trading patterns, but the nationalities of masters and owners and the home ports of ships are not easy to determine. Most of the customs accounts supply only the master's name, and we should be careful about drawing conclusions from these about ship-ownership and origins; individuals may have ranged quite far from home in search of business. In a few cases references in the judicial and administrative records of the city of London and of central government provide details of owner, master, origin, cargo, or destination, and where this information survives it suggests a complex state of affairs. In 1386, Hugh Richardesson of Southampton, master (*custos et gubernator*) of the ship called *le Marie* of Exeter, was called to account to the ship's owner John Bedon of Calais for the money received for freighting goods from Middelburg to London.[52] Richardesson's surname suggests a Low Countries origin (names in this form being uncommon in England at this date), though he is said to be 'of Southampton', while Bedon, in English Calais, may well have been English rather than French. In any case, the port-name, Exeter, attached to the ship's name, gives no clue to the ship's sphere of activity.

The accounts for the New Custom on alien wine imports sometimes record a place-name with the ship's name: in the 1340s ships from Dordrecht, Sluis, and Brill dominated the traffic in Rhenish wine, while ships from Antwerp, Axel, Bruges, Harderwijk, Hulst, and Zwin also participated. One English ship, la Margarete of London, carried 42 pipes of Rhenish wine in 1372, and a ship of Dunkirk is mentioned in 1381.[53] In 1392–5 five of the fifteen ships carrying alien-owned Rhenish wine were said to be of Dordrecht, but the majority were identified only by the master's name.[54]

The origins of ship-masters are no more certain, though some guesses can be made on the basis of name-forms. The customs accounts were kept in a simple Latin, heavily influenced in structure and vocabulary by English and French. Christian names were partly Latinized and often abbreviated or suspended, so the original forms of common names are often lost (Peter, Pierre, Piers, Pieter, Pedro, all tend to become Petrus or Petr'); surnames are usually given in full, though their spelling is idiosyncratic. In these circumstances it is hard to distinguish English names from Dutch and German ones; even Spaniards and Italians may be concealed under unfamiliar spellings. There are some markers, however: the Christian names recorded as Albright, Arnald, Bast', Boldwin, Clays, Copin, Dederik, Frowin (possibly a woman's name), Gislebright, Herman, Heyn', Issebright, Keyser, Lambert, Mews, and Tidman are not normally found in England, and appear to be Dutch,[55] while surnames incorporating 'van' or 'van der' or ending in -son or -ssone can also probably be safely assumed to indicate a similar origin. A few instances where masters' origins are given help to justify this assumption.[56]

Though otherwise uncommon in London, at least forty different surnames of this kind occur in the particular customs accounts for the 1380s and 1390s, some of them borne by up to twelve different individuals.[57] On the same rough and ready basis, using both surnames and given names, at least 102 of the 340 masters in the subsidy account for 1390, or 30 per cent of all masters, were probably of Low Countries origin. A rather higher proportion (45 per cent) of the 289 masters of ships liable to the Petty Custom in 1390–1 had names of this kind.[58] Among the remainder of masters, some are identifiable on other grounds as Hanseatic or Spanish, and the Italian ships and galleys also stand out, but this leaves nearly half without a national attribution. Some of these were probably also Netherlanders, but a good many must have been English; in the 1480s English and Low Countries ships were about equal in number,[59] but there can be no certainty about the 1380s and 1390s.

Merchants did not necessarily ship with compatriot masters, and indeed it would have been impossible for many of them to do so: Italian and to a lesser extent Hanseatic merchants seem to have shipped goods from their Low Countries depots to London with English and Netherlandish masters. English merchants could have chosen English masters for preference but it is not certain that they did. In any case, though brokers and clerks were available for drawing up contracts and agreements, there must have developed a lingua franca for handling ships and cargoes. London English certainly borrowed Flemish and Dutch words, especially in connection with the river and the sea, and with fishery.[60]

Several of these Netherlandish masters were frequent visitors to London, and must have been figures familiar to the port authorities; others, though they came only once or twice in any one year, nevertheless reappeared in London over periods of ten or fifteen years.[61] The dates at which custom was paid on import and export cargoes are not necessarily the dates of the ship's arrival or departure, but turnaround must have been quick in order to enable several visits a year, so the frequent visitors may not have spent more than a few days in London at a time. Very little is known of what they did in London, where they stayed, and how they carried on their business. Masters and mariners, unless overtaken by misfortune or litigation, rarely appear outside the customs records, since they did not buy or lease property, hold civic office, or pay taxes, and were unlikely to make wills in London. Taverners and innkeepers probably provided them with temporary accommodation, and may have acted as business contacts too, even if not always reliably: Ernold de Bruyn, a taverner, was accused of robbing one Baudewyne, master of a ship of Brill, of fifteen gold coins, in 1365.[62] Resident or naturalized Netherlanders may also have offered hospitality, but possibly transient mariners had more in common with men of the same trade than with the immigrant craftsmen who made up the bulk of the settled alien population.[63]

However fleeting the visits of individual ships, it is clear that the frequency and volume of cross-channel trade meant that late-fourteenth-century London was in constant contact with the trading community, language, native products, and everyday culture of the Low Countries. The cargoes noted above to illustrate other points also demonstrate the range of goods available in London. There was clearly a high demand for a wide range of imports, which drove trade to the extent that some ships could find no export cargoes in London and apparently left without one.[64] Londoners drank Dutch beer and perhaps some Rhenish wine, and ate imported apples, pears, onions, and garlic. They cooked on stoneware bakestones, imported in their thousands every year, and with Dutch earthenware and metal pots and pans bought in the Low Countries. Tables were laid and meals served with imported napery. Londoners dressed themselves in

Netherlandish and German linens, and Londoners, Dutch, and Brabanters wore woollen gowns of English broadcloth and perhaps of Flemish rays and motleys. Londoners could improve their vision with imported spectacles, protect their feet with imported 'pattencloggs', and their heads with Flanders or Paris kerchiefs. Households in London and in the cities and towns of the Low Countries also had access to the products of more distant lands: Mediterranean spices and drugs, Spanish fruit and oil, French wine and salt, Baltic timber, fur, wax, and metals. The main raw materials and tools for manufacture came from these distant areas, but the Low Countries supplied some woad and madder and also teasels and fullers' earth.[65]

In few cases (except perhaps for linen) were the quantities of any of these imports sufficient to have supplied more than a small number of households, but they made a contribution to daily life and perhaps influenced taste and techniques of production. Dutch beer evidently created a demand in London which was afterwards met by beer brewed by Dutchmen in London, just as in the fifteenth century imported printed books may have helped to establish a market and readership on which Caxton's business could subsequently prosper.[66] Archaeologists have found it difficult, if not impossible, to distinguish imported knives or dress accessories from London manufactures.[67] Almost everything of this kind known to have been imported was manufactured in London as well, but London craftsmen may have learned ideas and products from imported goods.[68] By the later fifteenth century the flood of small manufactures was so great that London craftsmen petitioned to keep out a wide range of goods from ribbons and spurs to pins and playing-cards.[69]

Very few items of obvious artistic merit or value are mentioned in the customs accounts to indicate that skilled Netherlandish craftwork was also in demand. Fine armour and silk brocades were probably products of south Germany and Italy. The dozens of paternosters of glass and horn, little images of wood or lead, glass beads and mirrors were given very low customs valuations. Arras was a rare but valuable import, especially when woven with gold or silver thread,[70] but the only real *objet de vertu* recorded in these accounts is a crystal cup and cover, gilded with silver, worth £17. It was imported by Herman Gowell in the ship of Clays Dederikson in 1390, among a cargo of beer, flax, baselards, apples, and Rhenish wine.[71]

The 'cultural contacts' between the ordinary people of London and the Low Countries were the result of a flourishing and sustained trade in items of modest value for everyday use. It would be wrong to overstate the extent to which trade integrated the material culture and consumption patterns of the two areas, but mutual influences were strong, and it is striking how many elements in the domestic setting, in dress and household furnishings, items of food and drink, and even objects of devotion, were common to urban communities on both sides of the Channel.

## Notes

1   The paper derives largely from material discussed in chapters 3 and 4 of V.A. Harding, 'The Port of London in the Fourteenth Century: its topography, administration, and trade' (unpub. Ph.D. thesis, St. Andrews Univ. 1983), and on some further archival research. I am grateful to Caroline Barron for encouraging me to write this paper.
2   *The overseas trade of London: Exchequer customs accounts, 1480–1*, H.S. Cobb (ed.), (London Record Society 27, 1990), pp. xxxiii–xliii.
3   N.J.M. Kerling, *Commercial relations of Holland and Zealand with England from the late thirteenth century to the close of the Middle Ages* (Leiden, 1954), esp. pp. 110–18.
4   N.S.B. Gras, *The early English customs system* (Cambridge, Mass., 1918).
5   J.L. Bolton, *The Medieval English economy, 1150–1500* (1980), p. 292.
6   E.M. Carus Wilson and O. Coleman, *England's Export Trade, 1272–1547* (1963), pp. 122–3, 138–9.
7   Figures for wool and cloth from Carus-Wilson and Coleman, *loc. cit.*; for wine, P(ublic) R(ecord) O(ffice). Exchequer, Various Accounts, E.101/80/22.
8   P.R.O. Exchequer, Enrolled Customs Accounts, E.356/13.
9   Harding, 'Port of London', p. 235; E. Power and M.M. Postan, *English trade in the fifteenth century* (1933), p. 343. The reduced level of the subsidy valuation (between £68,000 and £78,000 in 1407–9) may partly be attributable to the exemption of denizen and Hanse cloth exports, which were apparently included in the 1370/1 figure. Denizen and Hanse exports made up 65 per cent of London's total cloth export in 1407–9, but less than 8 per cent of Southampton's: Power and Postan, *op.cit.*, pp. 328–9, 343.
10  P.R.O. Exchequer, Particular Customs Accounts, E.122/71/4; E.122/71/23, 25.
11  P.R.O. E.122/71/13. In all, 78 ships paid export duties without being recorded as entering. Forty-two of these left before the end of June, and many of these must have arrived before the account begins in March; 36 left after 1 July, and few of these are likely to have arrived before March. The 35 to 45 ships estimated above as arriving without a dutiable cargo had probably come from another English port with English goods only, since arrivals from foreign ports loaded only with gravel or chalk for ballast, or from an English port with duty-paid foreign goods, would almost certainly have been noted.
12  P.R.O., E.122/71/16. The Subsidy and Petty Custom accounts overlap for some months in the autumn of 1390: the former records 150 ships (excluding wine-ships) to the latter's 102. If allowance is made for the wine fleet, and for some ships arriving from other English ports, as above (say 80 to 100 ships in all), as well as for those arriving with denizen-owned foreign imports only, the total is around 730 to 750.
13  P.R.O., E.122/71/8. By way of comparison, in 1368 about 680 ships made over 1,000 visits to Lübeck: J. Schildhauer, translated K. Vanovitch, *The Hansa, History and Culture* (Leipzig, 1985), p. 150.
14  P.R.O. E.356/14; E.122/71/4; E.122/71/23, 25. Over 90 per cent of denizen-owned wool exports went to Calais in the period 1371–6: T.H. Lloyd, *The English wool trade in the Middle Ages* (Cambridge, 1977), p. 252.
15  P.R.O. E.356/8.

16   P.R.O. E.122/71/4, 23, 25.
17   Harding, 'Port of London', pp. 172–91. For details see P.R.O. E.101/77/18; E.101/78/4–20; E.101/79/1–25; E.101/80/1–25.
18   Their relative shares of the Gascon wine trade in that year were 29 per cent and 71 per cent: P.R.O. E.101/80/22.
19   P.R.O. E.122/70/18; E.101/80/18.
20   P.R.O. E.122/71/13.
21   *Cal(endar of select) P(lea and) M(emoranda) R(olls of the City of London preserved among the archives of the corporation of the City of London at the Guildhall, a.d.) 1381–1412*, A.H. Thomas (ed.), (1932) pp. 98–9.
22   *Ibid.*, p. 102.
23   J.H. Munro, 'Industrial Protectionism in medieval Flanders: urban or national?', in *The medieval city*, H.A. Miskimin, D. Herlihy, and A.L. Udovitch (eds.), (Yale, 1977), pp. 229–65.
24   P.R.O. E.122/71/8, 13, 16.
25   P.R.O. E.101/79/3.
26   *Cal(endar of) P(lea and) M(emoranda) R(olls preserved among the archives of the Corporation of the City of London at the Guildhall, a.d.) 1364–1381*, A.H. Thomas (ed.), (1929), pp. 269–70.
27   *Cal. P.M.R., 1381–1412*, pp. 98–9, 102, 125, 127–8, 140–2.
28   'Bakestones' could possibly have been bricks or tiles, perhaps the 'Flemish tiles' used in ovens, but are I think more likely to have been flat pieces of terracotta or stoneware, used as heat-distributors in cooking. M. Hazan, *The second classic Italian cookbook* (1982), pp. 32–59, discusses their use in Italian cooking. The large numbers imported in the Middle Ages suggest that they were both useful and rather breakable.
29   P.R.O. E.122/71/8.
30   P.R.O. E.122/71/13: Clays Blunke, 13 March, 22 March, 20 April, 9 May; Michael Mys, 13 March, 22 March, 20 April, 13 May; Henry Sonesson, 28 March, 6 May, 13 June, 1 Sept. Several others brought two or three cargoes of fish.
31   P.R.O. E.122/71/4.
32   P.R.O. E.122/71/13.
33   P.R.O. E.122/71/4, 8, 16.
34   P.R.O. E.122/71/4, 8.
35   P.R.O. E.122/71/8.
36   Harding, 'Port of London', pp. 292–8. In 1390 Peryn or Peter de la Rassch and John Derling bought a ship in London, on the value of which (£46 13s 4d) they had to pay export duty; de la Rassch appears to have been its master, while Derling owned part of the cargo of flour and cloth it carried when it left London. Peryn de la Rassch reappeared in London three months later, with an import cargo of iron and wine, and left with a load of cloth, points, and small wares: P.R.O. E.122/71/13: 16 June (export), 6 Sept. (import), 20 Sept. (export).
37   The topic of ship-size and capacity is more fully discussed in Harding, 'Port of London', pp. 236–54. For the size of ships in the Gascon wine trade see P.R.O. E.101/80/22. 25.
38   P.R.O. E.122/71/8: 18 July (import), 7 Sept. (export).
39   P.R.O. E.122/71/4: 30 Jan.; E.122/71/13: 2 Nov.
40   P.R.O. E.101/80/22–5; E. 122/71/4, 23, 25.
41   P.R.O. E.122/71/8: 18 July. The weighty or bulky elements in the twelve cargoes were: (1) 7,000 lb flax and 2 barrels oil; (2) 10,000 bakestones; (3) an empty chest; (4) 30 tuns wine, 6 barrels tar and 3,500 lb madder; (5) 7,000 lb flax, 3,500 ells of linen, 3,000 lb and 13 tuns of woad, 1,500 lb copper, 2 butts of malmsey wine, and a horse; (6) about 8,000 ells of linens and canvas and 400 lb flax, and 750 lb *baterie*; (7)

165 weys of wax, about 2,500 ells of linens and canvas, 3 tuns or woad and 1,500 lb flax; (8) 2 tuns of Rhenish wine, 2 barrels of beer, 110 lb flax, 8 barrels of steel and 2 pairs of quernstones; (9) a last of beer, a last of quernstones, and 13 barrels of saltsmolt; (10) 25 chalders of alum, 4 tuns of woad, 1,500 lb copper, and 2,500 horns for lanterns; (11) 20 weys of wax and 4,000 lb flax; (12) 20,000 lb flax, 2,500 lb copper, 2,000 lb thread, and 7,000 (?salt) fish.

42  P.R.O. Chancery, Miscellanea, C.255/4/12, m. 10.

43  P.R.O. E.101/79/10, 24; E.122/190/12; E.122/191/28.

44  *Cal. P.M.R. 1364–81*, p. 269.

45  For a discussion of these ship-terms (hakebot, crayer, farecost, shout) see L.C. Wright, *Sources of London English: Thames technical vocabulary* (Oxford: Clarendon Press, 1994). I am grateful to Dr Wright, and through her to Karina van Dalen Oskam of the *Vroegmiddelnederlands Woordenboek*, for comments on these names.

46  *Calendar of Wills proved and enrolled in the Court of Husting, London, A.D. 1258–1688*, R.R. Sharpe (ed.) (1889–90), Vol. 1, p. 611; *ibid.* Vol. 2, p. 233; *Memorials of London and London life in the XIIIth, XIVth, and XVth centuries*, H.T. Riley (ed.), (1868), p. 380. The *kraier* was also known in the Baltic, as was the *schute*: J. Schildhauer, translated K. Vanovitch, *The Hansa, History and Culture* (Leipzig, 1985), p. 150.

47  *Munimenta Gildhallae Londoniensis*, H.T. Riley (ed.) Vol. I, *Liber Albus* (Rolls Series, 1859), pp. 343, 374.

48  *Munimenta Gildhallae Londoniensis*, H.T. Riley (ed.) Vol. II, Part I, *Liber Custumarum* (Rolls Series, 1860), p. 407; D. Burwash, *English Merchant Shipping, 1460–1540* (Toronto, 1947), p. 123 and *passim*.

49  Harding, 'Port of London', pp. 251–2.

50  *Waterfront archaeology in Britain and northern Europe*, G. Milne and B. Hobley (eds.), (Council for British Archaeology Research Report no. 41, 1981), pp. 13–16.

51  P.R.O. E.122/190/12.

52  *Cal. P.M.R. 1381–1412*, pp. 121–2.

53  P.R.O. E.101/79/2, 6, 8, 10, 12, 24; E.101/80/22; E.101/80/23, m. 3.

54  P.R.O. E.101/80/25.

55  I am grateful to Karina van Dalen Oskam for comments on these. The name Conrad, which also occurs among shippers and masters, may be German; two names apparently recorded as Fremd' and Outr' are of uncertain origin.

56  E.g. John Dederikson of Brill (P.R.O. E.122/71/13; export, 28 Aug. 1390); Clays Comynson of Dordrecht (P.R.O. E.101/80/25; 19 Nov. 1392); John Outresson, master of a ship of Flanders, 1370 (*Cal. P.M.R. 1364–81*, p. 119).

57  P.R.O. E.122/71/4, 8, 13, 16, 23, 25. There were at least twelve Johanssones, twelve Pieressones, eight Clayssones, and five Jacobsones. Cf. Harding, 'Port of London', p. 286.

58  P.R.O. E.122/71/13, 16.

59  *The Overseas trade of London: Exchequer customs accounts, 1480–1*, H.S. Cobb (ed.), (London Record Society 27, 1990), p. xxxviii.

60  Cf. L.C. Wright, *Sources of London English: Thames technical vocabulary* (Oxford: Clarendon Press, 1994).

61  Ships of Henry Peresson, Lodowik Henrykson, and Henry Johanssone occur in customs accounts from 1380 to 1391; the ship of John Yonge, who may be English, occurs in all the accounts from 1380 to 1398: P.R.O. E.122/71/4, 8, 13, 16, 23, 25.

62  *Cal. P.M.R. 1364–81*, p. 21.

63  S. Thrupp, 'Aliens in and around London in the fifteenth century', in *Studies in London history presented to P.E. Jones*, A. Hollander and W. Kellaway (eds.), (1969), pp. 251–72.

64  In 1390 eight masters paid a nominal export duty on chalk *pro lastagio* (for ballast), but

some of these also carried a few other goods: P.R.O. E.122/71/13.

65   P.R.O. E.122/71/8, 13. See also Harding, 'Port of London', pp. 202–6, 217–32.

66   S. Thrupp, 'Aliens', in Hollander and Kellaway (eds.), *Studies in London history*, pp. 259–60, 265–6; Cobb, *The overseas trade of London, 1480–1*, p. xxxvi.

67   J. Cowgill, M. de Neergard, and N. Griffiths, *Medieval finds from excavations in London: 1, Knives and scabbards* (1987), pp. 8, 17–24, 32–4; G. Egan and F. Pritchard, *Medieval finds from excavations in London: 3, Dress accessories* (1991), pp. 269–71, 297–304.

68   M. Rhodes, 'A pair of fifteenth-century spectacle frames from the City of London', *Antiquaries Journal*, lxii pt. 1 (1982), pp. 65–6.

69   Cobb, *Overseas trade of London, 1480–1*, pp. xxxvi–xxxvii.

70   See also S. McKendrick, above, ch. 2.

71   P.R.O. E.122/71/8, 13. The cup arrived on 20 April 1390, in the latter account.

# 8

# Trade between England and the Low Countries: Evidence from Historical Linguistics

Laura Wright

*University of Hertfordshire*

Recently, the trend in the study of historical linguistics has been to celebrate variation, to rejoice in the multiplicity of spellings, words and grammatical constructions found in single texts, rather than to attempt to reduce them to one *ur* script, dialect or language. Hence Milroy[1] infers a polyvalency of phonetic reality from the plurality of letter graphs in historical texts, and concludes that social context may explain their presence. The present article will look at business writing produced in London in the fifteenth century, because such texts display an amount of linguistic borrowings from the languages of the Low Countries. The aim is to present one or two hitherto untreated words that are now obscure to us, and to attempt to reconstruct the direction of influence – from the Low Countries to London, or the other way round? I will also trip over the semanticist's besetting hazard, that of metaphorical extension, and show how others have fallen into the pothole of taking etymology literally (and perhaps fall into it myself). Ultimately, I too will seek refuge in the central reservation of social context – but with certain reservations. While historical linguistics cannot always solve the sort of problems outlined in this article, the information unearthed *en route* may be of passing interest to the social or cultural historian.

The current-day language situation in the Low Countries displays considerable variation. Far from reflecting the 'one country, one language' state nationalists yearn for, the expanse from the Frisian Islands to the French border is multilingual, and multidialectal. Leaving aside the modern imports due to the effects of colonialization and *gastarbeiters*, historically the area has always been linguistically heterogeneous. This is partly due to its being the meeting point between the Germanic and the Romance families, and partly due to its fluctuating political divisions. Further, it is no easy matter to distinguish between dialects and languages, whether Germanic or Romance. There are no cut-and-dried criteria for distinguishing between dialects and languages; rather their linguistic status correlates with their political status, past or present.

When classifying languages, historical linguists usually invoke a

metaphor of genealogical descent. The relevant criteria are shared
characteristics, so if two languages have many features in common, it is
deemed likely that they are closely related and stem from a common parent
language. This is the case with English and Dutch. The earliest attested
forms of English and Frisian have certain features in common,[2] which
mark these two languages off as close siblings from the rest of the West
Germanic parent family. Dutch is another member of the West Germanic
family. Historically, the West Germanic branch had at some point been
united with its North and East siblings in Common Germanic, and the
Germanic family and the Romance family had a common parent, Indo-
European.

The two main languages spoken to the south of Frisian in our period
were Middle Dutch, and Middle Low German,[3] also members of the West
Germanic parent family. Low German is separated from High German by a
particular sound change, which accounts for Modern English *ship*, Dutch
*schip*, Low German *skip*, but German *Schiff*; and English *apple*, Dutch *appel*,
Low German *appel*, but German *apfel*.[4] Drawing a distinction between the
various Germanic languages of the Low Countries is a rather arbitrary
exercise, as linguistically speaking they are all related dialects, with a
continuum of mutual intelligibility over the entire area. A speaker from the
north of the Netherlands speaking Frisian cannot nowadays necessarily
easily understand somebody from the south of Belgium speaking Flemish,
but there is no point in between where an inhabitant cannot understand the
people in the next town. Romance dialects are also spoken in the area, and
it is equally difficult historically to determine where one French dialect left
off and another one started. The pattern is further obscured by the
predominantly Northern French dialect into London in 1066, which then
continued to develop and grow for several centuries, cut off from its
continental roots. As happens with any language, once a section of speakers
is separated physically from the parent body, their form of the language will
quickly change and develop into a distinct dialect. While it is arguable
precisely how long Anglo-Norman continued to be a spoken language in
London, it is certain that the language continued to have life and
momentum as a written medium in legal and business contexts for at least
another four hundred years, and this form of the French language continued
to exercise an influence over the development of London English.[5]

In the fourteenth century, business writing in England was not, as a rule,
written in English. It was written in a mixture of Medieval Latin and
Middle English, or Anglo-Norman and Middle English. During the
fifteenth century this pattern began to change, and by the last decades
monolingual English records were produced. But for most of the period,
we can reckon with an admixture of Medieval Latin and Anglo-Norman.
However, the Medieval Latin of business records was not quite like the

Medieval Latin of sermons, and the Anglo-Norman of business records was not identical to the Anglo-Norman of romances. Rather, it was a particular sort unto itself – by and large, the prepositions, conjunctions and articles were in a Romance language, and the nouns and verb-stems were either Romance or, optionally, Germanic. Another way of characterizing this is to say that the prepositions, conjunctions and articles occur in the prestige language (Latin or Anglo-Norman), and the nouns, and to some extent the verbs, can occur in the vernacular.[6] I make this distinction because this type of business mix occurs in other European languages. Further, the ends of the words, which often carry a grammatical suffix, were frequently abbreviated, or represented by a suspension mark, and some of the internal letters of the word could be abbreviated or suspended too. Example (1) illustrates this kind of language, here demonstrated by a legal text:

### Example 1

*It'm dicunt qd' apud dokheytis sunt tres Route posite p' quos ignorant &c' Et dicunt qd' om'es & singuli d'ci ffirmarij wera' Routa' isto eodem anno armanerunt weras illas cu' wasis virgis & ramis clatis herdellis & alijs ingenijs ligneis tam firmit' & stricte int'ligatis necnon cu' rethibz de crine vocat' Beerdis beerdpottis & hokenettys ac alijs rethibz & machinis de tam stricta ap'tura & meschia confect' . . .*
Corporation of London Records Office MS Liber Dunthorn[7] fo 347 (*c.* 1474); copied from a document now lost from the beginning of the fifteenth century.
(And they say that at Dog Eyot there are three routes, positioned by whom they do not know, etc. And they say that all and every single one of the said renters of weirs and routes this same year have equipped their weirs with wases twigs and branches, lattices, hurdles and other wooden devices so tightly and closely intertwined, and also with nets of hair called beards, beardpots and hooknets; and other nets and contraptions made up of such narrow aperture and mesh . . .)[8]

In other words, a particular type of business language evolved, probably primarily as a written rather than a spoken language, and it is attested in London as early as the eleventh century.[9]

There were quite a few advantages to this system of recording information, which occurred in many of the European languages. It was rapid to read and write, and took up little physical space due to the heavy use of abbreviation. It was geographically flexible, as the practice of mixing a Medieval Latin base with the local language, be it Middle Low German, or whatever language local merchants used, meant that accounts could be understood – to a degree – by other merchants throughout Europe. The names of commodities often pertained to their place of origin, or retained their local name when they were traded. Further, the user could have been very experienced in reading and writing, or only partially practiced at reading, and yet still have been able to get some use out of reading business accounts, because much of the potentially opaque information (the Latin case endings, for example) was represented by abbreviation marks, which the reader could have chosen to ignore. This kind of manuscript will display vernacular features, but they may well not all be from the same vernacular. This is because no language is racially 'pure', but will borrow from neighbouring speakers. From checking the non-Latin terms for goods entered in London business accounts in Middle Dutch dictionaries, whole areas of Dutch predominance can be discovered. Most of these are expected; they include areas such as shipbuilding, making fishtraps and curing fish, and riverside construction activities such as driving piles and building watermills.

If Middle Dutch and Middle English are so closely related, how is it possible to know whether a word found in Dutch and English documents is Dutch or English, or just historically common to both? The answer is not particularly satisfactory – there are not many ways to distinguish. One way is if a word shows evidence of a distinctive sound-change; something that happened in one language but not in the other. Another is by looking at the referent or meaning of the word. Sometimes a whole group of words seems to have meant pretty much the same thing, so presumably the speakers of that language were quite good at whatever it was, and exported the vocabulary along with their expertise. In fact, distinguishing rare Middle Dutch words from rare Middle English words in business documents can be fraught with difficulty. Melchers[10] notes how wary scholars have been in attributing Dutch influence, because of this difficulty: 'In contrast with his presentation of the Scandinavian and French loans, Wakelin[11] is extremely hesitant in definitely ascribing his examples to Dutch/Low German and the short section abounds with modal expressions such as "may", "possibly", "seems to".'[12]

While reserving the defence that further data may prove me wrong, I venture to assert that two such areas of Dutch expertise in our period were boatbuilding and brewing beer, and that they have influenced English boatbuilding and brewing terminology.

To begin with boatbuilding: in London manuscripts of the fifteenth century there occur several words denoting types of fibrous material wedged between seams of a boat's hull to make it watertight. They include *canvas* < AN, *goathair* < *OE,[13] *mapple* < ?L, *thrum* < *OE, ?MDu, *tow* < ?MDu, ?ON, *oakum* < OE, *wiveling* < ?MDu.[14] This last term is of especial interest as it has been mistranscribed in *O.E.D.* and entered under *Windling* sb. 1., and hence no etymology could be given. From the contexts *wiveling* can be defined as a type of such fibrous matter:

Example 2

*It'm solut' p' wyuelyngge empt' p' batell' p'dc'o xvd'* . . .
C.L.R.O. MS Bridge House Account Roll 1 m 7.20 (1381/2)
(And paid for wiveling bought for the boat aforesaid 15*d*)

*It'm solut' p' Wyuelyngge empt' p' eod' Batell' vjd. It'm solut' p' Wyuelynge empt' p' eod' Batell' iijd'* . . .
C.L.R.O. MS B.H.A.R. 2 m 9.29, 30 (1382/3)
(And paid for wiveling bought for the same boat 6*d*. And paid for wiveling bought for the same boat 3*d*)

*Item Solut' p' wyuelyng & j olla terrea p' pice liquend'. viijd'* . . .
C.L.R.O. MS B.H.A.R. 12 m 8 (1392/3)
(And paid for wiveling and 1 earthenware pan for melting pitch 8*d*)

*It'm sol' p' wevelyng ponder' j petr' empt' p' les shippcraft / &c' vd'* . . .
C.L.R.O. MS Bridge House Weekly Payments first series 1 pp. 102, 103 (1406/7)
(And paid for wiveling weighing 1 stone bought for the shipcraft etc 5*d*)

*Die sabb'ti xxiij die april' sol' p' j petr' de wevely'ng' empt' p' f'cura j batell .v.d'* . . .
C.L.R.O. MS B.H.W.P. first series 1 p. 330 (1411/12)
(Saturday 23 day of april paid for 1 stone of wiveling bought for the manufacture of 1 boat 5*d*)

*It'm p' pil' vocat' wyvelyng' empt' p' ead' ijd'* . . .
C.L.R.O. MS B.H.W.P. first series 2 p. 187 (1416/17)
(And for pile (hair) called wiveling bought for the same 2*d*)

There was an adjective found in thirteenth-century Dutch texts,[15] *wevelin*, meaning 'made of cloth woven from wool that is less tough than usual', derived from the Middle Dutch noun *wevel*, 'woollen cloth woven from delicate wool'. It seems likely that the English term *weveling* was a borrowing from Dutch, with a diminutive suffix *-ing*, giving the sense of 'small piece of fine woollen cloth'. Notice that several of the 'oakum' terms do refer to types of cloth: *canvas; mapple* (< ?L *mappa manula*, 'hand towel'); *thrum* < ?OE 'ligament', but c.f. MDu *drom, drum* 'endpiece, remnant'. The term *tow* referred to unravelled or unworked fibre, probably of flax, hemp or jute. The other terms listed, *goathair, oakum* < OE *ācumbe* 'off-combings' (OE period); 'untwisted rope fibre' (ME period and subsequently) seem to have originally denoted types of animal hair.

However, it is not adequate to simply derive the terms from their immediate etymological parent and conclude that they held the same meaning as that parent. While the etymology of *wiveling* may lead us to a root signifying a type of wool, the attestation given for the financial year 1416/17 makes it explicit that *wiveling* was a type of hair.[16] Just as *catgut* today does not refer to the gut of a cat, or *moleskin* to the skin of moles, we cannot assume that *goathair* literally referred to the hair of goats, although it may have done. The term *goathair* is not attested in any dictionaries so far as I know, but the contexts again make clear the usage:

Example 3
*It'm p' j oll' p' pice & goteshere empt' p' le Shoute vjd' . . .*
C.L.R.O. MS B.H.W.P. first series 2 p. 309 (1418/19)
(And for 1 pan for pitch and goathair bought for the shout[17] 6*d*)

*It'm sol' p' Gotehere empt' p' le Shoute iiijd' . . .*
C.L.R.O. MS B.H.W.P. first series 2 p. 310 (1418/19)
(And paid for goathair bought for the shout – 4*d*)

*It'm p' ij patell' t'rr' p' pic' & p' Goteshere empt' p' dict' batell' iijd' . . .*
C.L.R.O. MS B.H.W.P. first series 2 p. 346 (1418/19)
(And for 2 earthenware pots for pitch and for goathair bought for the said boat 3*d*)

It is possible that it is indeed hair that is being referred to; compare the following entry concerning non-specific hair:

> *. . . for xi lb of towghe xid for heere and mapoltis[18] to the repa'con of the boottes vd . . .*
> C.L.R.O. MS B.H.R. 4 fo 127v (1491/2)

Working from the data we have uncovered so far, it is not possible to know whether *goathair* is semantically transparent, or whether it has undergone a metaphorical extension of semantic scope. With regard to *wiveling*, it might seem somewhat paradoxical that a Middle Dutch etymology and hence by inference Dutch expertise can be posited for a noun that is, in fact, only attested in English in London manuscripts. Either this is one way in which historical linguists can aid the endeavours of historians, or this is the point at which historians stop believing in historical linguistics. Ultimately this kind of problem can only be resolved by finding more data embedded in explicit contexts.

To continue with the theme of metaphorical extensions: much of the Middle English brewing terminology came from Middle Dutch, but not all the meanings of obsolete terms are now recoverable. One such problematical term is the word *tabard*, now famous as the name of the inn in *The Canterbury Tales*. From the following contexts it appears that a tabard formed part of a brewery's equipment:

Example 4

*In primis vno < > plumbo stant' in fornac' It' j taptrogh de plumbo It' j massfato It' j yelton' It' j clensyngton' It' iiij wat'fatt' It' xxxviij kemelyns It' lij kyldekyns It' iij fferdekyns It' j tabard' de plumbo It' j molendino equino cu' toto apparatu . . .*

C.L.R.O. MS Mayor's Court, file 3, 167 m 2 (1442/3)

(And firstly one lead ? standing in the furnace. And 1 lead taptrough. And 1 mash vat.[19] And 1 gyle tun.[20] And 1 cleansing tun. And 4 water vats. And 38 kimelins.[21] And 52 kilderkins.[22] And 3 firkins[23] And 1 lead tabard. And 1 horse mill with all apparatus)

*I' quibz expend' in ij taberd' plumbi p' le masshyngtu'ne & le yelyng tu'ne remanenc' in ten'to vocat' the Cokke ad finem de Ivy lane ponder' iij qrtr' C xij lb' . . .*

C.L.R.O. MS B.H.R. 3 fo 196 (1471/2)

(And from which spent in 2 lead tabards for the mashing tun and the gyling tun remaining in the tenement called the Cock at the end of Ivy Lane weighing 3 quarters of a hundred and 12 pounds)

*It' in j tabarde p' le growte leede in d'ce ten'te vocat' the Cowpe j quartr' xij lb' . . .*

C.L.R.O. MS B.H.R. 3 fo 244 (1474/5)

(And in 1 tabard for the grout lead[24] in the said tenement called the Cowpe 1 quartern and 12 pounds)

There are a few other instances where a tabard formed part of the equipment of a fifteenth-century brewery.[25] The contexts show that the term *tabard* was also used in context of kitchen cisterns, lavatory cisterns, window-sills and roofs, and was made of lead. It seems to have signified a kind of small leaden tank, used to hold ale or rainwater, or perhaps act as lagging or a cover for such a tank. This would then make sense of the pub name in *The Canterbury Tales* as something like 'The Ale Tank' or 'The Tank Lid'.

It is possible that this word *tabard* is the same as the term *tabard* derived from Old French meaning 'short coat, sleeveless jerkin' which is still in use today, and was being used in a metaphorical sense. As we now speak about a jacket round a boiler, possibly *tabard* was simply an earlier metaphor. So far, only the clothing sense has been signalled in students' editions of *The Canterbury Tales; viz* Robinson (1979) p. 651[26] 'The sign of the inn was a tabard, or short sleeveless coat, embroidered with armorial bearings. The word came also to be applied to the laborer's blouse or smock.'[27] This definition has not in essence changed from that given in 1603 by John Stow (1971 reprint, vol II p. 62):[28] '. . . the Tabard, so called of the Signe, which as we now tearme it, is of a Iacquit or sleeuelesse coat, the whole before, open on both sides, with a square coller, winged at the shoulders: a stately garment of old time, commonly worne of Noble men and others, both at home and abroad in the warres, but then (to wit in the warres) their Armes embrodered, or otherwise depict vpon them, that euery man by his coate of Armes might be knowne from others: but now these Tabardes are onely worne by the Heraulds, and be called their coats of Armes in seruice: for the Inn of the Tabard, Geoffrey Chaucer, Esq . . .' However, Stow was not aware of the Corporation of London manuscripts usage.

Etymologies cannot tell us about metaphorical senses, but they can perhaps alert us to a possible presence of other language speakers in the generation of a text. This is why mixed-language business documents are so valuable for the historian: each merchant, dealer or clerk who had a part in the transaction has potentially left his mark in the language of the resultant account, regardless of the origin of that language. The other conclusion, that the pot-pourri accrued by so many traders inputting their linguistic experience has created a separate, business register, brings us back to subject of social context mentioned in the introduction. Either one could argue that if a word of non-Latin etymology is present in a mixed-language London business text, then its very presence must indicate its status as a loanword into London English at that point. Support for this would be the function of the text: how can a business text − which has to be checked by auditors − or legal text − which may prohibit people from actions, or record their criminal activities − function, if the non-Latin elements are also non-English? Who would understand such a text − and if traders on the one hand and criminals on the other couldn't, then how did the text have any force at all? Or, one could argue that such mixed-language texts had a separate social function from other texts, that their very mixedness constituted their identity, and that therefore one should *expect* them to differ from other contemporary spoken and written usage. At no point need any of their constituent parts reflect contemporary speech, because their difference connotes a separate register to the reader. Hence a strange word appearing in a business or legal text (and, for example, *wiveling*, by its rareness, could be deemed a strange word) might have no currency at all outside this particular text type.

These arguments seem quite contradictory. The social context hypothesis as applied here would explain the many words in business and legal texts which have etymologies from Low Countries languages (and elsewhere) as being loans into this particular text type, without necessarily filtering through into other text types or speech. Such a hypothesis would allow for several synchronic synonyms, each connoting a slightly different register and hence with a slightly different pragmatic force. The function of the text hypothesis would simply explain the many words with Low Countries etymologies as being synchronic loans into London English. My reservations are that both hypotheses seem attractive, but neither can be proved. If the same examples were to be found embedded in non-business or non-legal types, this would then support the function of the text theory. Alternatively, if a plethora of synonyms (i.e. *not* the same examples) were to be found in other text types, this would support the social context theory. Either way, considerably more data is needed.

## Notes

1    James Milroy, *Linguistic Change and Variation* (Oxford, Blackwell, 1992) pp. 113, 124–8, 142–5, 154–7; see also April M.S. McMahon 'Underspecification theory and the analysis of dialect differences in Lexical Phonology', *Transactions of the Philological Society*, Vol. 90, No. 1 (1992) pp. 81–2.

2    For example, the sound-change known as first fronting.

3    'In its heyday in the fourteenth and fifteenth century, Low German was the administrative, diplomatic and trading language of the Hanseatic League, with a distributional reign stretching from what is now Holland and Belgium on the North Sea, east all around the Baltic including the Scandinavian kingdoms, Finland and part of Russia, with Luebeck as its administrative centre and Lubic law, written in Low German, the recognized code of judgement. During that period Low German was perhaps the most unified and standardized of all Germanic languages.' Wolfgang Wölck, 'Language Use and Attitudes among Teenagers in Diglossic Northern Germany', *Language Contact in Europe*, eds. P.H. Nelde *et al.* (Tübingen, Max Niemeyer, 1986) p. 98.

4    John A. Hawkins 'German', in Bernard Comrie (ed.), *The Major Languages of Western Europe* (London, Routledge, 1990) p. 103.

5    See for example William Rothwell, 'The Problem of Law French', *French Studies* (1992): 'Thanks to the widespread acceptance of the convenient myth that after about 1250 insular French degenerated into an incoherent gibberish, of which Law French was considered a striking example, there has been no incentive for philologists to take account of the great volume of perfectly intelligible insular French documents of all kinds produced in the later thirteenth and fourteenth centuries.'; 'The "Faus Franceis D'Angleterre": Later Anglo-Norman', *Anglo-Norman Anniversary Essays*, ed. Ian Short, Anglo-Norman Text Society Occasional Publications Series No. 2 (1993) p. 310. 'The Anglo-Norman origins of a great many English words are still not recognized by the O.E.D., and the active and useful role played by Anglo-Norman right up to the threshold of the fifteenth century is not generally appreciated.'; 'The French Vocabulary in the Archive of the London Grocer's Company', *Zeitschrift für Französische Sprache und Literatur* Band CII, Heft I (1992) p. 24: 'A study of his [Chaucer's, L.W.] vocabulary will reveal time and again that its extensive and very obvious French component may be traced back not solely to continental French, as commentators have invariably done up to the present time, being in the main ignorant

of insular French, but at least in part to the Anglo-French in which he must have been thoroughly steeped.'; and 'From Latin to Modern French: Fifty Years On', *Bulletin of the John Rylands University Library of Manchester* Vol. 68, No. 1 (1985) p. 193: 'a plentiful supply of evidence is available to show that this "faus franceis d'Engletere" was very far from being either a "dead" or "degenerate" language until well after the age of Chaucer'. See also 'The Missing Link in English Etymology: Anglo-French', *Medium Aevum* Vol. LX, No. 2 (1991).

6   That this mixture is deliberate and not due to ignorant scribes or the decadence of Medieval Latin is addressed in Laura Wright, 'Macaronic Writing in a London Archive, 1380–1480', Matti Rissanen *et al* (eds.), *History of Englishes* (Berlin: Mouton de Gruyter, 1992), pp. 762–70 and Laura Wright, 'Early Modern London Business English', Dieter Kastovsky (ed.), *Studies in Early Modern English* (Berlin: Mouton de Gruyter, 1994, pp. 449–65.

7   I am grateful to the Corporation of London for permitting me to print extracts from their manuscripts.

8   *Route* 'fish trap ? formed from lattice-work' < ?OF *route* 'track', ?MDu *ruit* 'chequered, diamond-shaped'. *Weir* 'fixed support for fish traps' < OE *wer* 'dam'. *Wase* 'fish trap of meshed straw, reeds, twigs positioned on a weir' < MLG *wase* 'faggot, brushwood'. *Hurdle* 'wickerwork frame' < OE *hyrdel*. *Berd* 'fishing net of hair and thread' < ?OE *beard* 'tuft' > ME 'barb'. *Berdpot* '?fish trap with a barbed wicker basket' < ?OE *beard* 'tuft' > ME 'barb' + OE *pot(t*. *Hooknet* '?net with hooks attached' < OE *hōc* + OE *net(t*. *Mesh* < ?MDu *maesche* 'mesh'. These terms are further discussed in Laura Wright, *Sources of London English: Medieval Thames Vocabulary* (Oxford, Clarendon, 1996), and the terms and their context is addressed in Laura Wright, 'Medieval Latin, Anglo-Norman and Middle English in a Civic London Text: An Inquisition of the River Thames, 1421', David Trotter and Stewart Gregory (eds.), *De Mot en Mot: Essays in Honour of William Rothwell* (Cardiff, University of Wales Press, 1997).

9   See the Billingsgate customs in N.S.B. Gras, *The Early English Customs System* (Cambridge: Harvard University Press, 1918) p. 154; and Laura Wright, 'A Hypothesis on the Structure of Macaronic Business Writing', Jacek Fisiak (ed.), *Medieval Dialectology*. Trends in Linguistics Studies and Monographs 79. (Berlin, Mouton de Gruyter, 1995) pp. 309–21.

10  Gunnel Melchers, 'On the Low German and Dutch Element in Shetland Dialect', *Sprachkontakt in der Hanse*, ed. P. Sture Ureland (Tübingen, Max Niemeyer, 1986) p. 303.

11  Martyn F. Wakelin, *English Dialects. An Introduction* (London, The Athlone Press, 1972), p. 14f.

12  Melchers (1986) p. 303: 'He is particularly careful when suggesting the very interesting possibility of voiced initial fricatives in south-west England owing something to Dutch influence, as in *food* (cf. Dutch *voed-*.) TH Stopping (cf. J.C. Wells *Accents of English* (Cambridge, Cambridge University Press, 1982)) is another characteristic which "may owe something to Low Dutch influence". The local [Shetland, L.W.] pronunciation of *thistle*, for example, corresponds to Dutch *distel*.' The C.L.R.O. documents show both of these features in words connected with areas of Dutch expertise, such as bridgebuilding (e.g. OE *f éol* > London ME *vyle* 'file; tool for smoothing' (C.L.R.O. MS Bridge House Rental 3 fo 34v, 1461/2); OE *stapolung* > London ME *stadelles* 'starling; the outwork of piles surrounding the pier of a bridge' (C.L.R.O. MS B.H.R. 3 fo 41, 1461/2)).

13  The asterisk denotes a reconstructed form not actually attested in the earlier period.

14  For etymologies here and below see *Middle English Dictionary*, H. Kuhn *et al* (eds.) (Ann Arbor, University of Michigan Press, 1953) and *The Oxford English Dictionary*, J.A.

Simpson, E.S.C. Weiner (eds.) 2nd ed. (Oxford, Clarendon, 1989). Laura Wright, *Sources of London English: Medieval Thames Vocabulary* (Oxford, Clarendon, 1996).

15    I am extremely grateful to Dr Karina van Dalen-Oskam of the *Vroegmiddelnederlands Woordenboek* for this information, and for her interest in Middle Dutch beer.

16    Providing, of course, that *pil'* itself had not undergone a semantic amplification at this date to include other types of fibre.

17    A type of flat-bottomed boat used on the Thames; derived from MDu.

18    i.e. mapple.

19    'Malt mixed with hot water to form wort' (*O.E.D.*) < OE *mǣsc*.

20    'A tun used for fermenting wort' (*M.E.D.*), first attested *O.E.D.* 1743, < ?Du *gijl* 'pulp from brewing'.

21    'A tub used for brewing' (*M.E.D.*) < ?OE (*O.E.D.*).

22    'A cask for beverages' (*M.E.D.*); 'fourth part of a tun' (*O.E.D.*) < Du or LG.

23    'Half a kilderkin' < MDu *vierdekijn (*O.E.D.*).

24    Grout: 'an infusion of malt, wort of the last running; a kind of thick, dark ale' (*M.E.D.*) < OE *grūt*, corresponding to MDu *gruit* 'coarse meal, peeled barley or rye, malt, flavouring for beer, yeast' (Mod Du *gruit* 'dregs' (*O.E.D.*)). Lead: 'a large pot, cauldron, or kettle; a large open vessel used in brewing' < OE *lēad* (*O.E.D.*).

25    See Laura Wright, '*O.E.D.*'s Tabard, 4.(?)', *Notes and Queries*, Vol. 39 New Series No. 2 (June 1992) pp. 155–7 for further treatment of this term.

26    F.N. Robinson (ed.) *The Complete Works of Geoffrey Chaucer* (Oxford, Oxford University Press, 2nd ed. reprint 1979).

27    I am grateful to Dr Jonathan Hope for reminding me of this point, and for his interest in Belgian lager. I am also grateful to Professor William Rothwell for corresponding with me on this term.

28    John Stow, *A Survey of London,* ed. Charles Lethbridge Kingsford (Oxford, Clarendon, 1908, reprint 1971).

# Index